On Th In Jersey

by R C Henwood

Published in 1999 by
Foley Publications, St Helier
Falmer
Manor Park Road
La Pouquelaye
St Helier, Jersey
Channel Islands

Printed by
Bigwoods Premier Printers Limited
4 La Rue Martel
Rue des Pres Trading Estate
St Saviour, Jersey
Channel Islands

ISBN 0 9525316 3 1

Foreward

In compiling this book the intention has been to include the everyday events, as well as the dramatic. The one page allotted to each day of the year contains a slice of Jersey's past, whether it be of historical importance or merely reflecting the society of the era. It tells of murders, battles fought, individual achievements and social changes, what was and was not acceptable, and the punishments thought appropriate at the time.

It has only been possible to give a brief synopsis of the more major historical events. Likewise, an entire life's achievements cannot justly be condensed into a few paragraphs. But it is hoped that this easily digested taste of Jersey's past will arouse the reader's curiosity sufficiently that a more complete explanation will be sought. To that end a comprehensive bibliography has been included at the back of the book.

No historical event occurs in a vacuum and the inclusion in this book of the trivial, as well as the historical, is intended to give the reader as broad a spectrum of Island life as possible, whether it is read from cover to cover or, as is more likely, is dipped into from time to time.

RCH
6th September, 1999

01 January

1820

The local newspaper *Le Constitutionnel* was founded. Party politics had broken out in Jersey and *Le Constitutionnel* was published for the Laurel party.

The division between the Laurels and the Roses, the other party, was incredibly bitter. Supporters were said to be at war with one another and the Island's population was split. Opposing parties often physically attacked each other.

Elections at this time were not by secret ballot. Votes were given audibly in the church porch after Sunday service, which allowed intimidation.

At one Jurat election in St Martin the first man to vote Rose was beaten with fists and umbrellas. The next two were treated more violently and the fourth was beaten to the ground and kicked. The Laurels won by 232 to 11.

1894

A newly arrived Jesuit priest, Marc-Antoine Dechevrens, began meteorological recordings on this day. Encouraged by his superiors, Dechevrens planned and built an observatory at Maison St Louis, including a tower 150 ft tall, to record wind speed and movement. Annual reports were published, containing data on meteorological and magnetic activity in Jersey.

1919

The law adopting English weights and liquid measures came into effect. Until this point Jersey had gone its own way.

1960

Jersey's last independent bus company, Joe's Bus Service, passed into the control of the JMT. Joseph Manning, the company's founder, had died four years earlier and his sons, who had carried on the business, eventually decided to leave the field of public transport to the company that had gradually swallowed up its many rivals, the Jersey Motor Transport Company.

02 January

1875

The States had decided to build a large deep water harbour. However, the English engineer who designed it had not realised the strength of the local tides and 200 feet of pier had already been washed away. On this day the wave action removed more of the works.

It is interesting to note that 120 years on the lesson had still not been learned as problems with the strong tidal flows were encountered during the construction of the Elizabeth Marina.

1937

On this day a letter was written from the States' Greffe to Jersey Railways and Tramways Ltd, offering to buy from them the railway track running from St Helier to La Corbiére. The sum offered was £25,000 and the sale was later agreed. As well as the track and the land on which it stood, the old stations, hotels, bridges and various rights were included in the price.

The railway had been in decline for years and a fire in 1936 which destroyed much of the rolling stock had been the last straw. The track was removed and the Railway Walk created.

1966

George Reginald Balleine died on this day. Born in 1873 Balleine went into the church and enjoyed a successful career in the ministry.

He is, however, better known locally as an historian. Balleine was appointed Honorary Librarian to the Société Jersiaise shortly after returning to his native Island in 1938.

With this archive at his fingertips, he went on to chronicle Jersey's history with a clarity and depth which remains a benchmark that few others have reached. *The Bailiwick of Jersey* and *A History of Jersey* are reference books that read as easily as well-crafted novels and are tomes few true Jerseymen would be without.

03 January

1848

The town drainage system was continuing at a great pace and on this day work in Charles Street began. Bath Street's drains were now complete and the scheme intended to connect up all the streets in the district, including Ann Street and Simon Place. It was noted that 'thorough-drainage was the greatest of all blessings to a thickly populated neighbourhood'.

1898

Euphrasie Eugenie Virginie Renault was brought before the Magistrate, charged with assaulting her husband. The court heard that Jean Marie Buhot, her spouse, often had to call the police for protection. He admitted that he too sometimes hit his wife but he only did so 'when she irritated him to such a point that he lost his patience'. The court ordered them to 'keep the peace towards each other'.

1931

Major C J M Riley and Mrs Yvonne Robin, née Lempriere were married at a midnight ceremony in the chapel at Trinity Manor. The chimes of Big Ben were relayed to the congregation and the ceremony began. Electric lights illuminated the chapel and the proceedings were conducted by F D Moat, the private chaplain to the Manor. Once wed, the couple's guests were served refreshments in the Manor's dining room, with Mr and Mrs Riley leaving for their honeymoon in St Brieuc the same morning.

1974

During the oil crisis, restrictions on heating and lighting were imposed in an attempt to reduce the Island's energy needs. Fines of £400 and three months imprisonment were punishments those who ignored the regulations faced. Street lighting was reduced, illuminated signs were forbidden and heat and light were reduced in schools and business. Lighting an empty room became an offence.

04 January

1870

Twelve young men went before the court, charged with breaking into St Lawrence Parish Church and ringing the bell on Christmas Eve. The group had rung the bell all night, permission for which would have been given if they had asked. During the entry windows had been broken and it was only when the men would not pay for the repairs that the Constable took them to court. Eight of the group were discharged but the four leaders, one of whom was Mr Martel, a Constable's Officer, were fined and ordered to pay damages. If they failed to pay the fine, Martel would go to prison for 15 days, the other three for a week.

1897

It was reported that the Jersey Savings Bank had received deposits of £64,925 1s 8d for the year ending 1896. The books showed a cash surplus of £5,284 15s 3d and it was pointed out that the sums involved were larger than those dealt with by many English provincial banks.

1977

A proposition to compensate dairy farmers for their losses during the previous year was lodged in the States. The industry was to be given £100,000 aid after the drought in 1976. Farmers would receive a subsidy of 1p for every pint of milk produced between July and December. The lack of water had meant that milk yields were reduced and feed costs increased. The £100,000 was intended as an emergency measure while the whole cattle industry was reviewed.

1986

A 32-year-old waiter, Joao Sepeta, was found dying on St Ouen's beach, having been battered about the head and then dumped in the incoming tide. A week later fellow waiter José Nelio Izilio was charged with his murder. It transpired that the two men had got into a fight. Izilio had then panicked, taken the then unconscious Septa to Les Brayes and left him on the beach.

05 January

1900

Forty-two passengers and 31 crew members were aboard the *Ibex* when she struck rocks off Guernsey on this day. The weather was clear, the sea calm and Captain Baudains was a local man with years of experience.

It was stated that had the *Ibex* completed her journey it would have been in record time and this may have been the reason the vessel took a course closer inland than usual.

All escaped uninjured, except one seaman who 'perished by his own fault'. Personal effects were lost but it was hoped that a diver could retrieve the mail bags that the 265-foot long ship was carrying.

1943

The German ship *Schottland* sent out a distress signal when she struck rocks off Noirmont Point. The 1,500 ton ship had set sail with another, the *Holland*, and they were awaiting the arrival of an escort ship for their journey to France.

Those aboard were mostly soldiers on leave and a number of boats went to their rescue. But of her 370 passengers, only 40 survived the sinking, the remainder being washed ashore along the south coast over the next few days.

Leslie Sinel notes in his *Occupation Diary* that after the war he was contacted by a Spaniard who claimed that a friend, a Todt worker, had made a bomb and placed it aboard the *Schottland*. So it is possible that it was no accident but sabotage.

1979

One of the heaviest snowfalls Jersey had seen caused chaos throughout the Island. The snow drifts, some over six feet deep, blocked the roads so thoroughly that even with the aid of mechanical diggers some minor roads remained impassable for many days. Schools and some workplaces closed, the Island remaining in a state of suspended animation for several days.

06 January

1781

The Battle of Jersey, and Major Peirson's part in it, is probably the best known of the Island's military episodes.

The French Baron de Rullecourt had landed at La Rocque with 600 men and proceeded to St Helier, where he captured Major Corbet, the Lieutenant Governor. Major Corbet signed an order to surrender, believing that the invasion force numbered 4,000 men, with another 10,000 troops on their way from St Malo.

However, the Island forces headed for St Helier, ignoring the order to surrender and engaging the French. Major Peirson, who commanded the 95th Regiment, was killed, as was Baron de Rullecourt, in the short fire fight which destroyed the French force.

Major Corbet came out physically unscathed, but was court-martialled, found guilty, and pensioned off on £250 per annum for previous good service.

1872

A meeting was called by a group named The North Western Railway Company, at which they proposed the building of a new railway from St Aubin through St Peter, St Ouen and St Mary to St John. The proposition went to the States but like the proposed railway from Grouville, via Longueville, Colomberie, Beaumont, St Peter's Church and St Ouen's Manor to a terminus at L'Etacq Hill, little more was heard about it and the enthusiasm and money for these grandiose schemes gradually waned.

1922

It was revealed that a British company had plans to run electricity through the whole Island. The firm, Hunter & Co, of Edinburgh, were prepared to fund the cabling themselves if the States allowed them to cover all of Jersey. Their proposals included taking over both railways and electrifying them. Hunter & Co were hoping to have the franchise on electricity in Jersey for a fixed period of time after which the States could acquire the network at an agreed price.

07 January

1868

The 130-horsepower single screw steamer, the *Caesarea*, was launched from the St Malo shipyard where she had been built. In sea trials she attained a speed of 13½ knots and entered service soon afterwards. The *Caesarea* maintained a regular service for the islands until June 1884. It was then that she sank while 10 miles off Cap de la Hague, having been in collision with a cargo boat full of Jersey potatoes bound for England.

1897

The Constable of St Lawrence, Edward Voisin, offered a reward of £1 for the capture and conviction of the thief who on New Year's Eve had stolen a bicycle, a Globe Dunlop, no 1934, belonging to J E Esnouf.

1906

At this time it was common practice for people to take their bean crock to a bakehouse in the evening and then collect the cooked food the next morning for their breakfast.

On this day a thief with bravado claimed a crock, paying the penny for the cooking of it, and it was only when the genuine owner appeared that the fraud was discovered.

The following morning the empty crock was found outside the bakehouse. The cheeky thief, content with his breakfast, had returned the bowl.

1943

St Aubin's Bay used to have three Martello towers defending it, the first being, not surprisingly, at First Tower, the second at Bel Royal and the third at Beaumont. The German occupying forces required more modern defences and on this day they blew up the Bel Royal Tower to make room for their own concrete fortifications. However, our ancestors built things to last and as the dust cleared half the tower remained standing.

08 January

1793

The General Hospital opened on this day. Fifty two years earlier Mrs Bartlett had left the bulk of her fortune 'to build at St Aubin's a house for poor widows, fatherless children and ancient people of the Island'.

Between then and the opening of the hospital, first Mrs Bartlett's relatives tried to have the will set aside and then permission was needed to change locations as no site at St Aubin could be found.

Once the building was completed, it was requisitioned as a barracks until the gunpowder store within it blew up. Eventually the structure was rebuilt and after 52 years the poor at last received some benefit from Mrs Bartlett's generosity.

1959

Tons of sand were removed from Grève de Lecq beach by haulage contractors. After recent storms the sand levels on this north coast beach were particularly high. And as Grève de Lecq was a 'free' beach, large quantities of sand were allowed to be removed. On this day several dozen lorry loads were taken with the aid of a mechanical digger, an activity that was prohibited the following week as a result of the hauliers' excessive actions.

1980

Albert Victor Bedane died on this day. Born in 1893, Albert had joined the Medical Corps in 1914 and saw action with the British army in Siberia, a posting that was to prove most useful during the next great conflict.

During the Occupation large numbers of Russians were brought to Jersey as slave workers. And being an island, fleeing prisoners had few chances of escape. But Bedane was ready to help.

At great personal risk Bedane hid a number of escapees, the few words of Russian he had picked up previously being of great assistance. In 1965 Bedane was one of twenty people honoured by the Russian government for assisting their countrymen.

09 January

1825

The year after the foundation of the Lifeboat Service, four members of a Jersey crew were awarded medals for the rescue of 13 people when the *Fanny* struck rocks near Elizabeth Castle. On this day two trips were made, ferrying people ashore. However the vessel broke up, drowning the five people who were awaiting the lifeboat's third trip. Three years later, on 1st January 1828, a ship of the same name, from the same port and commanded by the same captain, struck rocks a mile off St Helier, drowning 11 passengers and two crew. The second *Fanny* was later salvaged.

1915

Samuel Falle, St Helier's Rector, appealed to Islanders to help Serbian children. The request for unwanted clothing to help 'our brave allies' was made through local churches as well as through the press. The First World War was raging at the time and Yugoslavia's Serbs were fighting against the German forces. On the same day the Serbian legation thanked the Island for the £55 recently sent.

1928

James Joy pleaded not guilty to the charge of driving while under the influence of drink, with insufficient lights and at a dangerous rate, knocking down Robert Lamerton and causing him injuries from which he later died. Joy claimed that Lamerton had been lying in the road when he drove by, having been in a fight but he was found guilty. The Bailiff said that an example needed to be made, as it was high time that motorists understood that other people had rights as well. Joy was sentenced to a year's hard labour, with his licence being revoked for 12 months from the date of his release.

1969

The last of the high metal railings that had surrounded Parade Gardens, limiting access to it, were removed as a part of the implementation of a new policy of public access. Everyone was invited to 'walk freely along the paths and make use of the benches' but 'there must be no walking on the grass'.

10 January

1695

Charles Dumaresq and James Corbet gave the Chapelle de la Madeleine to the parish of St Helier to use as a poor house. At the same time the Island's first prison was under construction at Charing Cross. It straddled the road of the only western entrance to town, forcing all traffic to pass underneath, through a gloomy tunnel.

1781

Major Peirson, who had died during the Battle of Jersey, was buried in the town church. He was a Yorkshireman, but his father preferred that he should be interred close to where he had fallen.

1905

Paul Le Petit and his maid, Marie Le Heron, were going to milk the cows in his St Clement stable. Le Heron went in first, at which point the door slammed shut and she was shot twice. Le Petit rushed in and was shot in the side.

Despite wounds to her head and chest Le Heron fled, pursued by the assailant, Jules Louis Paillardon. She got away, at which point Paillardon shot himself in the temple.

Le Petit's braces had saved him, the bullet hitting their metal buckle. But the other two underwent surgery, with Paillardon dying in hospital on this day.

The reason for this bizarre shooting was jealousy, as Le Heron had broken off her relationship with Paillardon.

1939

The Jersey Electricity Company opened its new building in Broad Street, where the old Mercantile Hotel had previously stood. The Electricity Company had been formed 15 years earlier, when there had been 200 initial subscribers. However by 1936, 5,857 people relied on electricity rather than gas lighting and by the time the showrooms opened the number was over 9,000.

11 January

1750

St Helier Harbour's foundation stone had been laid in 1722. On this day the States decided to raise funds to continue the building project by the use of a lottery.

1886

The leading Island bank was the Jersey Banking Company, known as the States Bank. But on this day it suspended payments. The bank's manager, Mr Gossett, had for years been the States Treasurer and naturally had put the Island's money with his own firm. It turned out, though, that Gossett had been gambling wildly with the funds and the bank had been insolvent for some time. The collapse left 1,500 depositors with a heavy loss and drove a number of established businesses into bankruptcy.

1902

An election for Roads Inspector in St Ouen had three candidates standing for the two positions. James Syvret received 64 votes and was thus elected. However, Philip Powell and François Hamon both got 54 votes. So the Constable, Henry d'Auvergne, used his casting vote in favour of Hamon, despite having already voted.

Powell asked to see the list of votes and saw that not only had the Constable voted twice, but Mr Le Cornu had also voted, despite being ill in bed, and St Ouen Deputy James Le Brocq was recorded as having voted for Hamon, when he had in fact voted for Powell.

On this day Powell went to the Royal Court, asking for the election result to be put aside and for the £50 costs to be paid by the Constable, which the court agreed to.

1962

Hurricane force winds and a 34-foot tide combined to cause flooding from the abattoir to First Tower. Gigantic waves pounded the sea wall, leaving Victoria Avenue under water and many cars had to be abandoned as roads became impassable.

12 January

1857

The first election for Deputies was held. Fourteen seats were available, three for the more populated parish of St Helier and one in each of the other parishes. These changes encouraged the Reform Movement. However, only three of their candidates were elected while the other eleven new States members were very traditional in their views.

1906

Three workmen were rescued after being stranded overnight on the Demie de Pas beacon. A gale and heavy seas had stopped their own boat from collecting them, so the lifeboat had to be used. After a number of attempts, a breeches buoy was successfully launched and the men were pulled one by one through the breakers to the safety of the lifeboat.

1979

The Island's authorities appealed to householders not to hoard food when a strike by UK lorry drivers had cut food deliveries. Some foodstuffs had already run out and there was concern that panic buying would exacerbate the situation, some shop shelves being already bare. Arrangements were made to import stocks from France, while negotiations with union officials in England attempted to agree a dispensation and allow food for the Channel Islands through the blockade.

1981

The Lieutenant-Governor, Sir Peter Whiteley, joined the Transport and General Workers Union. The offer of membership was made by René Liron when the Queen's representative visited Union headquarters and the Governor accepted his honorary membership 'with great pride'. Fortunately Sir Peter's unionisation never required him to go on strike nor to join a picket line.

13 January

1666

Fear of a French invasion lead to the Governor, the doddering old Lord Jermyn, being pensioned off and Sir Thomas Morgan, a military man, replacing him. Louis XIV of France had declared war on England in this year and spies in Paris reported that Jersey would be the first to be assaulted. The attack didn't come but if it had 4,000 men and 200 horses were waiting to repel it.

1843

Thirty feet of the steeple of St Peter's Church were damaged when it was hit by lightning. And this was not the first time the spire had felt 'the Hand of God'. In 1612 lightning had completely destroyed the steeple as parishioners were entering the church.

In 1843 the parish met the cost of repairs by issuing 275 special one pound notes on the security of the parish. The damage was repaired but five years later the saying that lightning never strikes the same place twice was again proved very wrong.

1954

F. Le Gallais and Sons' shops, stores and workrooms were completely gutted by fire for the second time in five years. When the blaze was eventually extinguished, after 300,000 gallons of water had been used, barely a shell of the Bath Street building remained.

The initial estimate of damage done was over £1 million and some adjoining buildings had also sustained considerable damage.

Arson had not been ruled out and a Home Office expert arrived to help with the investigation. A week later, having inspected the remains, the verdict was that one of the Island's worst fires was accidental.

1986

It was announced that the Chase Manhattan Bank was buying two buildings on the site where the Forum cinema had previously stood for £10 million.

14 January

1915

Francis Le Bredouchel appeared in court charged with stealing two rabbits. Mary Kennedy, the Lady Superior of Bagatelle, had found her rabbit cages forced and the animals missing. Centenier Marett soon tracked down the culprit, who only admitted to stealing one rabbit. His meal was to prove a costly one, as he was sentenced to one month's imprisonment with hard labour.

1923

A mass meeting demanding political rights for women was held at West Park Pavilion. The meeting was the result of an incident at the Town Hall a month earlier, when Mrs Trachy's nomination for election had been refused by the Constable of St Helier. Ruling her ineligible to stand, he claimed that the law stating 'every British subject aged 20 enjoying civil rights will be eligible for the office of Deputy' only referred to the male sex. The well-attended and good-natured meeting which took place on this day was intent on bringing Jersey 'out of the dark ages'.

1950

A fire on this day at the Jersey Optical Co Ltd premises in Hill Street was the 15th arson attack by a firebug, who caused untold damage to buildings and businesses between 1948 and 1950. A store in James Street, Cleveland Garages, Normans timber mill and Martlands Store were among the many victims.[1]

1981

It was election day in St Brelade and a high turn out was expected. The post of Constable had become vacant with the retirement of Max de la Haye and for the first time in 142 years more than one candidate was standing, with Len Downer and Alf Vibert contesting the position. The result of the 50.86% turn out was a landslide for Downer with 2,478 votes and 820 votes for Vibert.

---

[1] See 5th October for further details.

15 January

1906

James Clarke and Alice Denman appeared in the Police Court, charged with keeping a disorderly house. The house in question was in Cabot's Yard, Payn Street, and had previously been declared out of bounds to the local garrison. But a soldier had been seen entering the house and when the police arrived, they found him in bed.

Denman told the Magistrate that if given a chance she would leave the Island. But as she had said the same thing the last time she had appeared before the court, the pair were remanded in custody while the Magistrate decided what to do with them.

1946

The States were informed that the British Government was opposed to the Island introducing retrospective legislation to 'deal with reprehensible conduct not amounting to treason or treachery'.

In the months that followed Jersey's Liberation those accused of collaboration and collusion with the enemy had been investigated. However, although some Islanders' behaviour had been 'scandalous and disloyal', it was not deemed to be criminal.

It had seemed unfair to many Islanders that those who had assisted the Germans were not to be formally punished. The problem was that there were only two charges on which suspects could have been tried and both carried the death sentence.

1986

On this day a charge of theft was added to the charge of arson already facing Ian Drew. Ten days earlier Drew, who worked at the Museum in Pier Road, had attempted to burn the historic building down.

Drew had for some time been stealing various items, including ancient coins and a Victoria Cross, which he had sold in England. With the imminent arrival of someone due to examine the missing coins, Drew decided to cover his tracks by setting fire to the building. His plan failed when closed doors meant a lack of oxygen stifled the fire.

16 January

1853

Peter Le Sueur died suddenly, aged 41. Born in Broad Street, opposite the spot where his memorial obelisk now stands, Le Sueur was responsible for a great many improvements to Island life.

He had studied law in Paris and returned to a brilliant career as an Advocate before being elected Constable of St Helier. He was re-elected four times and while in power started St Helier's underground sewer system, widened old street and prosecuted slum landlords. A fire brigade was formed and St Helier rapidly became a cleaner, safer and more pleasant place.

Although a great reformer, Peter Le Sueur used his brilliant legal mind to defend Jersey's independent constitution. On his death over 400 people attended his burial.

1923

A brand new motorised fire engine arrived in the Island. It had originally been proposed that as the country parishes would benefit greatly from its acquisition, they ought to contribute to its cost on a pro rata basis. Surprisingly enough they agreed and with a donation of £200 from the Jersey Mutual Assurance enabling extra machinery to be purchased, the fire brigade were now using state of the art equipment, with a Dennis engine that had a top speed of 25 mph.

1944

One of the Island's largest, and most expensive fires, with damage estimated at over £100,000, broke out in A De Gruchy and Co at about 10.30 pm. During the Occupation the pumps that maintained mains water pressure only worked intermittently and water had to be pumped from a tank within the museum grounds until mains pressure could be obtained. In the meantime, the blaze destroyed the whole arcade area, bakery, restaurants, warehouse and workshops, as well as 2,000 German uniforms and other equipment in the stores used by the occupying forces.

17 January

1781

The commander of La Rocque Tower, Sergeant Falle, along with eight of his men, was taken before the court, charged with neglect of duty following the French landing and subsequent Battle of Jersey. Falle was imprisoned and his men cautioned.

Another man found to be absent from his post was Mr Godfray of the St Lawrence battalion, who was sentenced to 15 days imprisonment on bread and water.

1897

On this day a duel was fought at the St Ouen's racecourse. The reasons were uncertain but must have been important to the participants, as one had travelled from Berlin and the other from Toulon to meet in combat.

Swords were drawn and the tournament was fought in a series of rounds, twelve in all. The combatants apparently went at each other with great enthusiasm, but it was only on round eleven that Lieutenant Buchard drew blood, and then only a few drops.

Lieutenant d'Agoult fought on and in the next round sliced open Buchard's left forearm. At this point the doctors attending the tournament stepped in and stopped the contest.

1901

A number of amendments to the Taverners' Law were brought before the States on this day, the new clauses including:

- 'every publican holding a special, ordinary or boarding house licence shall keep a register in which he shall inscribe the name of the persons residing in his establishment, together with the date of their coming and of their departure, under pain of a penalty of £1 for each contravention',
- 'publicans shall not allow dancing or any other amusements whatsoever in their establishments, without obtaining a written order from the Chief Magistrate',
- 'it is forbidden to sell spirituous liquors to young persons under 16 years of age and to young persons under 18 years of age for consumption on the premises'.

18 January

1592

Advocates were ordered by the court to pay for the customary Assize d'Heritage dinner, a decision which proved unpopular with them.

1638

William Prynne arrived in Jersey and was imprisoned in Mont Orgueil Castle. Prynne was well known as a Puritan and wasn't released until November 1640, after intervention by the House of Commons. The following year his verses about his castle prison were published.

1799

With the ever present fear of a French attack, it was decided to set up a series of signal stations. Once established, news of a French fleet sailing could be flashed via lookout ships to Mont Orgueil, then on to Grosnez, Sark and Guernsey, where the British fleet was stationed. In trials it was proved that news could reach St Peter Port within a quarter of an hour.

1908

The 1907 St Ouen Deputies election was annulled and a new one ordered by the Royal Court. Jean Priaulx had ousted sitting Deputy James Le Brocq by three votes. But a dispute arose as to whether people who had recently moved into the parish were entitled to vote. John and Arthur Le Feuvre had been refused ballot papers, while St Helier resident Philip Hamon was allowed one.

In his judgement, the Bailiff quoted from the law which stated that an election should be 'carried out in accordance with the spirit and intention of the law' and he decided that it had not been in this case. He then asked Jurat Malet de Carteret to act as returning officer, as he had done during the original election. De Carteret refused, stating that he would not do so at any public election in the future as he disagreed with the judgement.

The new election was again won by Priaulx, who this time increased his majority to four.

19 January

1687

With the Island's land becoming divided by the planting and building of hedges, accurate land measurements became important. On this day the States fixed the length of a yard, and three hundred years on the actual measure, kept in the States Building, is still used.

1824

Shipbuilding was still a big industry in Jersey and on this day the *Aurora* was launched. Built by George Deslandes and Co near La Folie, the 107 ton brigantine was the first of about forty vessels that were to be built locally to that design.

1875

The railway service around St Aubin's Bay was disrupted for two days when a ship blocked the track. Shipbuilding was still a big industry around the coast of Jersey at this time and when permission was given to construct the various railway lines a clause guaranteeing unhindered access to the sea for ship builders was stipulated.

The ship that stopped the trains had been built by Messrs Deslandes and Le Sueur in their yard on the land side of the line and was in the process of being launched when it stuck fast across the tracks.

1883

The *Hilda* had been built especially for the Channel Islands shipping route and on this day she made her maiden voyage. The single screw steamer could travel at 14 knots and had cost £33,000. She serviced the islands until October 1890 when she was transferred to the Le Havre service. The *Hilda* remained in local waters, finally meeting her end in St Malo in 1905. Attempting to enter the harbour in fog, the vessel struck rocks and was lost, as were 128 of those on board.

20 January

1854

On this day the Petty Debts Court sat for the first time, brought into being as a result of pressure for reform exerted by the British authorities. It was presided over by Jurat Philip Le Gallais.

1908

John Mollet was not best pleased when, on returning home, he found men had lopped the branches off an oak tree which stood outside his house. A fellow resident of the Royal Crescent had instructed the workers to remove the branches as they were blocking the light to his house. When Mollet found the workers intended to do the same to the five other trees in the garden, he raised the Clameur de Haro to stop them.

More often than not the Clameur is raised incorrectly, but Mollet was the Commis au Greffe of the Royal Court and knew how and in what circumstances the Clameur could be called. Mr Herivel, who had ordered the work, apologised in court and said he would employ a gardener to care for the tree, thus ensuring its recovery. A doubtful Attorney-General wondered how the severed limbs could be replaced, before the court fined Herivel for the offence.

1939

What was said to be a miniature tornado struck the Bagot area of town. The whirlwind caused particularly terrific damage to greenhouses, with most of the glass being torn from them. Iron stanchions were wrenched from their foundations and blockwork also damaged. Two workers in the greenhouse worst affected were said to have 'run for their lives'. The cost of repairs was estimated at over £1,000.

1983

Jersey's Arts Centre in Phillips Street was opened by the Bailiff, Sir Frank Ereaut. The States had donated the site, which previously had been the catering college, but £500,000 was still needed to finish the project. At the opening, Sir Frank hinted that the States might like to help.

21 January

1915

The States, having previously passed a law allowing corporal punishment of women, were now faced with amending the legislation, as the Privy Council had refused to accept it.

During the debate, which seems to have centred around madams procuring young girls as prostitutes, Deputy Le Cornu stated that no punishment on earth was too great for those who ruined young and innocent girls, a view that was echoed by a number of Members.

Deputy Cory spoke against corporal punishment for women, saying 'if you whipped half a dozen devils out, you whipped a dozen more in'. He hoped the States were not 'German enough to pass such legislation' and doubted if anyone would be prepared to whip a woman with the cat 'o nine tails. But Jurat Payn argued that if the money was right someone could easily be found to inflict the punishment, although it was generally agreed that only a woman should whip another woman.

When it came to the appel, the vote was 15 to 25 and the proposal to abandon corporal punishment for women was adopted.

1926

Island telecommunications took a leap forward with the inauguration of a new central telephone exchange. Users in the town area were advised that it was no longer necessary to use the generator handle. The new system allowed the client to lift the micro-telephone and be automatically connected with the exchange, whereupon the operator could then connect them with the party being rung.

1963

It was cold. Very, very cold. Twenty degrees below zero, the lowest temperature ever recorded in Jersey. And the spell lasted until 24 January. Reservoir pipes froze, as did the fountain in the market and a great many water pipes. The ice was thick enough to allow cycling across St Ouen's pond, as was pictured in the *Evening Post*. And most unusually the sea froze, the intense cold killing a number of conger eels.

22 January

1825
The States ordered the construction of a public weighbridge which was sited on the area where the bus station now is.

1848
A daring roadside robbery occurred on this day. John Monck, a butcher, was returning home to St Peter's in his cart when he noticed a man clinging to it. Monck gave chase, but the man made good his escape and upon inspecting his cargo, the butcher found he was short 40 lbs of beef, as well as some fish and other produce.

1931
The States voted in favour of doubling the price of the dog tax. The cost of owning a dog was to rise from 2s 6d to 5s. The money raised, £322 10s the previous year, had always gone to the Hospital Committee and this too was changed, as the funds would now go to the parishes.

The dog tax had been introduced in 1863 and although some members were concerned that the increase would affect the poor, Jurat Le Boutillier pointed out that in real terms it should have risen to 10s. He noted that in 1863 a good carpenter earned 1/3 per day and now, in 1931, he could earn 15/ per day.

One Member asked what was paid in England. When the House was told 7/6, they voted in favour of the increase.

1957
A hoard of 500 Armorican coins was discovered at Le Câtillon, Grouville. A large stone had lain in the corner of a field, constantly causing a nuisance to machinery. On this day, 17-year old Peter Langlois decided to remove it after it fouled the plough. Beneath the large lump of granite lay a flat stone and under that was the cache of coins. Armorican coins date from around the time of Christ and although not valuable as bullion, the copper coins proved of great historical value and interest.

23 January

1753

On this day Jean Martel died. Aged 59, he left a 33-year old wife and nine children. Martel, born in St Brelade of an old Jersey family, had, when aged 24, set up as a brandy merchant at Cognac. It proved to be a lucrative venture, exporting brandy to the Island from where it was then smuggled into England and America. On his death, the business could have folded but his wife proved to be a brilliant manager. Under her direction Martel became the leading house in the brandy trade, a position it never lost.

1794

The French Committee of Public Safety ordered the Channel Islands to be captured and so sent an army of 20,000 men to St Malo for the purpose. However, the Republican government was unpopular in Brittany and, aided by British and Jersey forces, the invaders were kept too busy even to cross the Channel to Jersey.

1900

At 5.30 pm the alarm was raised when flames were seen issuing from the Town Arsenal. Despite the best efforts of the Fire Brigade, the building was completely destroyed. The flames, which were visible for miles, had drawn a large crowd, but once the ammunition stored within started to explode, they soon dispersed.

1902

Two brothers went before the court for refusing to maintain their mother. Mrs Channing had seven sons, one a cripple, one just starting work and three more who would give her 1 shilling a week, but not unless the last two also paid. William, aged 43, had a wife and ten children; 24-year old Thomas had a delicate wife and large doctor's bills. So neither wanted to pay and the case was dismissed.

1973

Sixty thousand wooden posts were sunk into the sea bed near La Rocque, to become Jersey's first mussel farm. It was envisaged that each post would produce 30-50 kg. But it was not a success.

24 January

1959

Two skeletons and three human skulls were unearthed at a building site at Bel Royal. Mr A Le Bailly, who worked for builders Charles Le Quesne, discovered the bones while levelling the ground around a house being built for H E Godbolt.

They were thought to be very old, as none of the skulls had received any dental work on their teeth. However, the position in which they were uncovered, not far from the German sea-wall suggested the possibility that they were Russian slave workers who had been buried where they had died.

At the inquest two weeks later, Dr Edward Geal, the States' Pathologist, ended the speculation by stating that although they may have been buried as little as fifty years earlier, it was quite likely that they had been dead for as long as 200 years.

Of the bones, one set were said to be female, the others male.

1975

Golfer Tony Jacklin and family arrived in the Island, joining the growing band of British tax exiles. Jacklin had won both American and British Open titles and intended to buy a property at Grève de Lecq as a base from which to travel the world.

1981

Woodlands Hotel in Grouville was destroyed in what was described as Jersey's worst fire for 10 years. The hotel was closed at the time but the previous day builders had carried out work on the building. The blaze is believed to have started on the ground floor and spread quickly. Sparks flew hundreds of feet into the air and the flames could be seen for miles. Immediately after the fire there was talk of rebuilding the hotel but eventually a block of apartments were built on the site instead.

25 January

1641

The ex-Governor of Brittany, the Duke of Vendome, took refuge in Jersey. He had been accused of trying to poison Cardinal Richelieu, of Three Musketeers fame. Throughout history Jersey has tended to see an influx of French nationals seeking refuge whenever French political power fluctuated. Later it was the Huguenots who were to have an influence on the way Jersey developed.

1854

Five days after the Petty Debts Court had first sat, the same Jurat, Philip Le Gallais, presided over the first sitting of the Police Court. This was one of the many law reforms which has occurred throughout Jersey's history.

1916

A new law was adopted by the States to stop the importation of substandard alcoholic liquors. The regulations were similar to those already in force in England. Spirits now had to be at least three years old and were to be inspected by the Impôt. These changes, as well as the adoption of selling spirits in a standard measure, were intended to reduce drunkenness, as well as other heath problems.

1939

A St Helier Parish Assembly asked its rate payers for an additional £4,000 for the parish poor. Originally, £25,415 had been allocated from the parish coffers and the Constable assured parishioners that the money had been spent wisely and well. A bad winter had caused hardship and the medical officer had found more people in need of milk, all of which had cost the parish.

It was also pointed out that children born in the hospital of poor parents automatically became chargeable to St Helier until they were 21 years old. 'If St Helier could send their poor to the country to give birth, the town would save thousands', it was said.

26 January

1782

Anne Dumaresq had been sent to a convent in Caen to be educated. In 1762 news of her death, including a certificate, arrived in the Island. Twenty years later a woman came to Jersey, claiming to be Anne. Was she genuine and entitled to part of her now dead father's estate or was she an impostor? Two men questioned her, one accepting her story, the other rejecting it. A long legal case ensued but the matter was never properly settled.

1901

A schooner, the *Germaine*, had lost her foremast and was being driven ashore in heavy seas off St Ouen. The lighthouse keeper at La Corbière telegraphed a message to the lifeboat, which left the boathouse a short time later. A team of ten horses took two and a half hours to pull the lifeboat to La Pulente but when it arrived it was not launched as it was high water and the schooner's crew signalled that they would not leave her. Edward Touzel volunteered to swim out to the vessel because it was proving impossible to communicate with the stranded crew. This he did and as the tide fell, all came ashore, aided by the lifeboat.

1954

The States were asked for £2,250 to build a bandstand in Howard Davis Park. To some Members the amount seemed surprisingly high, St Helier's Constable commenting that a couple of houses could be built for that sum. Two bandstands had previously been built in the park but a combination of weather and children had meant their lives had been short. The new bandstand was intended to be a permanent structure, which could be used for plays as well as concerts. The States accepted the argument and voted the money.

1972

The issuing of Jersey's first £10 notes was reported. They were purple in colour with St Ouen's Manor pictured on the back. Despite this high denomination's release there were 'no specific plans to have £20 notes printed'.

27 January

1921

The Education Committee resigned after the money they had requested from the States was reduced. They had asked for £62,176 but Deputy Gray wanted £13,000 less spent on teachers' wages, saying that although not opposed to education, it should no longer be absolutely free. And amid applause, he went on to point out that the Education bill said it should be free 'only in exceptional circumstances'.

It was noted that Guernsey were spending only £26,770 on education and many thought £62,176 far too much. A head teacher earned 30/- to 40/- a day and it cost about £10 per child per year to attend elementary school, which the bulk of States Members thought was too much. When it came to the vote, 24 to 23 went in favour of reducing costs.

1938

The question of the cost of keeping people in prison was raised in the States when the Prison Board asked for £660 towards their upkeep. Jurat Bree asked how much it cost to keep a lad in borstal and was informed that it was £3 per week. An adult prisoner cost £161.16.6 per year, slightly more than £3 per week. Jurat de Gruchy found it strange that the convicts worked all year and yet the States had to pay 'as much as it would cost to keep a labourer, his wife and family for a year'. But despite this, the money was granted.

1986

Vernon Tomes was sworn in as Deputy Bailiff in the Royal Court. It had been exactly 17 years earlier that he had, in a similar ceremony, been sworn in as Solicitor General. The Bailiff, Sir Peter Crill, in welcoming Mr Tomes to his new position, stated: 'I shall regard you as a second Bailiff. It is a partnership, although the Bailiff must be the senior partner.' The Bailiff referred to the position of Deputy Bailiff as 'leaving the turbulent waters of Attorney-General to the calmer waters of Deputy Bailiff'. But none of the dignitaries in attendance could have known just how turbulent the waters were to be, with Mr Tomes being removed from his post in 1992.

28 January

1469

Edward IV rewarded Jersey for her loyalty to him by ordaining by charter that Islanders should be free from all tolls, customs and subsidies payable to the Crown. In the centuries that have passed, succeeding monarchs have renewed and endorsed this charter, leaving Jersey in a very special position.

1873

La Société Jersiaise was founded on this day. Its intentions were to study the Island's history and language, the preservation of antiquities and to publish historical Island documents.

1909

The States unanimously voted in favour of making money. There were a lack of coins in the Island and to rectify the problem it was decided to issue £3,000 worth of copper coinage. Pennies, half pennies and farthings were to be circulated and it was hoped that this would reduce the amount of French coinage being used.

With the introduction of gas meters and such, where money was out of circulation for long periods, coins in sterling, which fitted the meters, were in short supply.

The States had last issued copper money in 1904 and, before that, in 1888. It was a profitable activity as £2,000 worth of copper coins cost only £554 to produce, giving a return of nearly 300%.

1937

The Education Committee asked the States for £3,000 to buy the property Hautlieu. The money would be used to secure the building, its nine vergées of land and to cover the extinction of seigneurial rights. Jurat Baudains, who brought the proposition, explained that the Committee's intention was to build a new school on the land to replace the one in Brighton Road. The cost worried some Members, Jurat Le Feuvre warning that if the land was bought, the Education Committee would soon be asking for £20,000 to build the school. He insisted on lodging the proposition, thereby deferring the debate.

29 January

1649

Marie Canivet was executed on this day. She was a widow living in the house of Jean Picot, a married man. It was suspected that she had been pregnant but no child was seen. Canivet denied this but an examination proved that she had recently given birth.

Finally, admitting it was true, she retrieved the child's body from a casement where it had been for fifteen days. Canivet now claimed that the father was an Irishman who had raped her. The court, however, sent for Picot, who fled the Island.

Canivet denied that she had killed her child, asserting that it had been stillborn. The Judge didn't believe this and sentenced her to be hanged. Neighbours had also claimed that Canivet had been pregnant on two or three other occasions. After sentencing, Canivet confessed that she had had three children by Picot, the other two having been buried in the garden, one stillborn, the second dying a few hours after birth.

1887

One of the fastest ships at this time was the iron paddleship *Brighton* which was built in 1856. Unfortunately the Brays Rocks were as hard as she was fast and when the two met the *Brighton* sank within 15 minutes. All on board were saved, although the mail was lost, as was a coffin containing a body which was due for burial in Guernsey. The local currents being what they are, some time later the coffin, along with its occupant, was washed up in Alderney.

1946

Deputy Ed Slade of St Martin apologised to the States and particularly to the Attorney-General following what was described as his breach of privilege. The Deputy had accused the Attorney-General of having, during the Occupation, 'caused the Constable and/or Centeniers of the Parish of St Martin to arrest or apprehend and to hand over to the German authorities a Russian national who was being harboured in the parish'. In his statement to the House the Deputy conceded that his remark had been 'entirely false and without any foundation'. He went on to withdraw it unreservedly.

30 January

1879

Jane Mourant and Mary Lock appeared before the Court of Correctional Police, charged with assaulting Mary Osborne. The three women lived together and Osborne had gone to get some food. When she returned the other two were dissatisfied with her efforts and set her alight. The pair were remanded in custody but at their next appearance Mourant became abusive and was sent to prison for a month, charged with contempt.

1897

The statistics on deaths in the Island during 1896 were published on this day. 990 people had died in that year, the greatest number, 110, being attributed to paralysis and other diseases of the nervous system. Close behind were heart and circulatory problems, claiming 94 victims, while phthisis and tuberculosis took 93. No one had died of small pox or measles and only four had been taken by influenza and four by typhoid fever. Whooping cough had claimed 18 and the disease no one can avoid, old age, dealt with 84 people.

1969

Three French fishing skippers were each fined £75 after they had been caught fishing within the Island's three mile limit. All denied the charge but the Magistrate said that they had 'taken a chance' and unfortunately for them, had been picked up on radar.

1995

Gerald Durrell died on this day. Born in India in 1925 and brought up in Corfu, Gerald had always been fascinated by animals. At 16 he had joined Whipsnade Zoo as a student keeper and later financed his own animal collecting expeditions. Being short of funds he began writing about his exploits and *The Overloaded Ark* was the beginning of a successful writing career. The money he made from his books enabled him to open his own zoo in the grounds of Les Augres Manor in 1959. The Zoo's philosophy is to specialise in species which are in danger of extinction, to breed them in captivity and later release them back into the wild.

31 January

1660

Marie Le Dain was the last person to be executed for witchcraft in the Channel Islands. She was sentenced on this date, after being found guilty by '24 good people' from her home parish of St Ouen.

1911

A St John Parish Assembly was held to discuss the proposed building of a parish hall. Plans had been on view at St John's Hotel prior to the meeting, which was being held in the school. Constable Herbert Falla produced a report, with the cost being estimated at £2,000. H Vibert stated that although in favour of a hall, he thought the plans were too elaborate and said that £2,000 could not cover the cost of the building. Concerned that a rise in parish rates would be needed, Vibert proposed instructing the architect to design something less elaborate. The vote was taken, with 16 in favour of a rethink and 17 for the grand hall.

1934

On this day five passengers arrived in Jersey and eight departed, bringing the month's 'carried' numbers for Jersey Airways to 296. Landing and taking off from the beach at West Park, tide permitting, 120 people had arrived and 176 had departed during January, about the same number carried in one modern jet. At this time Jersey Airways were negotiating to buy 100 vergées of land near Sorel, St John, with the intention of building a permanent aerodrome.

1971

The first Jersey resident to receive a kidney transplant did so on this day. A kidney had become available at lunch time and by 3 o'clock the unidentified woman was on her way to London aboard a specially chartered Aurigny plane. By 7 pm she was in the operating theatre at St Mary's Hospital and by 10 pm the surgery was completed. Prior to the transplant, the woman had had to travel to London twice a week for dialysis until the Island's first kidney machine had been bought by a local company for her use.

01 February

1380

The Treaty of Paris decreed that the Channel Islands should be entirely depopulated, every house destroyed, every tree cut down and nothing left but a blackened desert. The French were upset that the islands were being used as a base from which the English launched raids on Brittany.

Jean de Vienne, a French admiral, arrived in March with 2,000 men and in a few days had captured the castles and the islands. However the islands were not put to the torch, as de Vienne intended to keep them for his own benefit. He sold Jersey in 1381 for 3,000 livres. Unfortunately for the buyer, the Channel Islands were recaptured a year later.

1793

Once again France declared war on England and once again Jersey became a pawn in the game. From 1790 onwards Jersey had received a trickle of French aristocrats fleeing the French Revolution but gradually the trickle had grown into a flood. By 1793 thousands of exiles were living in the Island, the numbers increasing even more with the arrival of over 4,000 expelled priests. At the time, St Helier was little more than a huddle of houses but the immigrants had brought money with them and before long a building boom trebled the size of the town.

1873

On this day the Mercantile Union Bank suddenly ceased trading. It had liabilities of £300,000 and assets of only £30,000. The bank's closure ruined a number of families and businesses. It also cost non-depositors, as £55,000 of now worthless mercantile notes were in circulation. The chairman was Josue Le Bailly, a man who had been highly respected and elected Jurat with a massive majority. However Le Bailly was sentenced to five years penal servitude when it was proved that he had been robbing his account holders.

02 February

1901

The statue of Queen Victoria at the Weighbridge was the centre of attention on this day, when the whole of Britain observed a day of mourning for the late Queen. Having previously been draped in black and purple, the statue now became a riot of colour as wreaths were laid around the Weighbridge Gardens. The weather was appalling, with heavy rain and a cutting wind, but Islanders went to mark their respect for their Duke's passing.

1923

On the site of the old town arsenal in Nelson Street a purpose built fire station was opened. It had been a long time in coming and had not been without its problems, the original builders having been dismissed for poor, slow work. However, the Fire Brigade were now able to leave their original premises at the Town Hall.

1939

The States agreed to increase the number of paid police. Although not to come into effect immediately, the bill allowed the force to be enlarged to 50 men when required. It was intended that twelve of the officers would be used at the harbours.

1956

Jersey was in the grip of icy weather, with temperatures not rising above freezing during the day. The usual chaos ensued, with frozen pipes and road disruptions. It had been thought by many that ice skating would be possible but the *Evening Post* reported that a tour of likely sites had shown that conditions were unsuitable.

1973

Television presenter Alan Whicker bought a property in Trinity. The house, Mont d'Olivet, cost £98,000 and remains the home from which his many world journeys have begun.

03 February

1843

Jeanne Gruchy made out her will on this day, her intention being to help the Island's poor after her death. She left 144 livres for the poor of each parish and a number of legacies to friends and relations.

The rest of her estate was to be divided equally between the twelve parishes, the money to be used to buy land, which would then be rented out and the income generated to be distributed among the parish needy. This money was to be given as well as, and not instead of, parish relief.

Jeanne Gruchy lived another five years and once her affairs were settled, each parish received the considerable sum of £725.

1955

The States voted in favour of buying local property belonging to the British War Department. For the money they were to get the Royal Engineers' store, workshop and yard at La Collette, the workshops at South Hill, the whole of Fort Regent, housing at South Hill, Green Street and Havre des Pas and a number of other areas.

The price being asked by the British Government was £40,000 and for once the States did not look the gift horse in the mouth.

The Fort was used by local merchants for storing coal, potatoes and wine, as well as confiscated derelict vehicles, for many years while a decision on its future use was awaited.

1981

Jersey was blacked out as the result of an Island-wide power cut. A fault in the switching mechanisms caused the turbines to shut down when they could not meet the required load. Parts of St Helier were without electricity for only ten minutes but it was nearly 1½ hours before the last sub-station was brought back on line. Various emergency generators at the airport and Hospital were used and firemen had to rescue residents of de Quetteville Court who had had the misfortune to be in the lift when the power failed.

04 February

1903

An article appearing in the national newspaper the *Daily Mail* on this day drew attention to the growing local hostility towards compulsory military service. Jersey law made every male aged between 16 and 60 liable to service and some local businesses were being sold or closed down due to the proprietors being called up. The States decided to look into the situation.

1910

A reward was offered by the family of Joe Picot, who had disappeared ten days earlier. They feared that 'in his wanderings he may have met with a mishap' and the notice promised that anyone recovering his body would receive a reward of £5.

1915

The St Brelade Fire Brigade held their fourteenth annual general meeting. The Brigade was funded by subscription and it was reported that the organisation was in an efficient state, having just acquired a cart to carry their hose. The treasurer announced a balance of £35 17s in hand, although the cost of the hose cart would reduce those funds.

The fire engine had originally been housed at St Aubin's harbour by the Piers and Harbours Committee for use on the ships but during the past half a century it had never been used. So it was given to the parish on the condition that they maintained it and this ancient machine was the centre around which the St Brelade Brigade had been formed.

1932

The La Moye Golf Course club house was destroyed by fire. The timber and corrugated iron structure did not last long, with just the ladies' room left standing. The one casualty was the club cat, which suffocated. The fire brigade seemed to be getting the blaze under control when their water supply failed, dooming the club house. It was estimated that the damage would cost about £2,000 to repair and it caused considerable disruption to club members.

05 February

1624

On this day a Jersey court condemned smoking as a great abuse.

1904

St Helier Vingtenier C J Le Feuvre left the Island without permission, an offence in itself. And when officials looked into Le Feuvre's affairs they found that he had absconded with nearly £800. Before departing he had locked and screwed his office door closed and the safe, which had been left open, contained only a bag with 40 farthings and one half penny in it.

A warrant for Le Feuvre's arrest was issued and Scotland Yard were alerted. A Parish Assembly decided to offer a £50 reward, with 'wanted' posters being circulated to every police station in the United Kingdom, as well as to ports in France and America.

Three weeks after his disappearance a female of Le Feuvre's acquaintance also left Jersey and was secretly trailed with the aid of Scotland Yard. After a number of train journeys she led police to Le Feuvre, who was arrested on a station platform.

1938

Two boys, aged 17 and 16, had stolen a number of cars over the previous weeks, driving them around until the petrol ran out. However, after a high speed chase around town, the police, in a commandeered doctor's car, caught the pair, who now faced the Magistrate. One mother told how her lad earned 23/6 at Allix's quarry and she gave him 5 shillings a week pocket money. The Magistrate was aghast, telling her that 'five shillings a week for a boy was ridiculous'. The other father blamed his son's lapse on reading books and, in fact, was unaware he could drive.

1951

An Anson carrying the Island's newspapers crashed on landing at St Peter's Airport. The aircraft overshot the runway and came to rest, without its undercarriage, on the southern boundary. Amazingly both pilot and radio operator escaped without injury.

06 February

1905

While returning to his farm, Mr Le Brun's horse bolted, taking the attached cart with it, and headed down St John's Road. The horse, in a state of panic, was unable to take the bend and instead ended up descending the 66 steps that lead to Queen's Road.

Amazingly both horse and cart were relatively unharmed, as was Mr Manning who, ascending the steps at the time, was forced to scale the wall to escape.

The event was recorded with illustrations that were later reproduced as postcards.

1933

A plot of land in Green Street was up for sale by auction. The large site was at that time a fruit garden. With few, if any building restrictions at this time, it was normal practice to buy a field and cover it with houses.

This particular parcel of land, between Rus-in-Urbe and Rockford, was in a convenient location and expected to fetch a good price. Bidding started at £200 and increased in jumps of £50. However the bidding stopped at £400, below the reserve, so George D Laurens retained the land.

1939

Jersey suffered a spate of sudden deaths with four post-mortems being reported on this day. Firstly a small boy had been accidentally killed by his father with a stable fork. William Glasgow had died suddenly in The Glen, Beaumont.

Thomas Le Cappelain died of his injuries, having been knocked down by a Lillywhite's Laundry van at St Aubin, and finally Edward Forster, a well-known stevedore, had collapsed and died. None of the incidents were connected but it did mean that the court had to deal with four different inquests at the same time

07 February

1644

It was the time of the English Civil War and on this day the Earl of Marlborough arrived in Jersey to consult with Sir George de Carteret over plans to conquer Guernsey on behalf of the Royalists. Jersey was at this time held for the Royalists, while Guernsey was Cromwellian.

1911

The States debated a proposition to alter the electoral law. Deputy Bois of St Saviour proposed outlawing the practice of giving refreshments to voters either before, during or after an election. Most Members were in favour of the bill. Deputy Crill of St Clement caused amusement by referring to the practice as a 'parochial fête'. It was also noted that these 'fêtes' were only held in country parishes. Deputy Cory suggested that all public houses should be closed on election day. It was pointed out by one long-standing Member that in the past banners reading 'Vote for ... and cheap beer' were not uncommon. The States decided to table the matter.

1914

The vraicing dates for the coming season were set in the Royal Court. The Bailiff proposed that 9th March be set for the winter harvest and was astonished when all the Constables agreed. This had apparently never happened before. The summer harvest was then agreed as 20th July. Vraic cutting on the east coast was to take place on 20th April and 7th May.

1950

An Irish motor coaster, the *Killurin*, was sighted among rocks off Noirmont Point by two fishermen. Seeing the vessel in trouble they set off in their boat and upon arrival at the scene picked up three survivors. A little while later the lifeboat pulled another three people from the sea, one of whom died before reaching harbour. A further search recovered the body of the ship's master but at least one crew member was never found.

08 February

1900

A move to have the English language adopted for use in the States was rejected. However an amendment allowing the use of English as an option in States' debates was passed by 26 votes to 15. A week earlier Deputy Renouf had tried to speak in English in the States' chamber which had not been allowed.

1923

New speed restrictions were adopted by the States. The new law stated that char-a-bancs, omnibuses and motor lorries were not to travel at more than six miles per hour when in town. Outside the limits of town, 10 miles per hour was the maximum speed allowed. The Constable of St Helier said, when questioned, that the restrictions did not apply to motor bikes as when they went too fast they usually came into contact with objects heavier than themselves and came off second best. Jurat Le Boutillier said that even three miles per hour might be dangerous and went on to say that the proposal was absolutely absurd. However, his fellow members disagreed and the proposition was adopted.

1938

Jurat Norman informed the States that there had been no further cases of foot and mouth disease and that his Agriculture Committee intended to remove some of the restrictions that had been imposed. However, this announcement proved to be premature when later in the day another outbreak was confirmed in Trinity. Stanley Le Brun's farm at Alfriston House had to be sealed off and his live stock destroyed. The stables were disinfected and the 'stay in' orders, whereby animals had to remain in their stables, were again imposed.

1944

American Joseph Kerbs had been piloting his single seater fighter when engine problems forced him to make a crash landing. Captured, he was taken to the town prison before being transferred to the German hospital at the Merton Hotel, where his minor injuries were treated. He was later removed to a POW camp in France.

09 February

1649

Sir John Poulet brought the news to Jersey that King Charles I had been beheaded. The information was met with disbelief but confirmed by letter on 16th February.

1924

The suspension of payments and the suicide of the Banque Massiot's director caused great loss for some Islanders. The French bank, which had a Jersey branch, went into liquidation on this day and a number of hoteliers and farmers lost a considerable sum in the crash. It was rumoured that one local farmer had lost £4,000 and his daughters their savings too.

1931

Emile Pierre Frigot appeared in the Police Court after the St Lawrence Parish authorities grew weary of supporting his seven young children. When Frigot's wife had drowned in St Ouen's Bay the parish had supported the children, with their father agreeing to contribute £2 per month towards their upkeep.

However, only £2 had ever been received from Frigot, while the St Lawrence rate payers had spent £253 over the years. The court had little sympathy with Frigot's claim of illness and said he could have a fortnight without worries, sentencing him to two weeks hard labour.

1938

Jerseywoman Jean Gilbert came fourth in the high diving competition in the Sydney Empire Games. She was following in the wake of Jersey's Dot Macready, who held the title but was not defending it at the championships. High diving was very popular in the Island in the first half of the 1900s, with the Havre des Pas bathing pool being the centre of activity.

10 February

1679

After successful lobbying by Sir Thomas Morgan, the States ordered the local militia to wear scarlet coats. During his time in office Sir Thomas had completely reorganised the Island's militia and defences in readiness for the always expected French assault.

1736

Philippe Falle, having previously given 2,000 books to start a public library, now donated £300 towards the building in which they would be housed.

1848

Heavy rains caused flooding and structural damage. A large wall owned by Mr Benest, the Constable of St Brelade, collapsed. It fell onto an old house, also knocking it down and damaging an adjoining property. No one was injured

1940

Arthur Woodhall was prosecuted at an Assize trial for publishing blasphemous libel. The case concerned a photograph of Woodhall which had been drawn on to make it look like he had been crucified. The photograph had been seen by a passport official, legally qualifying it as publication, and Woodhall had been arrested. Although he had not defaced the photograph himself, the prosecution claimed he was guilty for not destroying it. After 20 minutes the jury returned with a unanimous guilty verdict. There being no precedent for such a case, a sentence of one month's imprisonment was passed.[2]

1945

After the Normandy landings in 1944, the Island's meagre fuel supply was cut off and the bus service finally halted due to lack of fuel. Once off the road, buses which had been converted to run on charcoal were secretly changed back so that a bus service could resume as soon as possible after the war. This they did on May 12th.

---

[2] See 9th November for further details.

11 February

1650

On this day Charles II gave George de Carteret Smith's Islands off the coast of Virginia. Sir George renamed them New Jersey and shortly afterwards sent a party off to colonise the islands. However on their first day out the ship was captured by a Parliamentary privateer and taken to the Isle of Wight. That group of islands are nothing to do with what we now know as New Jersey.

1852

A powerful lobby of Englishmen were again pressing for the British Parliament to exert its authority (as they claimed) over Jersey. On this day the Privy Council issued orders for the Island to establish a police court, a petty debts court and paid police in the town. This so enraged Jersey's politicians and people that the Rose and Laurel parties, normally the bitterest of enemies, united in their refusal. After twenty months of negotiating the Council revoked its orders and Jersey implemented most of the Privy Council's original instructions voluntarily.

1876

Five years after deciding to build a grand new harbour the States decided to abandon the project. The breakwater from Elizabeth Castle had been built but the ¾-mile long quay from La Collette had caused problems. In 1874 200 feet of pier had been washed away. It was rebuilt but the following year the tide claimed another 300 feet. Further destruction the next winter caused the States to write off the £160,000 cost and implement dredging instead.

1967

Having conducted an opinion poll on what the recently introduced lottery's profits should be spent on, the *Jersey Evening Post* published its results. Topping the list was the rundown Fort Regent, followed closely by the public's desire for an indoor swimming pool. Third on the list was the restoration of La Rocco Tower, which was in an extremely poor state, the tower's surrounding wall having been breached.

12 February

1897

The steam ship *John Grafton* hit rocks in fog off the south coast and began taking on water. Fortunately a local fisherman was nearby and boarded the vessel. Using his knowledge of the area the ship was able to be beached off St Aubin's Fort.

The 158 ft long vessel, with its cargo of 500 tons of coal destined for the Jersey Gas Light Co, had been awaiting a pilot to navigate her through Jersey's treacherous waters, but she had struck the Pignouet Rock first.

The following day the coal was loaded onto barges and the pilot had been suspended.

1929

Eight degrees of frost and high easterly winds aided the snow in bringing Jersey to a halt. Rail and bus services ceased, with drifts over 6 ft deep reported around the Island.

1929

Lady de Bathe died of influenza in Monaco on this day. She was better known as Lillie Langtry, the daughter of the local Reverend Le Breton. Her body was returned to Jersey where she was buried in her father's old church yard of St Saviour.

1944

John Helier Lander died, aged 76. Lander was one of the finest painters Jersey has produced. Lillie Langtry gave him his first set of paints, an activity disapproved of by his parents. Considering it a waste of time, it was strictly forbidden for young Lander to paint, but he continued secretly.

At fifteen he was apprenticed to a watchmaker. However once his father found people were buying his son's art, the situation changed. Studying in England, John Lander went on to paint many of the leading people of the day.

13 February

1767

A permanent Customs Service was set up in Jersey. Islanders had a long tradition of smuggling goods between their home port, France and England. Avoiding duties and supplying scarce commodities had proved a profitable occupation for centuries and despite this new inconvenience, the local people continued their illicit activities as usual.

1794

Despite the dangers of attack from French vessels, a weekly ship service to Weymouth was started. Two Post Office packets, the *Royal Charlotte* and the *Rover*, cutters of about 80 tons, began a mailboat tradition that continued for nearly two centuries.

1845

The States bought three manual fire engines to be sited at the Island's major ports of St Helier, St Aubin and Gorey.

1848

Firearms were more prevalent in Jersey in the 1840s than they are today. On this day two men were approached as they walked along St Saviour's Road. A stranger had climbed over a roadside fence, pointed a gun at one of the walkers and shot him in the head. The attacker then escaped over the fence the way he had come. Fortunately the victim's head wound was superficial but calls for action to be taken were made as it was 'the third time that people have been shot at'.

1902

Louis Gustave Galliou was brought before the Police Court, charged with threatening Jean Gion with a revolver. While aboard the *SS Margaret* en route from St Brieuc to St Helier, Galliou had approached Gion and threatened to shoot him if Gion did not hand over his cap. The ship's mate later confiscated the gun after Galliou shot at another passenger. Found guilty, Galliou was sentenced to 15 days imprisonment with hard labour.

14 February

1254
On this day Prince Edward, son of Henry III, was granted the Lordship of the Isles. Edward sent two Bailiffs to run the islands for him, one in Guernsey, the other in Jersey. On becoming King, he gave the title and privileges to his friend Otho de Grandison. Otho held the lordship for more than 50 years but despite drawing taxes from the islands he was nearly ninety before he bothered to visit Jersey.

1934
Two motorcycles crashed into each other, both riders being killed. Reginald Brisset and William Sewell were travelling along St Aubin's Road near Westmount at 2 pm. The road was wide and empty and the conditions were dry, yet the bikes had met head on. The only reason suggested for the collision was that a Jersey Airways aeroplane had taken off from the beach and perhaps both riders had been distracted by it.

1965
Rock climbers discovered a previously unknown cave on the north coast. The chamber was 20 ft above high water and contained a number of stalactites. The historical importance of the cave was realised as it was obvious that when it had originally been excavated the sea levels were much higher. Subsequent excavations of the area revealed many interesting aspects of Jersey's prehistory.

1978
The States voted in favour of redeveloping the General Hospital. The £9 million scheme was due to take eight years but Senator Dick Shenton said that the final cost was more likely to be £14 million. Senator Ralph Vibert warned of a slow drift to bankruptcy, although some four years later he claimed Jersey had money coming out of its ears.

15 February

1794

Jersey's first Post Office opened in Hue Street with Charles William Le Geyt as postmaster. Prior to this, ships' captains had carried letters to the mainland in a private capacity.

1910

The price of wine, spirits and tobacco went up when the States increased the tax on them. Despite accusations of taxing the poor to pay for the maintenance of the roads for wealthy motorcar drivers, the measure was accepted by 30 votes to 15. At the same time those under 16 years would no longer be allowed to purchase tobacco.

1974

It was announced that a new secondary school was to be built at La Rocque in St Clement. The Education Committee had been looking for a site in the east of the Island to provide for the area's expanding population. It was hoped it would open in September of the following year, with a second section ready a year later.

1978

The Attorney-General, Vernon Tomes, made it clear that Jersey would have to give up birching. The Court of Human Rights was hearing a case against the practice involving the Isle of Man and although technically Jersey could still use the punishment, realistically it could not. It was stated that if the Island's authorities were to resist banning the birch, Jersey's independent status would be at risk, as Jersey had signed up to the European Convention on Human Rights 25 years earlier through the British government.

1980

It was announced that a tender of £964,158.51 had been accepted for the construction of a boat marina in the harbour between the Albert Quay and the New North Quay, a plan the States had approved in 1977. The facility would have 370 berths and it was hoped that the first yachts would be using it by the following year.

16 February

1643

During the English Civil War Sir Philippe de Carteret went to the States of Jersey with a commission from the King appointing him Lieutenant-Governor. Sir Philippe was an adamant Royalist at a time when the Parliamentary cause was increasing its support in the Island.

1797

Revolutionary pamphlets inciting the poor to rise up against Jersey's ruling class were being distributed across the Island and a worried States banned meetings that were likely to disrupt public order. Despite a £500 reward being offered for the disclosure of the ring leaders, the population neither informed nor revolted.

1875

The *Havre* was said to be the smallest and most uncomfortable steamer servicing the islands. She was 184 ft long and her 21 ft paddles could push her through the water at a speed of 13 knots. But the vessel only had to be endured by travellers for five years before she was wrecked off Guernsey on the Platte Bou rocks. All aboard were rescued, however, the captain was suspended for 12 months following an enquiry into the incident.

1907

At a sitting of the Royal Court the States' decision to abolish public executions was confirmed. The law was to come into effect from 18 February, the day before the execution of Thomas Connan for the murder of his brother-in-law.

1915

Posters were issued by the Town Hall, warning of possible air raids. They depicted both enemy and friendly craft, the idea being that Islanders familiarise themselves with the shapes. If then, at some later date, locals saw an airship overhead, they would know if it was wise to stand beneath it. As well as the silhouettes of zeppelins and other airships, aeroplanes and seaplanes were also depicted, although at this time planes did not have the range of airships.

17 February

1649

Having received news of King Charles I's execution, the Prince of Wales was proclaimed King in the Royal Square. Parliamentary forces ruled England and even Guernsey no longer recognised the office of King. Jersey was the first and, for a time, the only region of his realm to acknowledge King Charles II's accession to the throne.

Charles II started to count the years of his reign from this point, a fact that caused confusion for some historians. When on documents he wrote 'in the fourth year of my reign' it might have been dated well before his reign officially started in England.

1927

A proposition went before the States for the protection of wild birds. It was intended that rather than listing protected species, the unprotected birds would be listed. During the debate Jurat Lempriere noted, jokingly, that no protection existed for the crapaud and although they destroyed many pests, they were fast disappearing.

1927

At 11.20 pm the Island was hit by a severe earthquake. Although no one was harmed and there was no major damage, it did cause considerable alarm. Residents of the Grève d'Azette area took refuge on the beach, only returning to their homes when satisfied that the danger had passed.

1948

The States Gallery was packed by eager Islanders keen to see the electoral reform debate. It was decided that the States should consist of 12 Senators, 12 Connetables and 28 Deputies, all of whom were to be elected by popular vote.

This meant that the Jurats, Rectors and the Vicomte would cease to sit in the Chamber. The Dean, however, would be allowed to speak in the States, but not vote.

18 February

1539

On this day a man was fined for calling another a 'Normand et fils de Normand (a Norman and son of a Norman).

1683

Sir Edouard de Carteret died on this day while visiting St Ouen's Manor. Tradition claims that arrangements had been made to bury him in St Ouen's Church but, as the procession was about to start, thunder frightened the horses drawing the hearse. They bolted and sped off with the body. The mourners, who followed the stampede, found the hearse and horses stopped outside Trinity Church. It was considered a sign the Sir Edouard wished to be buried in his home parish. A new grave was dug and he was interred there.

1794

The *Royal Charlotte*, a cutter captained by James Wood, arrived in Jersey, heralding the start of a regular mail service to the islands. The 85 miles from Weymouth took 16 hours in good weather. Originally the ships sailed on Thursdays, but after a request from the States this was changed to Saturdays.

1939

Gathering a bit of vraic for the garden proved quite an adventure when the van belonging to A H Copp Ltd, of Waterloo Street, got stuck. It had been driven onto the beach between First Tower and West Park. However, the van soon became stuck in the soft sand and before it could be extracted, the tide came in and claimed it. When the water receded a lorry tried to tow the van out but it also became stuck. After some difficulty both vehicles were removed from the beach, with Copp's van comparatively undamaged.

1970

It was announced that Portelet holiday camp had been sold for £200,000. The camp, which had opened in 1925, had been owned and run by Major Oxenden. Shield Investments Ltd had bought the property but it was not known who was behind the company.

19 February

1881

The passengers on board the *Caledonia* must have been readying themselves to disembark as they steamed towards St Helier harbour en route from Guernsey. However they were destined to leave the vessel without quite reaching the quay. Striking Oyster Rock just outside the harbour, the *Caledonia* sank. All aboard were rescued, as were the ship's valuable engines, although they weren't brought ashore until six months later.

1897

A French couple, Ange Moulin and Jeanne Marie Rault, appeared before the Constable of St Helier on this day, because of their elopement. Moulin had allegedly enticed the young Rault from her home in St Brieuc some days earlier and they were being pursued by the French authorities. Having been discovered staying in a house in Hilgrove Lane, they were taken into custody and their fate was in the hands of the Constable. He decided to set Moulin free, while Rault was sent home to France.

1907

Thomas Connan was executed at 8 am within the prison walls after admitting to the murder of his brother-in-law.[3] The 29 year old Frenchman was hanged, dying instantly. Just before the sentence was carried out, Connan made a statement insisting that he had beaten Pierre Le Guen to death with a rock at the instigation of his sister.

1974

Jersey was declared an infected area when foot and mouth disease was confirmed. It was the first case for 17 years and affected ten cows on a St Ouen farm. Dogs were ordered to be kept on a leash and all animal movements were embargoed. The infected cattle were destroyed and most farmers sealed off their property.

---

[3] See 19th July for further details.

20 February

1934

The States debated a report on tourism. It was noted that each tourist was worth £1 of revenue and visitors should therefore be encouraged. Tourists also brought employment and although it meant crowded buses in the summer, without the visitors there would have been no bus service.

It was said that agriculture would receive £8,435 in States aid this year and tourism needed help too. Money was needed for an advertising campaign and the House was told that this was 'an art in which the service of experts had to be employed'.

A question of class was raised a number of times, with speakers concerned about the type of visitor to be attracted, and there was also concern over the lack of domestic servants in the Island.

When it came to the vote on whether to spend money on the advertising, it was tied, with 20 for and 20 against. The President used his casting vote against, explaining that ratepayers were able to vote money from the parish rates for advertising the Island and the bulk of them had declined to do so. He therefore had no intention of forcing them to pay.

1969

The Jersey Evening Post reported that there were 1,200 applications for Westaway shoes. A trust had been set up in 1901, with the interest to pay for shoes for primary school children. The effects of inflation had meant that this year only 350 pairs of shoes would be given out, despite the great demand. One aspect of the trust which upset some people was that only Protestant children were eligible, yet it was the Catholics who had more children.

1980

Gerry Cottle's Circus was in town - well, in the Gloucester Hall at Fort Regent. Today was the first performance, which included four Indian elephants, as well as lions and other animals. The Jersey Society for the Prevention of Cruelty to Animals had campaigned against the visit and called on Islanders to boycott the show. However, attendance was good, with queues forming for tickets.

21 February

1910

Mr G C Godfray appeared before the Royal Court, accused of libelling the States. Two weeks earlier, on the day of the election for Constable of St Helier, posters had appeared throughout the town. They had read 'Jerseymen insist on the laws of the Island being justly observed and protest against the outrageous decision of the States in the Mirehouse case' and 'Elect honest and independent men to represent you and who will draw the attention of the proper authority to the gross violation of the laws'.

Despite claiming privilege and presenting a robust defence, the court fined Godfray £10 and costs.

1939

Four teenage boys appeared in the Police Court, charged with a shooting offence. They had shot their airgun at a bus being driven by Alfred Tilling near Haute Croix and had then cycled off towards Queen's Road. A motorist had given chase and caught two of the culprits but they gave him false names and addresses.

Pc Shenton then tracked the boys down, and also another of their victims, Andrè Goaziou, who had been shot in the ear. Two of the boys were discharged with a warning, but the other pair were sentenced to six strokes of the birch. The fathers of the boys were allowed to mete out the punishment, with a warning from the Magistrate not to overdo it.

1949

A house was demolished in an explosion heard over the whole Island. At first it was thought that a German landmine had destroyed the St Brelade property and a number of cars. Mr Nicolle and his wife, although shocked, were unhurt and had been able to escape from their home before caught by the fire that had followed.

However two weeks later Mr Nicolle was arrested. It appears that a garden hose had been used to bypass the gas meter and this money saving fraud now proved to be very costly.

22 February

1902

A two to three week old baby was found abandoned on the hospital doorstep. Mr T J de Gruchy had found the child when he answered the doorbell, but apart from the baby boy, no one else was in sight. The child appeared to have been well cared for, was dressed and had a bottle of warm milk. He had been loosely tied in sacking and a sheet of brown paper had been laid down before the infant had been placed on the step.

1911

There was gold fever in the air. The valuable metal had been discovered some weeks before on land in Waterworks Valley but now the secret was out. The cotil on which the ore was found belonged to Mr F Garnier and when a tree had been uprooted a glittering substance had been discovered. A sample was sent to London and excavations were begun even before the assayers confirmed that it was indeed gold. A report at the time reminded readers that a seam of mica had been discovered when the Albert Pier's construction had begun and this had turned out to be fool's gold.

1927

Tim must have been a much loved cat, for when he went missing his owner, Mrs Briard, offered a £2 reward for his return. The advert appearing on this day describing the feline said he had been missing from 42 Roseville Street since 5th February. Had you found the cat and claimed your reward, £2 could have bought you eight pairs of silk, ladderproof knickers, a case of burgundy or two pairs of leather shoes.

1969

A milk shortage in Jersey caused queues in the Milk Marketing Boards market shop. The decision was made to import 3,000 gallons from England, which was to be added to local supplies.

23 February

1830

The Channel Islands paddle steamer, the *Meteor*, struck rocks off Portland on this day. The ship was the third of its kind to carry mail to the islands and had entered service less than two years earlier. The 190 ton vessel with 60 horsepower engines had previously run from Lisbon and Ireland but took over the Channel crossing from April 1828. On the night in question she struck the Church Ope Rocks in heavy seas. All those aboard were rescued. However, at low tide hundreds of people looted the stricken vessel and the now stripped *Meteor* became a total loss.

1838

This day is credited with being the one on which the Mont Ubé dolmen was discovered. Having survived over 5,000 years, this passage grave was now being used as a pig sty. Ten years later the capstones were broken up for use as building material. The uprights remained and can still be found above the woods to the east of Samarès Manor.

1865

The area known as People's Park at West Park was purchased from Francis Godfray on this day. The parish of St Helier put £2,000 towards it, with the £1,000 balance being given by the Lieutenant-Governor, the Bailiff and the Jurats.

1917

It was the time of the Great War and the units of the Jersey Royal Militia, who had kept watch over the Island's coastline since July 1914, were demobilised. The cost of the operation had been £99,356. In its place it was announced that all men between the ages of 18 and 41 were required to do compulsory military service. A Royal Jersey garrison battalion was to be formed now the militia were demobilised. Men who had been turned down on medical grounds were to be re-examined.

24 February

1768

Throughout history, Jersey has either led the way or been the last to fall in line. The Jersey Chamber of Commerce was established on this day, the first in the British Isles.

1902

An advert offering a reward of £10 appeared in the *Jersey Evening Post*. It stated '£10 reward for information that will convict and bring to justice the person who at the end of October and the beginning of November stole and carried away every stone of a granite built house, with two gables and two sexagon tall chimneys, which till then had stood in perfect condition on the property adjoining the Greenville Station, on the Corbière Railway'. Thieves were obviously more ambitious and daring a century ago.

1903

A St Helier Parish Assembly addressed the subject of unemployment. The Constable said that there were scores of good men out of employment and that he had put them to work planting trees on the slopes of Westmount. He was concerned as it was parish money being spent and he wished the assembly to know the situation. The men were being paid a starvation wage of between 9 and 11s a week. The parish, first having questioned whether the unemployed were local and from St Helier, accepted the Constable's decision to employ the men but it was suggested that they might be put to use cleaning the roads of mud.

1989

Senator The Reverend Peter Manton stated that he would not be resigning from the States. The former Rector of St John had been the subject of a police investigation involving sexual impropriety. Reverend Manton said he would be withdrawing from his priestly duties. However, over the following months and after a series of public meetings and court appearances, his position became quite untenable.

25 February

1794

The 4,000 Catholic priests who had been expelled from revolutionary France were only allowed to live in Jersey providing they did not attempt to make converts. On this day the States made it official and as the priests had nowhere else to go all but one obeyed the conditions. The one was a local man converted to Catholicism while in France. Mattieu de Gruchy owned land and didn't think the rules should apply to him. Complaints were made after a number of girls converted and he was hurriedly removed to England to the relief of the desperate refugee priests.

1798

Thomas Pickstock, a local man, was captain of the *Herald*. As she was cruising off the French coast three French privateers attacked. The battle went on for three hours with the *Herald* heavily out-gunned. But due to skilful seamanship, the French vessels were forced to withdraw, their hulls shattered and rigging damaged. There were thirty killed and wounded on the French side, whereas Captain Pickstock had not lost a man. That night a smaller boat attempted to take the *Herald* by stealth. The twenty-two men who attempted to board her went to the bottom, along with their boat.

1876

The States ordered all Jersey's old copper and bronze coins to be called in. It was decided to issue a new set of small denomination coins to come into line with England. Until this point, there were 13 Jersey pennies to the shilling whereas in Britain there were only 12.

1970

The tunnel under Fort Regent opened on this day. Costing an estimated £400,000, the project had been instigated nine years earlier. The Bailiff performed the obligatory ceremonial duties after the tunnel's vital statistics had been given. It was 830 feet long, 29 feet wide, 22 feet high, 50,000 tons of stone had been removed from under the Fort and 4,000 cubic yards of concrete used.

26 February

1661

Sir Philippe de Carteret, whose family had greatly assisted Charles II during the Civil War, was appointed Bailiff. At about the same time the group who had signed Charles I's death warrant were imprisoned in Mont Orgueil Castle, where they remained until their deaths. Some survived over fifteen years, until eventually succumbing to the confined conditions.

1946

The Parish of St Brelade accepted the States' offer to sell them the Terminus Hotel for use as a parish hall. The sum being asked was £2,000, which nearly all at the parish assembly agreed was a bargain. One dissenting voice belonged to Mr Cox, who claimed that the parish did not need a hall, that it would cost a fortune to convert and even more to maintain. Two thousand pounds was the predicted cost of converting it into a hall and offices, Mr Fiott saying that even if it were £3,000, it would still be cheap. The terms of the sale were that it was to be held in perpetuity by the parish, there were to be no sublets and an office was to be provided for States weighbridge officials. When it came to the vote, despite Mr Cox's vocal opposition, the proposition was carried by 26 votes to four.

1968

Jersey's first multi-storey car park opened for business in Green Street. It contained 600 parking spaces and was part of the plan to solve some of St Helier's traffic problems. Another two multi-storeys were to be built and each would cost around £200,000.

1978

Charles Dupré was appointed a Knight of St Gregory, the first Jerseyman to receive the honour, which is the highest papal award for services to the Roman Catholic Church. After the mass during which the medal was presented, a vin d'honneur was held by St Helier's Constable in Dupré's honour. The Bishop of Portsmouth, who had officiated at the ceremony, said that he expected only one such award to be presented in his diocese each year.

27 February

1897

A French ragman called Auguste Le Pavoux was arrested for stealing hay. Mr Laurens of St John had noticed that some of his hay was missing and had informed Centenier Le Couteur. The Centenier did not need to be Sherlock Holmes to follow the trail of dried grass which lead to La Tombette, St Mary, and Le Pavoux. Footprints found at the scene of the crime matched the boots of the Frenchman. Being a cross-border incident, St Mary police arrested Le Pavoux and charges were brought. This was not the first time hay had gone missing, as it was reported that several robberies of hay and roots had recently occurred in St John.

1905

Sixteen thousand ormers were declared unfit for human consumption and it was forbidden for them to be landed in Jersey. The *Six Soeurs*, a French fishing boat, had arrived too late for the market. So her cargo of ormers had stayed on board over the weekend. A large number of the fish had died by the time they came to be unloaded and the States vet, Mr Parker, condemned them after an inspection. They were banned from being off-loaded and a policeman was positioned by La Folie to see that the order was observed.

1946

Alexander Coutanche, the Island's wartime Bailiff, was knighted at Buckingham Palace. He had been sworn in as civil governor just before the Germans had arrived and had thus been given the task of surrendering the Island. Coutanche and the other States members, who acted as a buffer between the German army and the civilian population, were sometimes criticised for their compliance with the occupying force's orders. However, at the time they were unable to defend or explain their actions. Only when all the documentation is published will there be a true insight into the government Lord Coutanche presided over.

28 February

1660

A directive issued on this day by the Lords of the Council stated that no stranger other than British subjects should be allowed to set up shop in Jersey.

1912

Jersey's new lifeboat, the *William Henry Wilkinson*, was launched for inspection. At 10.30 am the maroon was fired, calling the lifeboatmen to action. And under the gaze of Mr Foote, the national inspector, and a large section of the public, the carriage was run down to the water's edge. Five minutes later, with the crew at their oars, the boat was launched. The *William Henry Wilkinson* performed well in the trials in St Aubin's Bay but concern was voiced about the need to lengthen the slipway and to keep it clear of pebbles.

1950

The States fixed 9th May, Liberation Day, as a public holiday. A number of Members had suggested that it should be on a Monday or Thursday, in the interests of commerce. However Senator Collas said that as 9th May was the actual day of the Liberation, that was how it should remain, sentiments that carried the day.

1987

Rowena Barthorp and Diana Cumberlege went for a horse ride on the beach in Grouville, becoming the focus of the international press. The two women, atop Dangerman and Monty, set off in misty conditions and became lost in what had become thick fog. Disorientated and surrounded by the incoming tide, the pair were fortunate enough to come across Seymour Tower, a coastal defence about a mile off the south-east coast. The horses were able to climb up the steep steps to safety, but it was later discovered that they could not walk down them. It was only after heavy machinery had built a massive ramp out of sand that, after 30 hours, the animals were able to descend. The whole operation was covered by a large press contingent and the story travelled the world.

29 February

1904

Helier Jenne and his employee, Jean Le Cosquet, were in court, charged with cruelty. The court heard how Mr A P Brophy, an officer of the Society for the Prevention of Cruelty to Animals had gone to Jenne's stables to examine a horse, having had information about the animal's state.

Beneath the saddle was a large sore which must have been open for over three weeks. The horse had been harnessed to a cart loaded with 22 cwt of cargo and the beast's general health was very poor.

When asked by the Magistrate if Jenne considered the animal fit to work, Jenne replied that he had seen 'horses worse than that'. The Magistrate retorted that Jenne 'must have been to the museum and seen skeletons'. Both the accused were sentenced to fines of £2 or eight days imprisonment.

Jenne paid his fine, while Le Cosquet went to gaol.

1916

The subject of banning the importation of cattle and fodder was raised in the States. For many years the importation of cows into the Island had been illegal. Now the Piers and Harbours Committee had banned the importation of fodder from England as well.

England had recently suffered a number of outbreaks of foot and mouth disease and Jersey's authorities were determined that it should not cross the Channel.

Their measures proved successful.

1964

The Maternity Hospital had their busiest day for some time, with nine babies being born. The three boys and six girls started arriving at 2.30 am, the last being delivered at 9.30 pm that evening. All were said to be well, but they now had to wait four years for their first birthday.

01 March

1483

Edward IV and Louis XI agreed that if there were to be another war between their two countries, the Channel Islands were to be neutral. The following year Pope Sixtus IV enforced this agreement with a bull (a decree) declaring that anyone who disobeyed the agreement would be eternally damned and have their goods confiscated. This privileged state of neutrality lasted over 200 years, halting raids and allowing commerce in the Island to flourish.

1631

Seven years after a Jersey court condemned smoking, the Privy Council banned the planting of tobacco in the Island. Its reasons were that it was injurious to the morals of the people.

1873

Strong winds and a spring tide combined to cause serious damage to the railway line between St Helier and St Aubin. At Millbrook, and particularly at Beaumont, undermining of the track had dropped the rails by three feet. Services were transferred to horse-drawn omnibuses for several days while repairs were carried out.

1939

A direct telephone link with France became operational today. Prior to this, all calls to the continent were routed via London. A cable laid for use during the Great War had now been reconditioned and enabled Islanders to get through to Rennes.

1957

The first pedestrian crossing in the Channel Islands was inaugurated on this day. St Helier Constable Mr F W Clarke was the first to push the button, thus changing the traffic lights at Snow Hill from green to red. It was hoped that the new crossing would prove useful in the tourist season and it had been pointed out that crossings were already in use in large towns on the mainland.

02 March

1915

'The proudest day in our history' was the headline about the departure of the Jersey Overseas Contingent. An enormous crowd had gathered to see off the enthusiastic young men as they boarded the mailboat. Bands played, flags flew and people cheered. The flags at the pier head were dipped in salute as the *Ibex* passed through and cannons were fired. The horrors of the First World War had not yet been reported and the event was viewed as an exciting adventure.

1922

The States were again debating education in the Island when the Constable of St Helier asked that free education be abolished. He said that if parents had to pay they would be more likely to ensure that their children attended school. The Rector of St Saviour agreed, saying that although he was in favour of compulsory education, he had never believed it should be free. One concern voiced was that if parents were charged, they would then want to know what the child had learned for that money. It was a close run thing, with the proposition finally losing by 18 votes to 21.

1959

For the first time myxomatosis was identified in the Island's rabbit population. The previous week a number of dead and dying rabbits had been found among the dunes in St Ouen. The carcasses had been sent to England for examination and on this day the presence of the disease was confirmed. It was believed that myxomatosis could wipe out the Island's rabbit population but, as in Alderney earlier in the decade, the rodents that survived proved to be immune to the virus.

1961

The States voted in favour of extending the 1954 Television Act to Jersey, allowing independent television to be broadcast locally. It was envisaged that a local TV company would be set up, both to make local programmes and to relay the ITV network's output to the Channel Islands.

03 March

1695

Jean Michelin, the French painter, was buried in St Helier on this day.

1799

Six men from the 85th Regiment attempted to escape to France while stationed near La Rocco, St Ouen, when the tower was being built. The potential deserters failed.

1832

A review of the Island's fortifications was ordered by the States. Advances in technology had made some of Jersey's defences obsolete and with the invention of steam ships, Jersey was more vulnerable than ever. The last of the coastal towers were now planned, these being shorter than the Martello towers and designed to carry large cannons. Kempt, Lewis, Victoria, La Collette and L'Etacq towers were constructed as a result.

1904

A fishing party of 'seventeen gentlemen' chartered the *Duke of Normandy* for a day's ormering. They travelled to the Minquiers on what was said to be an exceptionally low tide. As rocks that rarely saw the light of day were exposed, the catch was good and the size of shellfish caught large. Over 2,000 ormers were gathered and the only regret the party had of what had been a warm and sunny expedition was that no 'knight of the pencil' had accompanied them to record the day in sketch form.

1966

A British United Airways BAC 1-11 jet set a new record from Jersey to Gatwick. With thirty-two passengers aboard, the flight took just 34 minutes, the plane flying at an average of 418 miles per hour.

04 March

1902

Frenchman François Kerneff was in court, charged with being drunk in charge of a trap. Kerneff denied the charge, claiming that he had just fallen backwards by accident. A number of witnesses were called, all stating that the Frenchman had been drunk, and St Peter Vingtenier, W F d'Allain, had found Kerneff leaning against a wall in an inebriated state. A fine of £2 or two weeks in prison was sentenced. Drunkenness was prevalent at this time and cases of drunken riding of horses and bicycles and the driving of horse-drawn vehicles appeared in court most weeks, although it is said that people had to be in an extreme state before they were arrested.

1928

Quarryman Walter Audrain was killed in a fall at Ronez Quarry. It was common practice after blasting a rock face for men to climb over the cliff's edge, attached to ropes, to dislodge any loose rubble from the area. Audrain was in the process of swapping ropes while standing on what appeared to be a secure ledge. Unfortunately the granite crumbled and the young Jerseyman fell 180 ft to his death. An inquest the following day returned a verdict of accidental death.

1959

Sark's Royal coachman must have regretted travelling to the bustling metropolis of Jersey when he was robbed. The thieves stole his new raincoat, which he had just acquired from Burtons, £20 in cash and a package containing sausages and fish. Two young Irishmen were later arrested, the police becoming suspicious of the pair as one was wearing a brand new coat over extremely shabby clothes.

1961

Noel and Porter Ltd took first prize in the Bulb Growers Association window decorating competition. Most participating stores were in King Street, but a number of other shops entered into the spirit, with Midbay Stores, St Brelade, taking the second prize.

05 March

1664

On this day Sir George de Carteret presented Jersey with its first House of Correction. Sir George's generosity might be explained by the fact that in the same year he had been given the area in America he named New Jersey. A gift was also made to him of certain manors in Devon and Cornwall, as well as an area of Carolina and land in the Bahamas.

The House of Correction was intended for unlicensed beggars, drunks, all who refused to work for a reasonable wage and men capable of manual labour found working among women.

1882

Jersey's first English language newspaper was published on this day. As the number of English residents was rapidly increasing, their needs had to be catered for. The publishing industry was booming in Jersey and soon there were 10 weekly newspapers being printed in English, as well as all the French ones.

1949

The British Nationality Act was registered in the Royal Court. The law stated 'a citizen of the United Kingdom and colonies may, if on the ground of his connection with the Channel Islands or Isle of Man if he so desires, be known as a citizen of the United Kingdom, Islands and colonies'. This act, in effect, gave Islanders full British citizenship.

1964

The *Jersey Evening Post* reported that the parish of St Mary would not be entering a float in the Battle of Flowers. A meeting had been called to discuss the possibility of building a parochial exhibit. However, other than the idea's proposer and seconder, only the Constable and the parish hall caretaker bothered to attend. The four decided that they could not build the float on their own and the idea was abandoned.

06 March

1902

Cyril Le Marquand was born on this day. After leaving Victoria College, he worked for the family business, Le Marquand Brothers. Entering the States as a St Helier Deputy in 1948, he was one of eleven members of the newly formed Progressive Party to be elected. He is most widely remembered for his support of the introduction of social security in 1951. This new law was vigorously, and sometimes violently, opposed by the farming community, a community that Le Marquand came from and relied on as an animal feed and seed merchant. Many farmers stopped buying from his company but Le Marquand stood his ground and social security was introduced. After a long and vigorous political career, Le Marquand died in 1980, his name living on on one of the least attractive buildings in St Helier.

1906

An unfortunate case of mistaken identity led to the demise of a pair of prize-winning pigs. A local farmer had agreed to sell two pigs to a butcher. The butcher sent his men to collect the animals from the farm. Having found two pigs, they took them back to the butchers', where the animals were immediately turned into pork. When the farmer returned home, however, he discovered the mistake and hurried back to town. But he arrived too late to save his prize porkers. The unhappy farmer hoped to get substantial compensation for his loss by bringing a case before the court.

1915

Herbert John Le Moignan pleaded guilty before the Royal Court to charges of bigamy, forgery, robbery and false declaration of birth. Le Moignan had married Helen Pirouet in 1908. In 1914, under the name of Donald Labey, he had married Maria Hamon, registering her daughter as his legitimate child and obtaining £50 from her. When sentenced a week later, other offences were considered and the Bailiff told the prisoner that he was a lazy, good for nothing, hard-hearted man who had ruined two women and that he would be sentenced to penal servitude for three years and be fined £10.

07 March

1848

A lecture on astronomy was held at the Theatre, Royal Crescent, on this day. The lecture was illustrated by 'magnificent dissolving and moving orrery and diagrams, expressly prepared to explain the recent extraordinary discoveries in science'. The lecture would also explain 'the means by which the planet Neptune was discovered before it was seen'. And as well as 'the refutation of the nebular theory by means of the Earl of Roses monster telescope', there would also be a 'splendid series of dissolving views, illuminated by the oxy-hydrogen light'.

1945

The Palace Hotel, at the top of Mont Millais, where Palace Close now is, had been taken over by the occupying forces as a secret training centre. It was out of bounds to civilians, so when a small fire broke out in the late morning, the German soldiers attempted to tackle it themselves.

The result of this was that the small fire became a big one. Local residents called the Fire Brigade. But before they arrived, they, along with the Island's population, heard a massive explosion, the blast of which shattered all the neighbourhood's windows, as well as those of two Bath Street shops. The detonation of the explosives within the complex killed seven and wounded countless more. The Fire Brigade fought the fire until late the following day but, needless to say, little worthwhile remained.

1958

Joseph Blake of Aubin Lane, St Saviour, was formally charged with wilful murder. The previous evening the accused's father had heard screams. Hurrying downstairs he discovered his daughter-in-law dead and his son close by. Nanette Horn had been stabbed twice and Blake admitted to the police that he had killed her. The couple's three children were taken in by their grandparents, while Blake was remanded. It was later disclosed that he had a history of mental problems, having been certified four times during the previous decade.

08 March

1897

The Island's first singing competition was held at the Alexandra Hall. The Temperance Movement was very strong in the Island and to encourage people away from the demon drink, they offered a silver medal to the best singer. On the night there were nine entries, all but one 'of the fair sex'. Each contestant sang a test song, 'Never Too Late to Mend', before performing a song of their choice. The winner, singing 'The Little Green Leaf in the Bible', was Miss Kent.

1906

Pierre Le Bars was in court, facing a charge of using a horse without the owner's permission. Le Bars had been working for Philip Le Gresley of St Ouen for three weeks and needed to go into town to collect his clothes. Without getting Le Gresley's permission, Le Bars took the horse one evening and headed for town. The family, having heard a noise and found the horse missing, telephoned the Centenier, who intercepted and arrested the Frenchman at First Tower. The Magistrate took a dim view of Le Bar's actions, sending him to prison for eight days, with hard labour.

1958

Jersey gets snow so infrequently that when it does arrive it causes chaos. The blizzard that struck over night this time affected the Island's telephone system particularly badly. Sixty telephone poles, the lines being overhead at this time, were down and thousands of people were cut off. Although the snow was not particularly thick, it had been raining prior to the fall and the ice had weighed heavy on the lines. The thaw set in quickly and, although some hills were dangerous, for once public transport was not greatly affected.

1983

Scrap metal merchant Mr Picot was fatally injured at his Bellozanne scrapyard. Picot had been cutting open an old oil tank when the fumes within it exploded. Terribly burned, Picot was flown to Oddstock Hospital in the UK, but died the following day.

09 March

1874

Having arrived in Jersey aboard his 200 yd yacht *Red Gauntlet*, Edward Langtry gave a dance at the Yacht Club and met Lillie Le Breton. They were engaged six weeks later and on this day married at Lillie's father's church, St Saviour's. On reaching London, Lillie was acclaimed the world's loveliest woman, painted by many great artists and even Oscar Wilde published a poem in her honour. Lillie became an enormous celebrity, known world-wide. A town in Texas was even named after her. However, her husband, hating the attention, soon departed on long fishing trips to Ireland and America, leaving Lillie free to enjoy the lifestyle of parties that she loved.

1903

Annie Elizabeth Le Cornu, of 26 Great Union Road, appeared before the court, charged with selling adulterated milk. A number of witnesses testified that the milk Le Cornu sold was 'very poor' and it appeared that water had been added to make it go further. Le Cornu had formerly taken milk from Mr Chevalier but being dissatisfied with the quality had gone to Mr Pallot in the hope of a better product. Milk was delivered to her twice a day, 1½ pots every morning and 1 pot in the afternoon. At this time milk was delivered to shops in milk churns and the customer would take a jug, into which an amount of milk was measured. It was therefore not uncommon for a less scrupulous shopkeeper to increase the profit by adding water. Having heard the evidence, although it appeared that water was being added to the milk, it was uncertain which party was doing so. Le Cornu was liberated. Exactly forty years later, during the Occupation, John Luce of St Lawrence appeared in the same court on the same charge. In this case, though, he was fined £20.

1994

Jerseyman Graeme Le Saux played his first international game of football in an England shirt. The game at Wembley against Denmark was to be the first of many caps and Le Saux's team won 1-0. He acquitted himself well, watched by his club's boss, Blackburn owner and local resident, Jack Walker.

10 March

1832

Despite it being illegal, Jersey's Bailiff Sir John de Veulle fought a duel with Colonel Charles de la Garde. The Bailiff had described a petition signed by the Colonel as 'the work of a few restless agitators'. The Colonel, offended by the remark, challenged the Bailiff, who reluctantly accepted, not wishing to be accused of cowardice. Shots were exchanged on this day at Jardin d'Olivet, with both parties surviving.

1937

Jersey's airport was officially opened by the Bailiff, Alexander Coutanche. It was an event that had caused a good deal of controversy amongst the locals, as the States had banned them from the new complex. Letters and editorials appeared in the *Jersey Evening Post*, deriding the stupidity of the decision but the States stood firm, claiming the public might cause 'inestimable damage' to the building. The Airport facility had cost about £128,000 to build, with the terminal containing 120 tons of steel and 4,607 tons of concrete.

1980

The company Lockwood Foods Ltd announced that it was closing its canning factory in Jersey. The business, employing 38 people, canned Jersey new potatoes. But demand had declined and the parent company intended to transfer the operation to the UK.

1989

It was revealed that Bergerac actor John Nettles had been refused permission to buy a house in the Island. He had been hoping to be allowed to purchase a 1(1)k property, which could be granted on either economic or social grounds. The resulting publicity did little for Jersey's reputation and later the Housing Committee agreed that Nettles could buy a house as long as it cost more than £250,000. Nettles had been heavily involved in Tourism's advertising of the Island, the character Bergerac being known around the world.

11 March

1568

The Channel Islands were annexed to the Diocese of Winchester on this day. This had no immediate effect, as the islands did not recognise the orthodoxy of bishops. However, Jersey still remains part of the Winchester Diocese.

1838

Sir Thomas Le Breton, the first Bailiff to reside in Jersey for over a century, died on this day. He had resigned in 1831 due to ill health after holding office for 4½ uneventful years. His career had not always been assured, particularly when two years after being made Lieutenant Bailiff a scandal almost ruined his career. A blacksmith had threatened to sue him for damages for committing adultery with his wife. Fortunately the smith saw reason when Le Breton paid him £800 to forget the matter.

1939

An outbreak of swine fever was confirmed on this day. Mr Cory, who specialised in pig breeding, farmed at Garrison House on the Five Mile Road. He had called in Mr Messervy, a veterinary surgeon, the previous week. Once it was confirmed that the pigs were suffering from swine fever, all 63 animals were slaughtered and measures were taken to prevent the infectious disease from spreading to other farms. It was ironic that in the same newspaper which reported the swine fever, it was also reported that a bacon curing factory was proposed for the Island.

1958

At noon on this day Jersey light levels were so low that it appeared night had come early. Car lights were needed and both shops and ships in the harbour required illumination. It was reported that birds went to roost and a little later it snowed. It was said to be the darkest noon in living memory.

12 March

1339

It is recorded that a large army, on 35 ships and 17 galleys, arrived in Jersey. They had sailed from Normandy and descended on Mont Orgueil castle, demanding its surrender.

The garrison refused and seeing that the fortress was strong, the invaders decided against attack. Instead they ravaged the undefended parts of the Island, looting and destroying all they could.

1831

On the same day that Sir John de Veulle was sworn in as Jersey's Bailiff, another ceremony was held in King Street. A few shops had been fitted with gas lights and these were ceremoniously lit.

1926

While entering the harbour the steamer *St Helier* rammed the quay and damage to her meant that she had to be withdrawn from service. Her replacement was the *Reindeer* and as she steamed into St Helier Harbour she too rammed the pier head, in exactly the same spot. The *Reindeer* sustained similar damage to the *St Helier* and was also withdrawn from service.

1979

A British Airways Tristar jet arrived in Jersey to help clear the back log of passengers delayed by fog. It was the largest aircraft to land at Jersey Airport to date and carried over 300 people.

Word had got out that the massive jet was coming and people flocked to the already swamped airport to watch its arrival. The plane's turnaround time was slow because Jersey Airport was not geared up for such an enormous craft and the passenger steps also proved a problem.

13 March

1851

The *Don*, a steam tug built by F C Clarke at West Park, took to the water, becoming the first steam boat built in the Island.

1912

The first general meeting of subscribers to the local branch of the Royal National Lifeboat Institute was held. A large attendance was anticipated, however, only twelve people turned up. Despite Jersey being an island with a long association with ships and shipping, the Jersey Lifeboat Service was in constant danger of disbandment due to lack of support, as had happened some years earlier in Alderney.

1928

The Deputy of St Saviour proposed amending the law on firearms at the request, he said, of a large number of his parishioners. At that time there was no lower age limit for children to use firearms, and .22 rifles and shotguns could be legally used by anyone on their own property. The military authorities only allowed lads of 18 years and over to possess guns and the Deputy believed that the Island should follow their example by introducing an age limit of 17. Supporting the proposition, Deputy Le Quesne light-heartedly pointed out that a law protecting wild birds, colimachons (snails) and benits had been passed and that now perhaps they ought to protect children too.

1978

Housing president Senator John Le Marquand announced that his committee would build no more mass produced 'boxes' and that in future people would want to live, rather than have to live, in the housing his committee was responsible for. The change of policy was the result of a fact-finding visit to Chelmsford, where planners had built individual houses on an estate.

14 March

1656

Five Commissioners arrived in the Island to organise the confiscation of estates and fines on the various Royalist households. Cromwell had appointed the men and although their demands were not excessive (the richest man in Jersey was assessed at £110) the process caused more than a little resentment.

1881

Philip Le Brocq raised the ancient cry of the Clameur de Haro on this day, believing that Gautier de Ste Croix had encroached on his property. However, when the case came to court Le Brocq withdrew his action, as the Clameur had not been raised correctly. Le Brocq had failed to remove his hat when making the cry, thus making it invalid. The court accepted the withdrawal, but still fined Le Brocq because when the Clameur is raised, someone has to pay a fine.

1939

Work on building an air raid shelter at Westmount came to a halt on this day when the workmen demanded danger money. In the pre-war climate the authorities were taking measures for protection should the Island be attacked from the air. Work on excavating a disused copper mine ceased when the roof began to crack. Those doing the work left the area and the next shift refused to enter. The workmen claimed that as the work was dangerous, they should receive an extra payment.

1946

A long awaited review of divorce in the Island was presented to the States. The committee reviewing the law had been set up in January 1938 but the Occupation had caused delays. The proposals suggested altering who heard the case, changing the presumption of death - it would now be an absence of seven years, and the grounds for divorce - which would now include adultery, desertion for three years, cruelty, insanity, sodomy, bestiality and rape.[4]

---

[4] See 15th March for further details.

15 March

1869

Peter Tostevin and Nicholas Fallaize, at work knocking down a wall, were brought to an abrupt halt when the Clameur de Haro was raised against them by Thomas Baudains and his wife, who co-owned the wall which the pair were intent on demolishing. All parties agreed to settle the matter through arbitration, with John Coutanche and Francis Gruchy being appointed arbitrators. When the Clameur is raised there is always a fine. If those who have had the Clameur raised against them have acted improperly they are fined, if they have not, the party who raised it is fined for using it inappropriately. In this case all parties were found to be equally guilty and all were fined.

1906

A report on Jersey's fishing industry was put before the States. It claimed that £9,431 8s 8d approximately of fish had been caught by local crews and that there were 250 professional fishermen. It was noted that the seagull population was increasing, 'destroying large quantities of small fish'. It was also reported that locals were having problems around the Minquiers and Les Ecréhous with French fishermen who were damaging or stealing the Islanders' fishing gear.

1950

A new divorce law came into effect on this day. Three people, intent on being set free from their spouses, were waiting outside the Royal Court, under the impression that a divorce could be granted immediately. They were, however, disappointed and told that no date had yet been set for the court's first sitting.

1961

For only the second time in half a century an inquest failed to reach a verdict. This time the court was looking into the death by gas of an 18-year old, an illegitimate child born during the Occupation who now lived at a boys' home. A psychiatrist said the boy longed for a family but whether he had gassed himself deliberately, the jury could not decide. It may have been that while listening to a fight on the radio he had intended to make a hot drink and had left the gas on.

16 March

1825

John Piquet was born on this day. At the age of 12 he was apprenticed for five years to a chemist. He remained in the shop as an assistant for a further five years. During those ten years he worked from 6.30 am until 11 pm and never had a holiday. Piquet's chief interest was botany and he soon became recognised as the Island authority on local flora. He studied seaweed and ferns in particular, but was knowledgeable about most local plants. A dedicated swimmer, Piquet swam regularly until he was 86 and was co-founder of the Jersey Swimming Club. He died on 5th September 1912.

1918

A German submarine put an end to the eventful career of the steamer *South Western* by torpedoing her while en route to St Malo. Her first Jersey run had been in 1875 and in her time she had collided with a Norwegian barque and also with the *Bay Fisher*. In 1910 she was one of the first ships to be fitted with an experimental radio.

1978

The oil tanker *Amoco Cadiz* ran aground on the Brittany coast with 200,000 tonnes of crude oil on board. For the following few weeks Island authorities waited and prepared to battle the oil slick as it advanced on our shores. Chemical and physical defences were made ready as the Brittany coast became swamped with the thick soup. However wave action and favourable wind and tide conditions saved Jersey. Although a number of seabirds and small oil deposits were washed ashore, relatively little damage was done.

1982

Radio Jersey started broadcasting to the islands at 7 am on this day. The presenter was Peter Gore, whose programme lasted until 8.15 am, when Radio 2 took over. At 1 pm local radio again came on air for just seven minutes. The medium wave transmissions were soon extended from the initial 82 minutes per day. On Sunday mornings the broadcasts lasted a little longer, with programmes called Jersey Jaunt and Talkback.

17 March

1870

The *Normandy* must have been an impressive ship when she was launched in 1863. She was 210 feet long, had 130 passenger berths, was capable of carrying 200 tons of cargo and had a top speed of 15½ knots.

However, the ill-fated paddle steamer was to remain afloat for less than 7 years. During a stormy crossing to the islands on this day, she collided with a Baltic trader, the *SS Mary*, and sank within 20 minutes.

The captain and fifteen crew were lost, as well as 17 of the passengers. The mail bags were also lost but were later found afloat and the letters were delivered.

A memorial to this tragedy can be found by the junction of Victoria Place and Mount Bingham.

1926

The combined forces of two fire crews and a number of soldiers from Fort Regent were unable to extinguish a fire at Normans Ltd at Commercial Buildings, with the result that the building was gutted.

1941

François Scornet, a twenty year old Frenchman, was shot by a German firing squad in the grounds of St Ouen's Manor. Scornet had been the leader of a group of young Frenchmen who had set out to cross the Channel from occupied France, hoping to join the Free French Forces in England.

The unfortunate party landed in Guernsey by mistake, thinking it was the Isle of Wight, and the men were caught by the Germans and sent to Jersey for trial. Scornet took full responsibility for the group's actions and so was sentenced to death.

The oak tree in front of which he was stood for execution is now a focal point in the annual commemoration of his death.

18 March

1847

The foundation stone of the Albert Pier was laid. The quay was built by Thomas Le Gros and Francis de la Mare for the sum of £549,000. Jersey's fishing fleet was growing rapidly, especially with the trade in cod caught off the Newfoundland coast, and the Island's harbour facilities were in desperate need of improvement.

1958

The inquest into Mary Hescott's death returned a verdict of accidental death. The Jersey Electricity Company had been digging up the pavement in Kensington Place when Mrs Hescott, a resident of that street, fell into the trench. She suffered a fractured femur and her age, she was 85, and the shock proved too much for her. The inquest heard that no barriers had been put around the excavated area, although the engineer in charge had ordered this safety measure just prior to the accident. In more recent times the company would most likely have been severely fined, but in 1958 the authorities were not even critical.

1965

The States rejected the proposed development of Fort Regent into a hotel and casino complex by 34 votes to 15. Deputy Jeune, having presented a petition against the project the previous year, pressed the Special Committee to resign, which they resisted. Having bought the Fort in 1958, a great debate as to its future raged for many years with car parks, bowling alley, swimming pool, winter gardens, hotel, and theatre being just a few of the ideas suggested for its use.

1975

The States gave the go ahead for the construction of an aquarium at Fort Regent. It was claimed that it would be 'the finest public aquarium in Britain'. It was to be paid for and run by a private company, although the States were to outlay the capital cost which was to be repaid by the company. It was proposed that 'staff will regularly go into the tanks in order to hand feed the larger fishes and this will certainly be a sight to watch'.

19 March

1549

The Reformation had led to a lot of land and property being confiscated. A commission was appointed on this day to sell on behalf of the Crown all ecclesiastical property in Jersey which had been seized.

1872

Official permission was given for the construction of the Eastern Railway, running from Snow Hill to Gorey, with a possible extension to St Catherine's in the future. Certain conditions applied, among them that the maximum fare was 1½d per mile in first class and 1d in second class, and there had to be a minimum of four services a day. Also, if the company failed to run a full service during 60 days in the course of a year, the railway would be considered abandoned and the States would get everything.

1981

Seven cattle were slaughtered and the phrase 'foot and mouth' was the hitting the headlines. A farm at Les Augerez, St Peter, was isolated and road blocks were set up to keep vehicles away from the area. This infectious disease had not been seen in Jersey since 1974 and farmers were advised to keep their animals inside. The seven infected animals, once slaughtered, were immediately buried in an enormous pit and covered with earth. Island farmers waited anxiously but the prompt action seems to have been effective.

1982

Nine people were in hospital after a gas tanker exploded. Liquid petroleum gas had leaked as the tanker was being unloaded, causing alarms to go off. As the fire brigade and gas workers were attempting to deal with the problem the gas ignited. A huge fire ball erupted, catching both firemen and gas men, who suffered considerable burns. A Channel Television crew were on the scene to report on the alert when the explosion occurred and caught it on tape. Residents were evacuated and the incident highlighted the dangers of having enormous volumes of gas stored in the centre of town.

20 March

1872

The States voted by 22 votes to 13 to proceed with the construction of La Corbière Lighthouse. It was estimated that running costs would be £500 per annum, including the salary of the two keepers. To help fund the cost a harbour due of 1 penny a ton on all vessels arriving in Jersey was proposed. This clause caused some discussion. It was argued that as passenger steamers did not travel at night they should not pay. It was then pointed out that with the lighthouse they could travel on to Jersey in darkness instead of staying overnight in Guernsey, as was their practice.

1900

The States of Jersey, having originally offered to supply the British Government with a field battery to assist in the South African war, were put in a difficult position by the British response to the offer, which was debated on this day. Her Majesty's government had said that they would rather have the money with which they would buy machine guns. This was not at all what had been intended but to save their dignity the States unanimously agreed to fund the purchase of 20 machine guns.

1915

Five hundred and ninety-six German prisoners of war were landed at St Helier Harbour by *HMS Lydia*. They were transported by train to Blanches Banques, where a prison camp had been prepared. Two days later about five hundred more arrived and they too were housed at the St Brelade camp. Many of the prisoners worked on the docks, being taken to and fro by the Jersey Railway Company, until their departure from Jersey in February 1917.

1928

A meeting decided to revive the Battle of Flowers, which had ceased in 1914. The project was to be underwritten by Springfield Entertainments Ltd, who were to receive 75% of the profits. After considerable discussion 2nd August was the date chosen, despite it clashing with a swimming gala.

21 March

1906

One of Jersey's most colourful residents, Lady Otway, held a dinner party for the Island's elite. The musical evening was attended by the Lieutenant-Governor, as well as most of the Island's dignitaries. Lady Otway herself was described as looking 'extremely well, in a superb toilet of geranium-hued velvet'.

Lady Otway was the centre of the local social scene. However, as with Lillie Langtry, scandal followed her, and she was involved in at least two blackmail episodes, one possibly involving her secretary.[5]

1911

Charles John Simmons was fined 2s 6d for not ensuring his son James, aged 11, attended school. Mr Simmons assured the court that he had done his best. He had left his work to take his son to school and even attempted to try a different school. It was said that 'he had thrashed the boy and treated him with kindness' without effect.

With the introduction of compulsory education families often found it difficult to comply with the law. Children were a vital source of labour at some times of the year and were kept out of school.

Cases of parents being brought before the court for this offence were fairly common at this time.

1989

It was revealed that 30 people had been arrested as police tried to break up a shoplifting ring. An enormous amount of clothing and other goods had been stolen from local shops, in one case 440 pairs of jeans in three months.

Police investigators uncovered the operation which was centred around a town pub, where items were stolen to order. Few locals were involved, the majority coming from the north of England. Many had come to the Island specifically to steal, the Island having a reputation of being a soft touch.

---

[5] See 12th October for further details.

22 March

1794

Concern that a French invasion was imminent was voiced among States Members. Spies were everywhere and word had arrived from France that 20,000 soldiers were in St Malo and that they would soon attack Jersey. But they never did.

1802

The Treaty of Amiens brought a temporary peace between England and France. A year later the war resumed, lasting another twelve years. Napoleon had become obsessed with Jersey, complaining that 'France can no longer tolerate this nest of brigands and assassins. Europe must be purged of these vermin. Jersey is England's shame'. And by all accounts Jersey richly deserved this praise.

1831

The first elections to be held on a weekday took place. Prior to this, voting was done on a Sunday in the church porches after divine service. Only male rate payers could vote and this was done audibly on leaving church. Because the votes weren't secret, intimidation was quite common and physical assaults had been known.

Political reform continued and two years later the general public were for the first time admitted to sittings of the States.

1938

The storm clouds of war could be seen on the horizon, even in a backwater like Jersey. On this day the Island's defence Committee requested £6,000 from the States' coffers to buy gas masks. As this was voted through without discussion, it is unknown how many the Committee intended to purchase and who was to have received one.

23 March

1643

On this day, with the English Civil War beginning, Sir Philippe de Carteret summoned the States. Having already attempted to make an unwilling population swear loyalty to the Crown, Sir Philippe tried to declare martial law, with himself in charge. However, Sir Philippe had made enemies and they attempted to arrest him, at which point he retired to the safety of Elizabeth Castle.

1861

Major Murchison was fined £5 for assaulting John Edwards. Earlier Edwards had arrived in church to find his pew occupied by Mrs Murchison, as the church was full. She declined to leave, despite Edwards demanding that she do so. Later that day Major Murchison had called at the home of his wife's abuser and punched him several times in the face, as he considered Edwards' behaviour had been ungentlemanly.

1914

A meeting at the Town Hall, attended by a large proportion of businessmen, agreed to a trial of midweek half-day holidays. The scheme would only work if all shops closed and all those attending the meeting said that if 75 percent of their competitors stayed closed, they would too. Once the Thursday half-day closing became accepted, it continued until the 1970s. Gradually the practice has died out, until by the end of the century only Hamons, the Central Market and a few others remain closed on Thursday afternoons.

1926

The Barreau Art Gallery, adjoining the Museum in Pier Road, was officially opened on this day, it's intended purpose being to display the works of Channel Island artists and works of local interest. Miss E A Barreau had founded the gallery in 1924, in memory of her nephew, Arthur Hamptonne Barreau, and the interest on her endowment of £5,000 was intended to fund the acquisition of paintings. She also founded an art scholarship of £100 per year, to go to a Jerseyman or Jerseywoman who was studying art.

24 March

1603

With the accession of James I to the throne on this day Jersey's Governor, Sir Walter Raleigh, was doomed. Accused of involvement in a conspiracy involving 600,000 crowns from Spain and the removal of James from power, Raleigh was arrested, dismissed from his governorship and condemned to death. He spent the next twelve years as a prisoner in the Tower of London.

1920

Mr W Whitaker Maitland, Secretary to the British Government, wrote to officials in the Channel Islands, informing them of a change in policy. It stated that from 29th March passports would no longer be needed by travellers journeying between the United Kingdom and the Channel Islands.

1973

After a surveillance operation, the police charged a man with living on the earnings from the prostitution of his wife. The police had received a complaint from one of the clients after money from his pocket went missing. When they entered the St Lawrence property, they found contraceptives, whips, underwear and photographs, as well as a telephone booking system. The man, who pleaded guilty, denied knowing that the men he taxied to his wife paid for the pleasure. This denial was undermined when it was heard that deals had been done over the telephone, the usual price being £3 for half an hour.

1975

Queens Valley and its proposed flooding hit the headlines. The idea was still in its early stages but the Jersey New Waterworks Company began drilling test holes and taking rock samples. Mourier Valley in St John was also being considered but the residents of Grouville were beginning to realise that they had a fight on their hands.

25 March

1372

Edmund Rose was named Keeper of Jersey and prepared against the ever present threat of French invasion. Mont Orgueil Castle's garrison was increased to 20 men-at-arms and 20 archers. The Island's defence policy was for the noblemen to take refuge in the castle and leave the peasants to look after themselves.

1805

La Vingtaine de la Ville decided to pave the public roads in it's district of St Helier. This was funded by the sale of Le Mont de la Ville for £11,280 to the British government for the construction of Fort Regent.

1912

George Turner suffered shotgun wounds while attending a wedding. At the time it was the custom in country parishes to salute newlyweds by firing shotguns into the air during the reception. Nineteen-year old Turner joined the party. However, when the trigger of his weapon was pulled, the gun exploded, blowing part of his left hand off. A doctor was summoned and the wound treated. Turner was expected to recover, which was not always the case in the days before antibiotics when a small wound could prove fatal.

1935

The Forum Cinema was opened by Mrs H de C Martell, wife of the Lieutenant-Governor. Edward O'Henry played the national anthem on the Compton organ as the party entered Jersey's newest theatre. It was reported that the carpets were so thick and the seats so quiet that latecomers, of whom there were a few even for the official opening, arrived unheard. The programme started with Pathe's news reels, followed by more renditions on the organ, then the feature 'Abdul the Damned'. It was noted that although 1,600 people were in the cinema, most of whom were smoking, the ventilation apparatus proved most efficient. West's Cinema also reopened on this day, having had a major refit. It was showing 'Bulldog Drummond Strikes Back' with Ronald Coleman.

26 March

1338

A short fat French admiral named Behuchet and his army attacked Jersey, landing troops and starting a reign of destruction that was to last for over six months. Behuchet burnt almost all of the Island's corn, an abbey and laid siege to Mont Orgueil Castle. Eventually the French withdrew, moving on to capture Guernsey, Alderney and Sark. Only Mont Orgueil remained under English control.

1904

A young Frenchman was severely injured when thrown from his bicycle. Pierre Liron had been cycling down St Saviour's Hill at a 'very rapid rate' when the front of the machine collapsed. Liron landed on his head and was knocked unconscious. He was taken to hospital, where his condition caused grave concern.

Four months earlier Liron had been cycling down St Saviour's Hill with his friend Leon François Fauvel when they had collided with a trap. Fauvel had been killed in the crash, which occurred at almost exactly the same place.

1931

A telephone link with England was inaugurated. At 2.31 pm the Home Secretary's voice came through and his message was relayed by loudspeaker to the various dignitaries present. Calls had to be booked and the *Evening Post* was the first to make a public call.

1966

The Jersey Milk Marketing Board introduced the tetra-pak. This pyramid shaped cardboard milk container proved less than popular. It didn't fit easily in the fridge and the cream Jersey milk is famed for tended to collect in lumps at its tip. The tetra-pak was a replacement for the glass bottle and within a week was being delivered Island-wide, much to the annoyance of Islanders.

27 March

1897

Jean Christie appeared in the Royal Court for not sending his son to school. He was a repeat offender who had previously been fined five shillings for his boy's non-attendance. The case was due to have been dealt with a week earlier, but Christie had gone fishing instead. The Bailiff found him guilty and followed the Solicitor-General's advice in sentencing. Christie was banished from Jersey for five years as 'the accused was not worthy of the privilege of residing in this country'.

1903

Twenty-month old Walter Pinel drowned in a container of sour milk. Having just learned to walk, he had apparently wandered into an outhouse at Warwick House, Mont à l'Abbé, and found a copper containing milk. It was assumed that the child had amused himself, dropping marigolds into the milk before falling in himself. At the inquest questions were asked by the Viscount as to whether the boy was insured and the matter of the height of the child in relation to the container was gone into before a verdict of accidental death was returned.

1935

Officially known as the 'Jersey Bus Service', Joseph Manning's buses were more commonly referred to as 'Joe's' by the public. Having started his service the previous year, Joseph Manning became another victim of the larger bus companies. He was forced to close, unable to pay his drivers. The two biggest bus companies, the JMT and the SCS, had divided the Island between themselves and proceeded to buy out rival smaller firms or to wait for them to fail. One owner-driver of the period ceased trading due to his habit of abandoning his passengers, many of whom had return tickets, while he went low water fishing. Manning, however, was not one to give up easily and seven months later he relaunched a successful town service.

28 March

1771

A small but important constitutional matter received Royal sanction. There had been an argument between the States and the court. The Bailiff claimed that the States advised but that he made the laws, while the States believed that they had the authority to make laws, with the court ruling if they were then broken. The decision finally confirmed the States as the Island's legislative assembly.

1928

74-year old John Le Dain died suddenly at home of suspected ptomaine poisoning and strain. His last meal had been of home-made brawn and although the rest of the family had also eaten the pork, only the septuagenarian had suffered any ill effects. At the inquest the doctor said that although the deceased had committed a 'dietetic indiscretion', no blame should be put on the butcher or cook.

1957

It was announced that petrol rationing would come to an end on this day. But supplies were still short and Islanders were informed 'that the supply of petrol is still limited' so they were 'expected to limit consumption'.

1960

The newly formed Federation of Master hairdressers decided to increase the cost of a haircut by 6d. Rising prices were blamed by the new organisation, who also criticised the use of foreign labour in the industry.

1966

The Russian government recognised the aid Soviet prisoners had received from some Islanders during the Occupation. The Russian embassy's delegation presented 20 gold wristwatches as memento to those who had assisted their countrymen. Among those who received one was Deputy Norman Le Brocq.[6]

---

[6] See 1st August for further details.

29 March

1899

Jersey's Theatre Royal burned down only hours after a rehearsal of the pantomime Red Riding Hood. A neighbour ran to the police station, having seen the flames, and assisted the two policemen in pulling the fire engine to the scene at Seaton Place. After two hours the fire was being brought under control and by 7 am the blaze was almost extinguished. Adjoining houses were evacuated, their furniture carried to safety, but the theatre itself was almost completely gutted.

1946

The British government announced that it was to give Jersey £4.2m towards costs incurred during the war. The Island had been bled dry by the Occupation, with expenses of just over £7.5m. Under the Hague Convention, Jersey had had to pay the expenses of the occupying army. At times 16,000 troops had been stationed here and their food, fuel, light and civilian staff all had had to be paid for by the States. In the last year of the war, the soldiers wages had been paid as well.

1968

Prince Charles arrived in Jersey to join the excavation of the prehistoric cave at La Cotte de St Brelade. The Prince was one of fifteen undergraduates working as part of the Cambridge team. He only stayed until 1st April, when he left on board an aircraft piloted by his father.

1977

A proposal to levy an annual tax of £10 on horses was rejected by the States. The idea had been brought by the Constable of St Ouen, who said that funds raised would go to the parish in which the horses' owners lived. The Constable reminded Members that 40 years before parishioners had had to work for their parish for a number of days based on the number of horses they owned. The States were told that St Ouen had spent £300 on road repairs and cleaning the previous year and were hoping to cover some of the cost.

30 March

1899

Stella was one of a trio of ships, but unlike her sisters, *Frederica* and *Lydia*, the *Stella* was to have a short life and a tragic end. She had started working the islands' route in November 1890. On this day thick fog did not slow the steamship on her crossing from Southampton. Competition between shipping lines was great and each vessel tried to cross the Channel faster than their rivals. Aware that the Casquet reef was approaching, the order was given to slow. However, almost at once, at 4.10 pm, the *Stella* struck the Black Rock, part of the Casquet reef, still travelling at full speed. One hundred and nineteen people were rescued but 105 lives were lost. One of these was Mary Rogers, a stewardess, who gave her lifebelt to a passenger and refused a place in the lifeboat.

1939

Mr Huelin, of St Brelade, often used a track which the Le Bas family claimed belonged to them. Huelin believed the track was a public road, as did the parish. On this day Huelin found a felled oak tree blocking the path, so he went to the Constable to complain. A party, consisting of the Constable, a Centenier, a Constable's Officer and two policemen went to remove the tree. They got to the scene to find that a man had barred Huelin's access to the path and Huelin had raised the Clameur de Haro. The tree was moved off the track and the case went before the Royal Court. Once there Huelin withdrew the Clameur, saying that he had not raised it correctly. This was accepted by the court and he was fined for his actions. However, the Constable, having ordered the tree to be removed after the Clameur had been raised, was charged with contempt. The Constable argued his case but to no avail and he too was fined

1982

The Island's honorary authorities unanimously voted in favour of introducing the radar speed gun, which the police had been using for two months as a trial. Up to this point speeders had merely been warned but with its official acceptance those now stopped were to face the court.

31 March

1763

Robert, Lord Carteret, was appointed Bailiff, a title which had become hereditary in the de Carteret family. However, Robert was to be the last. Neither he nor his predecessor ever visited the Island, leaving his Lieutenant, Charles Lempriere, to rule Jersey in his absence.

1811

A map of local defences was published, showing the positions and extent of the recent fortification work. The six arsenals and the Grève de Lecq Barracks had been built, as well as the batteries along all the coasts.

1834

The Jersey Agricultural and Horticultural Society held its first cattle show. The venue was the cattle market in Beresford Street, with the judging carried out under strict secrecy. A points system had been drawn up in January, with much emphasis being placed on the animal's conformation, ie, its shape and proportions.

1871

With the growth of the Newfoundland cod fishing industry the number of ships owned by Jersey firms had doubled in 30 years. On this day the States adopted the plans of Sir John Coode for the building of an ambitious new harbour to house all these new vessels. Forty-two proposals had been submitted but Sir John had a good reputation and was considered the most distinguished harbour engineer of the century.

1923

At midnight on this day the States of Jersey took over the Island's telephone system. Jurat Le Boutillier, who announced the purchase, said that although the public would expect great changes, they would not come immediately. But the acquisition would benefit Jersey in the long term.

01 April

1842

A civil register of births, marriages and deaths was established in Jersey. Prior to this these events were registered in individual parish churches.

1853

Jersey was struck by a minor earthquake.

1920

The vessel *Lorina* made her maiden voyage to the islands on this day. Her delivery to the London and South Western Railway had been delayed by the Great War. She plied the Channel for two decades, only halting briefly in 1935 after hitting a rock while leaving St Helier Harbour. She was withdrawn from the Channel Islands in 1939 and was lost at Dunkirk in May 1940.

1933

Charles Gaslande faced a number of motoring charges. He had taken a car for a test drive and while in Sand Street came to the notice of Pc Nicolle, as he was driving without lights. The policeman also noted that the number plate was only a trial one. Gaslande faced three charges, including refusing to obey a police officer, and was fined a total of £5 5s. The car he had been test driving was for sale for £2.

1978

A report in the *Jersey Evening Post* lead to many Islanders journeying to Sorel Point. The article showed a large hotel and leisure complex built, it was claimed, without planning permission. The photographs clearly showed the multi-million pound structure which had been constructed in Ronez Quarry. This report was, of course, an April Fool, but it was convincing enough for a steady stream of cars to visit the area. Less believable, yet memorable, April Fools of the past have included the discovery of a German soldier who was unaware that the war was over.

02 April

1374

Jersey residents were more than a little fed up with the regular appearance of French raiding parties, who left the Island ravaged and burnt. On this day a solution was agreed. Jersey's inhabitants would pay a ransom in return for a cessation of hostilities. These payments were made for two years, when a truce was signed.

1551

An order was issued to take down and sell all but one of the bells in each parish church to raise funds for the Island's defence. Work was underway strengthening a battery at St Aubin, as well as constructing a new one where Elizabeth Castle was later built, work for which Jersey people had already been commanded to provide money and labour.

1884

The RNLI had opened a lifeboat station in Alderney in 1869. After more than 10 years had elapsed without the boat being launched it was recommended to do away with the station. About this time the Jersey lifeboat was due for replacement and so on this day the *Mary and Victoria* was towed from Alderney to St Helier. When in September 1885 a new boat arrived, the *Mary and Victoria* had still not been launched on a rescue. It remained in the boathouse and was eventually sold.

1907

A law was passed by the States increasing the number of St Helier deputies to 6 and dividing the parish into 3 electoral districts.

1923

The Jersey Motor Transport Company Limited started to operate a bus service from the Weighbridge area. The minimum fare was 2d. The introduction of motor buses in the Island was to have a devastating effect on the already fragile railways. The Jersey Eastern Railway tried to compete by diversifying into the bus market itself but was doomed.

03 April

1803

Judith du Parq married Thomas Anley on this day and must have known from his reputation what she was getting. Anley was a man of action, as well as a learned one. He had been involved in the Battle of Jersey and had given evidence at Major Corbet's subsequent court-martial. In 1785 he had stood for Constable of St Helier, the result of which was disputed. Law suits flew and it was nine years before both parties finally withdrew, during which time St Helier had no Constable. In 1787 Anley's interference put paid to the local custom that on the Saturday following an execution the hangman collected three sous from everyone who brought goods to the market. Anley advised the market traders not to pay and backed them up when the arguments began. Always keen for a battle, in his time Anley was horsewhipped on the court steps, challenged James Pipon to a duel and in 1803 was finally elected Constable of St Helier. After his death in 1827, the States authorised a lottery for his daughter, a thousand £1 tickets being sold. First prize was a house in La Chasse, the second was a pew in the Town Church.

1900

On this day the *Alberta*, a twin screw vessel capable of 19 knots, was launched. She made her maiden voyage two months later, beginning a career that lasted over 40 years. During her life, she underwent a number of refits and modifications. Having served in the Great War, the *Alberta* returned to servicing the Channel Islands. In July 1920 she hit rocks off Guernsey but was patched and repaired to continue work. The *Alberta* left the Channel Islands route in 1929 and was sunk by German aircraft in 1941.

1968

The Housing Committee announced a tightening up on immigration. It was decided that from now on newcomers to the Island would not be allowed to purchase houses under £18,000. This rule would not apply to essential employees. At this time, £12,000 would get you a detached 4 bedroom town house or £18,000 a granite farm house with outbuildings.

04 April

1866

The Jersey Herd Book was formed. In an attempt to breed stronger, healthier and more productive cattle, 42 yearling bulls and 182 cows were chosen as foundation stock from which all pedigree Jersey cows can now be traced. The original animals were chosen for their desired characteristics and, after over 100 years, the selective breeding has resulted in the world renowned cow we know today.

1912

On this day John Rendall's daughter, while working in the family shop, accidentally mixed some coffee and chicory, a mistake that landed her father in court. The man who bought the adulterated coffee was Mr G Walker, the States Inspector, who sent it to be analysed.

Despite it being a mistake, the Magistrate told Rendall that an offence had been committed and fined the shopkeeper 20s, plus 6d to cover the cost of the analysis.

1923

Cashel J Craig died after fighting Jersey's heavyweight boxing champion, W Ralph, in a title fight. The two met at the West Park Pavilion to decide who would challenge for the Channel Island title, but when the fight began it was obvious Craig was outclassed. After 19 rounds both men were still standing, but at the start of the 20th Craig collapsed. He was taken to hospital but died later.

1959

A man who had been missing since Easter Monday was found buried on the sand dunes. Children picnicking with their mother were playing with their bucket and spade when they uncovered the toe of a shoe. They called their mother, who dug a little deeper, finding the shoe still contained a leg. The police were brought in. The victim, John Perree, appeared to have been shot.[7]

---

[7] See 10th September for further details.

05 April

1540

On this day Eduoard de Carteret was arrested and charged with murder. The 22-year old, although from a powerful family, had a reputation for violence. Previously he had struck a Jurat and had also beaten another man with whips and a dagger. Michael Sarre was one of the richest men in Jersey and had married de Carteret's cousin. It was claimed that Eduoard de Carteret had broken into Sarre's bedroom, where he and his wife were in bed, and attacked him. Dragging Sarre from his slumbers, de Carteret beat him savagely before locking him, almost naked, in a freezing room. De Carteret then spent the rest of the night with Sarre's wife. Two weeks after Michael Sarre's death, his widow secretly married her husband's alleged killer. Having been imprisoned in Gorey Castle for nine months, escaping twice during that time, de Carteret's father secured his release on bail.

1828

On this day the States of Jersey made a representation to the British government after the oyster war had flared up again. Despite being repeatedly warned to keep out of French waters, the English fishing vessels had continued to ravage the French oyster beds, Jersey's having already been decimated. When two French gunboats captured a poaching English boat, an armada of small vessels sailed across to France on a rescue mission. They boarded the French warship and brought back the English vessel. But in the fight several boatmen were killed and a number imprisoned. It is hard to see on what grounds the Jersey government complained, but they did.

1959

Twenty-six head of cattle were flown out, en route to America. At the turn of the century, Jersey's cows had fetched enormous sums, up to £1,000, with American ranchers attempting to improve their breeding stock. This trade had since died off to a great degree. With the export of these twenty-six pedigree cows it was hoped to revive Jersey's international trade in cattle.

06 April

1826

The mail packet, *Sir Francis Feeling*, was wrecked in a storm.

1926

Sir Jesse and Lady Boot put on a party for the children of La Motte School to celebrate the completion of the new building. The school's construction had been funded by the Boots, who also donated a number of other facilities to the Island.

At the celebration a concert was given by boys from Dr Barnardo's home, while other entertainment included a conjuring show and Punch and Judy. Food was provided by Birds, the bakers and perhaps best of all was that a copy of a photograph of the children was to be given to each child.

1944

At about 10 pm a damaged and burning German bomber flew across the Island, crashing in a field off the St Martin main road. Two of the crew were found outside the burning wreckage, both dead. The other two were trapped within, unable to be helped because of the heat and exploding munitions.

The plane's remnants caused a great deal of local interest, especially among children, and although a guard was put on the aircraft, its fragments became prized souvenirs among the younger generation of the area.

1981

Seven rare birds were killed and a dozen more injured when dogs attacked them in the grounds of Jersey Zoo. Two white-eared pheasants and five Cape Barren geese were slaughtered in the early morning as the dogs ran amok. Both species were endangered, the geese being particularly rare.

07 April

1673

Colourful is one word that describes the life of Mary de la Riviere Manley. Born on this day, either in Jersey or on a boat just arriving, she was the daughter of the Deputy Lieutenant Governor. When orphaned at 16, she was trapped in a bigamous marriage with her considerably older cousin. Deserted, she began to write plays in England and in the years that followed became mistress to a number of prominent men. More plays and a series of outrageous and libellous books were published. In her time she was arrested for forgery and making allegations about the establishment. When she died on 11 July 1724 she may not have been greatly loved, but she had shaken things up.

1817

Philip John Ouless was born on this day. Of French extraction, Ouless studied painting in Paris but later returned to Jersey, where he painted portraits, landscapes and shipping, as well as teaching painting. Generally agreed not to be a great artist, Ouless' gift was his ability to capture accurately the details of ships, costume and life of the period. Ouless died in 1885.

1838

The States had spent £4,000 to stock new oyster beds in Grouville Bay. But these areas were not to be fished until the oysters had grown. On this day, 120 boats set off from Gorey and trawled the area. The Constable of St Martin had followed in a rowing boat but had failed to stop them. On returning to shore the Constable arrested the ringleaders but four days later the beds were raided again.[8]

1964

A petition against the idea of a casino in Jersey, which contained 8,548 signatures, was handed in. It had taken less than three months to collect the signatures and had been backed by most church groups.

---

[8] See 12th April for further details.

08 April

1664

Josue de Carteret, the influential family's black sheep, was laid to rest this day. As a young man he had carried off Jeanne Le Feuvre, a child heiress, to Normandy. When the minister refused to marry them, due to her age, Josue travelled to Sark where he married his child bride. During the Civil War he attempted to use both sides for his own ends and very soon he was imprisoned by both Royal and Parliamentary forces in turn. This irrepressible character seems to have been content to cheat and lie to almost everyone to get his way and was considered a nuisance by most.

1885

Fifty years after the great oyster boom, oyster farming was attempted. A concession was granted to the Jersey Oyster Culture Company but the venture failed.

1925

On this day the Woman's Property Act was passed. Until this time any property owned by a woman became her husband's on their marriage.

1967

'Oil is so close' was the *Jersey Evening Post*'s headline as fear of pollution from the *Torry Canyon* increased in the Island. The oil tanker had struck rocks in the Channel and large oil slicks were heading towards the Islands. Jersey's authorities stayed alert for some weeks but although Guernsey was hit, Jersey survived fairly unscathed.

1970

The States approved the plans for developing Samarès Marsh by 37 votes to 13. Development of the area had been under discussion for some time and on this day the construction of the four 'skyscrapers' that now dominate the skyline on the south-east coast were agreed.

09 April

1912

The States decided not to buy Princes Tower (La Hougue Bie). The site was for sale and £168 5s was required to purchase the 'national monument' for the people of Jersey. The property consisted of an hotel and tavern, parkland, the Princes Tower itself and the as yet undiscovered Neolithic tomb. During the States' debate it was pointed out that the Island would have a surplus of £4,000 to £5,000 at the end of the year. Despite this, the proposition to acquire the site was rejected and it was left to the Société Jersiaise to later secure the historic site, recognising its importance to Jersey's heritage.

1915

The first steam powered boats to run to the islands were paddle steamers. As the technology improved, some ships were driven by screws or propeller. The *Guernsey* was such a vessel. Capable of 13 knots, she carried mail and cargo for over 35 years, but not without incident. In 1903 she was in collision off St Catherine and in 1913 she was seriously damaged when she hit rocks off Roscoff. Her run of bad luck ended on this day when she was wrecked on rocks off Cap De La Hague. Although there was a lighthouse to aid mariners, it wasn't functioning due to the war. Seven crew were killed.

1943

Canon Clifford John Cohu was sentenced to 3½ years imprisonment. During the Occupation it was forbidden to have a radio and Canon Cohu had disobeyed this order. Hidden in St Saviour's Church tower, the Canon and his sexton, Joseph Tierney, listened to the BBC on the wireless and then relayed the news to parishioners. Cohu was arrested and court-martialled. The length of his sentence, although reduced on appeal, meant it had to be served on mainland Europe. Tierney had also been arrested and the duo were deported, along with a number of others, in July. The party were moved to a number of locations, including Spergau concentration camp. By 1944 both men were dead, the result of exhaustion, starvation and general maltreatment.

10 April

1557

On this day Jean Mourant and Jeanne Reynauld drank to their marriage pact and in doing so it became legally binding, whether either party had second thoughts or not, which it appears Reynauld later did. The custom of eating or drinking together binding a marriage contract was recognised by the Ecclesiastical Court and infringements were punished with heavy fines.

1928

Jersey's new income tax law was adopted by the States by a narrow majority. The Island had a deficit of £31,000 and the proposed tax was intended to meet expected future deficits. Jerseymen are not easily parted from their money and did not intend to pay without a fight. A petition was organised appealing for His Majesty in Council not to confirm the law. Parochial meetings took place but to no avail. The tax was 'not to exceed a shilling on the pound' and even in the late 1930's it was only charged at nine pence on the pound.

1929

T B Davis was granted a Royal Charter from the King. The Howard Leopold Davis Scholarship Trust was set up with £50,000, in memory of his son who had been killed in the Great War.

1961

It was announced that a mammoth's skull had been found at La Cotte, St Brelade. Excavations in the cave had been taking place on and off for some decades but now a Cambridge-led team had reached the layer dating from when mammoths and woolly rhino had roamed the land that had not yet become an island The unearthed skull belonged to a young mammoth and was said to be 100,000 years old. As the excavation continued an enormous amount of material was recovered. More skulls and bones were found of both woolly mammoth and woolly rhino, as well as large quantities of worked flint. It appears that our ancestors used to drive the animals over the cliff and then butcher them in the cave where they had fallen.

11 April

1734

On this day five Jurats were dismissed after allegedly encouraging riots. This was the latest stage in the civil unrest that had engulfed Jersey for four years. After a bungled attempt to devalue French money, the States had unleashed an explosion of civil disobedience related to the payment of tithes. Feelings had become so heated that collectors of dues were regularly attacked and their property damaged. On one occasion Philippe Le Haguais' house had caught fire. Unfortunately the large crowd that gathered came to cheer, not help, because Le Haguais had supported the authorities after the Jurats had been dismissed for siding with the populous. The courts had ceased to function and in 1736 two accused murderers were released as there was no court to try them.

1933

A traffic jam of 30 cars received a mention in the *Jersey Evening Post*. Due to poor parking in Colomberie a bus was unable to get through and 'in a minute or two 30 or more vehicles were held up on both sides of the Grenville Street - Colomberie junction.

1947

The war against the Colorado beetle intensified with the arrival of Polish soldiers. A team totalling 160 men was to be employed spraying the potato crop against the insect. The veterans of Mont Cassino were greeted by representatives of the Department of Agriculture and housed in the Grand Hotel.

1983

In heavy seas the crew of a trawler were lifted to safety by helicopter while being battered in the Channel. Two local crabbers who heard about the crew abandoning the vessel over the radio set out to find her. When they finally came across the unmanned ship, the engines were still running. Managing to get a couple of men aboard, after some hours they secured a tow line, the engines having failed. The following day the two local crews arrived in St Helier Harbour with their salvage prize and toasted their achievement.

12 April

1597

Queen Elizabeth, always careful with her money, was aggrieved at the amount she had to contribute to Jersey's fortifications. £325 6s 8d was required for three months of supplies and wages for the Island's garrison. Earlier she had appealed to the Islanders for assistance and discovered that the people had not responded. On this day a stiff letter was received from her, rebuking officials for not doing as instructed.

1838

The oyster fishermen of Gorey were confronted with the town militia. Having raided newly seeded oyster beds twice already, the Constable of St Martin had appealed for help. When the boats again set sail for the forbidden area, a couple of cannon balls were fired among them, which quickly brought the boats back to shore. In the riotous conditions, 97 captains were arrested in what became known as the Battle of the Oyster Shells.[9]

1924

A law was passed increasing the number of Members in the States. The new law also allowed women over the age of 30 to stand as Deputies but this was fiercely resisted by the old guard. However, it was four years before a woman stood as a candidate and she was crushingly defeated. It was a further two decades before the first woman was elected.

1933

At 3.31 pm on this day the Island was again shaken by earth tremors. The two quakes shook buildings and caused pictures to move, but did little damage. Although the shocks emanated from the north west, Guernsey felt nothing. Jersey has been subjected to a surprisingly large number of earth tremors throughout the centuries, although they have so far always been quite mild.

---

[9] See 21st April for further details.

13 April

1603

The States decided to make Wednesdays market days. With no covered market, local trading took place in what is now known as the Royal Square.

1669

Permission was granted allowing duty to be charged on wine, spirits and cider. The money raised was to be used to fund a house of correction, the building of St Aubin's harbour and a school. £31 was spent levelling a site close to where Victoria College now stands, before the project was forgotten. Scholarships were also set up, but as Jerseymen were seen as barbarous, few colleges accepted them.

1912

John Eon and Auguste Le Vaillant went before the court, charged with blackmail. Fourteen years earlier Mr Leonard had been tried for the murder of a man named Francis and had been found not guilty. After over a decade the two accused had gone to Mrs Leonard, claiming to have found a confession written by her husband, who was no longer in Jersey, and they had demanded £4 to keep quiet.

The pair had themselves spent time in prison and claimed to have discovered the confession written in a book in the prison library. Mrs Leonard had paid up in instalments. However, a policeman, Pc Jouan, investigating a different offence, discovered the blackmail plot and took action. In their defence, the two accused claimed Mrs Leonard had 'forced the money on them'.

1959

Quick police action saw the rapid detention of two men who had attempted a smash and grab raid on tobacconist R E Binet in Broad Street. A milk bottle had been used to smash the plate glass window but neighbours alerted the police and Pcs Queree and Sutcliffe caught up with the pair in York Street. However, all their good work was for naught because while at the police station the thieves were left unsupervised and simply walked out of the headquarters unchallenged.

14 April

1925

On this day the *Ibex* left Jersey for the last time. After a long and eventful life the steamship was to be scrapped. In 1897 and 1900 she had sunk, only to be refloated.[10] In the Great War the *Ibex* had been missed by a torpedo and had sunk a German submarine. She had collided with, and sunk, a cargo ship and been swamped by a huge wave. Despite this, or perhaps because of it, the *Ibex* is one of the most fondly remembered of the old steam ships.

1965

A British United Airways Dakota struck a landing pole while trying to land in fog at Jersey Airport. The aircraft cartwheeled into a ploughed field and burst into flames with 23 passengers and four crew on board. A 22-year old French stewardess, the only survivor, was found lying beside the tail section. Her two broken legs kept her in hospital for a few months but she made a complete recovery.

1967

Rolf Harris flew in and played to a capacity audience at West Park Pavilion. As well as giving renditions of his chart-topping songs, including 'Tie Me Kangaroo Down Sport', Harris entertained his appreciative public with jokes, some of which were aimed at Island issues. His half hour encore proved how popular this flying visit had been, with Harris signing hundreds of souvenir programmes, each with a sketched self caricature.

1973

An ecological survey of Maîtresse Ile at the Minquiers was undertaken on this day to see if conditions would allow trees to be planted. Samples of the soil were taken for analysis and collecting apparatus were set to check the salt content of the rain water. A move to plant trees on Maîtresse Ile had been halted a few weeks earlier by the Attorney-General Peter Crill, who wanted assurances that any trees would not affect the ecology of the reef.

---

[10] See 5th September for further details.

15 April

1331

Royal Commissioners received a report on Mont Orgueil Castle on this day. Repairs had been undertaken and the report records the strength of the garrison. The castle was defended by 3 men at arms, each paid 12d a day; a constable with his attendant on 6d a day; and 30 foot soldiers on 2d per day.

1550

The Book of Common Prayer, having been translated into French for Islanders' benefit, was printed in London. The prayer book had a Protestant flavour, reflecting the religious changes Jersey and Guernsey had undergone.

1773

Jersey suffered a minor earthquake and no real damage was caused.

1809

This day saw the first publication of *La Gazette de Césarée*. This was just one of a multitude of newspapers to be printed locally in the first half of the 19th century. The local political parties, the Laurels and the Roses, each had their own paper, as well as 10 different weekly papers published in English. *La Gazette* ceased publication on 15th July 1820.

1832

Many of his old boys must have been glad when Eduoard Valpy passed away on this day. Born in St John, he was educated in England and later ran a school there. His scholastic successes were remarkable, with an unusually large number of boys going on to make their mark in various spheres of life. He was also a merciless flogger, with his school being described as a 'continual round of torture'. One boy recalled receiving a prolonged and brutal flogging for 'missing a word in saying the Greek verbs' until Valpy was 'unable to wield his cane any longer'.

16 April

1603

It was reported in the States that the Bailiff and some Members of the States had been refused entry to Gorey Castle where they had intended to inspect the fortification at the request of Sir Walter Raleigh. The matter was of great concern and the following week the party gained access only after presenting the porter with a letter from the Governor. What they found also caused concern. Gun carriages were broken and the garrison's strength reduced to such a state that an attack could not have been repelled.

1661

In the still uncertain times of post-civil war Jersey, the States decided that all men over the age of 16 should swear an oath of allegiance.

1897

The *Ibex* was one of the best known of the Great Western Railway Steamers to service the Islands. On this day, a Good Friday, she and the rival *Frederica* were vying to reach St Helier Harbour first. The *Ibex* struck rocks off La Corbière, causing a great deal of damage to her hull and propellers. The passengers were taken off by life boats. She was refloated and taken back to England for repairs, returning to duty in July of the same year. But this was not the last time that trouble befell the *Ibex*.[11]

1935

A crane crashed into the harbour, killing its driver. The 30-ton crane had recently been moved to Victoria Pier and was undergoing tests. Everything had appeared fine until the gantry, with a 30-ton load, began to move. Gathering speed quickly, the crane tipped into the water, trapping the driver in the cab. His apprentice was saved only because as the machine fell he leaped clear, suffering only a dunking and shock.

---

[11] See 14th April for further details.

17 April

1646

Prince Charles, on the run from the Parliamentarians, arrived for the first time in Jersey, staying until 25th June. One of the results of his visit was the strengthening of Elizabeth Castle and the building of the area known as Fort Charles. The work took about a year and created a self contained outpost, well armed and with a drawbridge.

1923

The parish of St Helier bought equipment to make tarmac. At this time roads were the responsibility of each parish. Most were just compacted dirt, with some of concrete. In the residential areas cobbles or wooden blocks provided a more permanent surface.

1961

One of Jersey's best known and popular residents was born in Switzerland. Jambo, the male lowland gorilla, delighted visitors to Jersey Zoo with his intelligent, noble expression and immensely powerful physique. The silverback was one of the most prolific male gorillas in captivity, fathering sixteen offspring by 1988.

1995

The *St Malo*, an inter-island catamaran, struck rocks off La Corbière. The ship, which was en route to Sark, had taken a course closer to the shore than usual and had rammed the reef which has claimed so many vessels over the centuries. Being a Bank Holiday Monday, a large crowd gathered on the headland and watched as the *St Malo* wallowed half a mile off shore. All the rescue services responded, as did the international press. Most of the passengers were taken onboard a Condor ferry which had manoeuvred close to the stricken boat. There were few casualties, with most injuries occurring during the transfer between vessels, although a number of passengers suffered from shock. By the evening the *St Malo* had been towed to St Aubin's Bay and beached there. The enquiry that followed was critical of the handling of the *St Malo*, but praised the emergency services' response and especially the captain of the Condor vessel for his seamanship.

18 April

1645

Three Royal Commissioners arrived in Jersey to adjudge on treason committed during the ongoing Civil War. Most Parliamentarians had fled and the few that were captured were saved from the gallows by a threat issued from England to execute three Royalists for every Parliamentarian killed in Jersey. The Commission did, however, confiscate land and money.

1810

The ever increasing number of Methodist converts in the Island's militia made the regular after church Sunday drill impractical. The Methodists maintained Sunday as sacrosanct, with work, dancing, game playing and other frivolity being out of the question. On this day the Sunday drill was finally abolished.

1822

The oyster beds at Gorey had been known about for centuries and had been fished moderately by local boats. But in the early nineteenth century, fishing companies from England moved in and cottages were built to house the thousands employed in the oyster industry. With over 300 boats, each one catching about 12,000 oysters a day, the stocks rapidly became over-fished and the fleet began to encroach into French waters. On this day a petition requesting protection for the British fishermen was presented to the King, after confrontations with the French had occurred.[12]

1969

One of the few water mills remaining in good condition was gutted by fire. Quetivel Mill in St Peter's Valley had been due to be handed over to the National Trust. The mill was owned by the Waterworks Company and used by the JF(T)U for storage. A similar fire broke out in a derelict farm in St John, about the same time, leading firemen to suspect arson.

---

[12] See 23rd May for further details.

19 April

1790

The foundation stone of St Helier Harbour's north pier was laid. Philip de la Mare was to build the structure but it would take 25 years to complete and cost about £80,000.

1906

Alaric East faced the Magistrate, charged with using a lame horse. East had been seen driving a trap in St Helier, having travelled from St Martin, when the horse was lame. The animal was said to have been covered in lather and looked as if it had just come out of the sea. A witness for the defence assured the court that East treated his animals well and with this in mind, the Magistrate imposed a light fine of 10 shillings.

1917

The Police Court Magistrate imposed the most severe sentence he could on Robert Bryant. Bryant had been seen driving dangerously down Bath Street. A Centenier followed the vehicle and found it at Grève d'Azette, with Bryant drunk at the wheel. As he was out of his jurisdiction, being in St Clement, he had no authority to make an arrest. However, when Bryant returned to St Helier he was taken into custody. The Magistrate decided to impose the maximum sentence, in view of the accused's appalling record. Bryant was fined £1 for dangerous driving, £6 for being drunk and he also had his driving licence suspended for three months.

1963

Motorist Anthony Hoare had his driving licence suspended for 25 years after being convicted of driving without due care and failing to stop and report an accident. The accused had already received a similar sentence from the English judiciary but the ban did not apply in Jersey. Hoare also received a month's prison sentence for using foul and disgusting language, all of which he intended to appeal against.

20 April

1042

A charter was signed mentioning the parish churches of St Mary and St Martin. Prior to this date the Island churches were little more than wooden chapels which were constantly being burned down and rebuilt. However, under the Norman influence, the parish churches were now being built of stone.

1873

François Amice Romeril died. Born in Jersey, he had lived in Paris in his early twenties, working as the proprietor of an exhibition of performing serpents. On his return to the Island, he had taken up journalism. It seems that life in the press was a dangerous one, with people regularly assaulted or sued for libel. Romeril escaped a potentially costly suit by claiming that the case was against François Romeril, whereas he was François Amice. The tactic rebounded when he was beaten up twice on the same day. He prosecuted his attackers but they escaped by using the same trick. They were charged with assaulting François Romeril, who the court had earlier ruled did not exist.

1894

François Voisin was probably the most travelled Islander when he died on this day. In April 1837, at the age of 20, he had opened a small shop in King Street. At that time the road was a narrow crooked lane onto which the backs of Broad Street properties opened. The shop, selling drapery, haberdashery and other goods, prospered. The following year Voisin took over the shop next door and later acquired land on either side and to the rear of his property. Content that his staff were well-trained and trustworthy, Voisin travelled the world for many years buying goods, furs from Russia, linen from Belfast, lace in Malines and silks from Asia. In 1878 he passed the business over to his sons.

1916

Owing to a shortage of men, because of the war, Jersey's first postwoman began to deliver the mail.

21 April

1608

A law was passed forbidding anyone over the age of 15 to knit during the vraicing season or during seed time and harvest. Knitting had become an enormous industry in Jersey. Men, women and children spent so much time producing woollen stockings and sweaters for export that work on the land was being neglected. The previous year a shortage of wheat grown had threatened a famine. Knitting was also banned from church as the clicking of the needles drowned out the minister.

1642

Sir Philippe de Carteret, having returned from a visit to England, presided over a meeting of the States. Now aware of the likelihood of a civil war, the States decided to order a public fast 'to divert the wrath of God threatened by the division in England'.

1692

Philippe Langlois had made a fortune trading between America, Europe and his native Jersey. Having settled in Salem, his comfortable life was shattered on this day when his wife, Mary, was arrested for witchcraft. It was the time of the infamous Salem witch trials and Langlois was soon also accused. He fled at first, but later returned to his wife. Twenty people had already been executed and a fair trial was unlikely so another escape was arranged. A diversion allowed the couple to flee on two fast horses, the shoes of which had been reversed to confuse pursuers. The couple found safety in New York but Mary's health had been damaged by her imprisonment and she died, something for which Langlois never forgave the Puritans.

1838

The 97 fishing captains arrested in the oyster riots were brought before the Royal Court on this day. Having destroyed the local oyster bed by overfishing, they had attempted to do the same in French waters. They then proceeded to decimate the young oyster stocks which had been sewn to help them. The court fined them for violation of the oyster fishery laws.

22 April

1373

The King, fearing a French attack on Jersey, ordered the sheriffs of Southampton to take action. They were to prepare soldiers, horses, munitions, victuals and supplies for immediate dispatch. However, none of this stopped the French invading the Island and laying siege to Mont Orgueil Castle three months later.

1922

Harry Thomas was sane and therefore sentenced to one month's hard labour. Thomas had been arrested for obtaining money under false pretences, claiming to be a steward on a steamer. When in jail awaiting trial, Thomas had tried to drown himself in two inches of water and had gone on hunger strike. Dr Le Brocq had declared him insane and he had been removed to the lunatic asylum. But doctors there had found him to be relatively normal, stating to the court that Thomas 'spoke freely and answered questions readily, if not truthfully'. Thomas wept throughout his court appearance and appealed to the Magistrate for one last chance. But he did not find it forthcoming, although the Magistrate was still thanked by the accused.

1935

A hoard of 12,000 Armorican coins was discovered in St Brelade. While digging, a workman had come across several stones. When removed, they revealed a cavity crammed with coins. Originally dating from about the time of Christ, the copper coins had been buried to keep them safe.

1981

It was announced that the Hospital would be serving its patients margarine instead of butter as part of a cost-cutting exercise. With the budget set and staff demanding a cost of living pay rise of over 13%, hospital managers were looking to make any saving they could. The introduction of marg was going to be done gradually and would not be at the expense of standards of health care.

23 April

1773

The second earthquake this year struck the Island.[13]

1788

In the House of Commons on this day it was claimed that Jersey's population was in the region of 20,000 people, of which half employed their time knitting stockings. Six thousand pairs were exported each week.

1794

Seventeen French warships were sighted near Jersey's coast, alarming an already nervous population. The militia was called to arms but the feared invasion did not materialise.

1897

A 10-year old shot his mother at their St Peter home. Young master Le Marquand had been taking an old gun to pieces in order to clean it, believing the gun to be unloaded. Unfortunately he had failed to check and the weapon discharged while it was pointing in his mother's general direction. The pellets hit her in the lower body and thighs, but the wounds were not fatal.

1903

Pierre Rabet was in court, facing charges of cruelty, having thrashed his horse so badly that it had lashed out, breaking its leg and subsequently having to be shot. Rabet, a 'dead cattle dealer' from St John, had on this day travelled to St Clement to cart away a dead horse. Having loaded the animal into his cart from the field where it lay, he then found his own horse was unable to negotiate a small hummock and he beat the animal. However, in court witnesses stated that although Rabet had hit the horse, it had not been ill-treated. Rabet was discharged.

---

[13] See 30th April for further details.

24 April

1914

A proposal to purchase a site at Gorey for the building of a new elementary school was discussed in the States. The law stated that there must be one or more public schools in each parish, large enough to take all the children. The population in the area was increasing and the proposed new school would accommodate 200 pupils. As to cost, the land was valued at £1,195 and the committee said that it was not intended to erect a 'monumental building, but a cheap, strong school on the best hygienic lines', costing under £2,000. Some States Members thought that the chosen site was inappropriate, as it was in a slum area and liable to unsanitary conditions. When the vote was taken, the proposal was passed by 20 votes to 18.

1952

The first load of this season's Jersey Royals arrived at the Weighbridge. Mr H Robert, of Warren farm, Beaumont, brought 2½ cwt of potatoes to town, where they fetched a good price. Before the advent of polythene sheeting, May was considered the potato season. In more recent times outdoor new potatoes can be obtained from as early as March.

1962

Mr R H Le Masurier was sworn in as Bailiff Delegate, as the law required, following the death of the previous Bailiff, C S Harrison, ten days earlier. Le Masurier was already Deputy Bailiff and so it was not required that a Judge Delegate also be sworn in.

1980

It was revealed in the *Jersey Evening Post* that St James' Church was likely to close. What had once been the garrison church for troops stationed at Fort Regent now had fewer than a dozen people in the congregation, and most of them were elderly. The Sunday School had been amalgamated with that of St Luke's, the church that Rev Jeffrey Hollis ministered, as well as ministering at St James'.

25 April

1550

A year after a previous Commission had been set up, a new group was appointed to sell, on behalf of the Crown, ecclesiastical property in Jersey which had been confiscated during the Reformation.

1838

The foundation stone of a new House of Correction was laid on land already adjoining the new prison in Newgate Street.

1867

Thomas Benjamin Davis was born at Havre des Pas on this day. Davis was the son of a ship's carpenter and was involved with the sea all his life. At fourteen, a snapped rope had cast him adrift in the North Sea. After being rescued by a passing vessel, he returned to Jersey, arriving during his own memorial service. His immense wealth was acquired through an empire of stevedoring services which provided labour at docks around the world. The money was used generously, founding a science university in Durban, a training ship for cadets, and a number of other worthy projects. However, most of Davis' gifts to the Island bear the name of his youngest son, Howard, who was killed at the Somme during the First World War.

1904

Richard Thomas Burrard was in court, charged with selling undersized fish. The fish in question were under the required 9 inches, some being as small as 5 inches. Burrard's defence was that he had bought the fish at an auction at the Lowestoft market, believing they complied with the English law. The inspector who had reported the case said that the fish had remained on sale despite his having warned Mrs Burrard, who had assured him that they would be withdrawn from view. The Magistrate said that he believed there to be 'a great deal of foreign fish on sale in the town' but that he must apply Jersey law. He fined Burrard 10 shillings.

26 April

1817

The Privy Council gave their judgement in a dispute between George Hooper and the Attorney-General. Hooper, a wealthy candle and soap manufacturer in the Island, had been a captain in the Militia. In 1816 the Lieutenant-Governor had promoted him to the rank of colonel, allowing him to hold the regimental colours. However, when a new Lieutenant-Governor arrived in the Island, Hooper was demoted back to Captain. Taking this very badly, he refused to hand over the colours. On this day the Privy Council ordered Hooper to pay a fine of £100 and to return the colours. The judgement was to be read to the whole regiment, in the hopes of encouraging Hooper to obey orders in the future.

1933

St Helier's new dustcart was displayed outside the town hall. The two-ton Fordson was motorised and was said to be a great improvement on the horse-drawn carts. The lorry was divided into six sections, with sliding lids to keep the smell and dust to a minimum. The ingenious opening mechanism was foot operated, allowing the dustman to use both hands to empty the bins.

1962

A prototype of a new car was demonstrated in Jersey on this day. The German built Amphicar was an open top tourer capable of 75 mph. It was also capable of travelling at 10 mph across the water. Expected to sell at around £1,600, this amphibious car appeared ideal for Jersey, as traffic hold-ups could be avoided simply by driving across the waters of St Aubin's Bay, into St Helier.

1967

Jersey Longlife Milk was introduced to the Island. Costing 1s 1d per pint, a penny more than ordinary milk, the product was not a great success. However 1,800 pints were exported that week, probably the best thing to do with the stuff.

27 April

1646

During the Civil War 107 Irish soldiers arrived. Their ship anchored off Elizabeth Castle but the men were not allowed to land because, as Jean Chevalier, the diarist, noted 'every nation detests the Irish'. A month later the Irishmen were still onboard and only after protests were they allowed to disembark. Not all were quartered in the castle. Sixty had to make do with straw bedding in a chapel. Each week these men collected their ration of biscuits, beer, lard and salt cod from Elizabeth Castle, but some seem to have supplemented their diet with stolen sheep.

1648

A new Court House was opened in St Helier. Built of granite from Mont Mado and paving stones from Swanage, the new building replaced the low thatched structure said to have resembled a barn.

1873

The Jersey Eastern Railway's first two locomotives arrived on board the schooner *Emma*. They were named the *Caesarea* and *Calvados* and each engine had cost £1,800. The first two passenger carriages had been landed a fortnight earlier and all were taken, with much difficulty, to the new sheds at Green Street.

1905

The first inter-insular football match played for the Muratti vase was held at Springfield. The crowd, numbering about 2,000, were partly made up of Guernsey and Alderney football enthusiasts who had travelled to Jersey by steamer for the occasion. The journey proved worthwhile as the Jersey team were beaten 1-0.

1936

Angry farmers gathered in the Royal Square to protest about the compulsory spraying of crops. The Colorado beetle, which had not yet arrived in the Island, had spread through France and was now just across the Channel. It destroys potato and tomato plants, both of which were cash crops that the Island exported.

28 April

1897

It is ironic that at a time when dockwork was particularly hazardous, docker John Scoone's death was caused by injuries received when he fell from a horse-drawn van, having caught a lift on it on his way home to lunch. Scoone's fall had been heavy and he was immediately taken to hospital where a fracture to the collar bone and the base of the skull were diagnosed. Scoone quickly slipped into unconsciousness and died soon after. Strangely Scoone had survived an almost identical accident seven years earlier and had been treated for a brain haemorrhage three years after, as a result of the first accident.

1906

The quick actions of a cabby saved a man's life, for which he was rewarded. At the corner of Broad Street and Conway Street a farmer had fallen from his cart, landing under the horses' hooves. The cabby had dashed forward and dragged the man to safety before he was trampled. The cabman then washed and bandaged the farmer's wounds and in turn was rewarded with a gift of one penny.

1964

Inter-island travellers now had the option of sailing on a hydrofoil, as Condor had begun a service between Jersey and Guernsey. Despite gale force winds, the inaugural trip took only 50 minutes. Having arrived at St Helier, the passengers were transferred to small boats for landing, as the pontoons necessary for berthing the hydrofoil, although ordered, had not yet arrived.

1978

Philip Malet de Carteret bought St Ouen's Manor for £400,000. Along with the property came the title of Seigneur, which had been in the de Carteret family for many centuries. Malet de Carteret bought the manor from his younger brother Reginald, who had suffered financial problems, thereby stopping the historic building from leaving the family. The new Seigneur intended to open the manor to the public.

29 April

1897

A charge of being drunk in charge of a horse, was laid against Jean Marie Gouyette. He had been arrested near St Mary's Parish Church, having just left a tavern. Gouyette was driving a horse and van which had narrowly missed a number of other vehicles, causing them to swerve out of the way. Once before the court, the Magistrate fined Gouyette £2 for being intoxicated while in charge of a horse and van, and 15 shillings for driving with negligence.

1947

An Island-wide referendum was held on the subject of electoral reform. Meetings were held at all the parish halls and votes were taken. The overall result was 64% for reform, 36% against. But this did not reflect many parishes' views, as St Ouen, St Mary, St John, St Peter and Trinity had all voted against it. The Constables' position in the States remained secure but the vote saw the removal of the Jurats and Rectors from the States Chamber.

1967

The first sea angling festival was held at St Catherine's. The three day event was supported by Jersey's tobacco distributors, who were giving out cigarettes. Over 100 boats took part and St Catherine's breakwater was a hive of activity.

1980

States Members came a step closer to becoming paid politicians when they voted themselves an increase in their allowances. Senator John de Carteret's proposition raised the guaranteed income of Members to £5,500 - £1,000 more than the Legislation Committee had suggested.

There was strong opposition to the move, particularly from Senator John Le Marquand, who saw it as further eroding Jersey's tradition of honorary service. However, the majority of Members voted to take the money.

30 April

1773

After two earthquakes had struck Jersey, the Royal Court sprang into action. A day of fasting and prayer was ordered in an attempt to avert more tremors.

1832

Philippe Syvret, Jean Grandin, Edouard Perrée, Jean Le Feuvre and Jean Vibert stood before the court, accused of kidnapping Jean Lucas. The abduction had occurred just before an election, the purpose being to stop Lucas voting. Having heard the case, Perrée, Le Feuvre and Vibert were acquitted. Syvret and Grandin were found guilty and sent to prison for one month, as well as Syvret being fined 100 livres and Grandin 50 livres.

These sentences were very light for their time, but it may have had something to do with the fact that Philippe d'Auvergne, the senior judge at the trial, was also the Commander of the north-west regiment of the Militia. The victim, Lucas, was a Methodist who years before had been imprisoned for refusing to do militia drill on conscientious grounds. His regiment had been the north-west regiment.

1980

Deputy Pierre Horsfall was elected Senator, to complete the late Cyril Le Marquand's term of office. The two-horse race was between Deputy Horsfall and Richard Manning, a political newcomer. There was a very low turnout, of just 12%, with Horsfall receiving 4,545 votes and Manning receiving 787.

1985

The States voted to follow England's example and made the wearing of seatbelts compulsory. The debate was a heated one and a number of petitions against the new law had been raised and presented to States Members. Some exceptions were made, notably for taxi and cab drivers. Following the debate the police announced that all vehicles registered after 1966 had to be fitted with seat belts immediately.

01 May

1643

The English Civil War came to Jersey when one of the King's frigates took refuge near Elizabeth Castle. The pursuing Parliamentary ships were then fired on by the castle's cannons, an act that clearly removed any possibility of the Island being neutral.

1779

A French fleet of three warships, two gunboats, two cutters and a privateer, as well as 42 small sailing boats carrying fifteen hundred men, was sighted off Jersey. The French force approached St Ouen's Bay, where the Island's troops were gathering, ready to defend. But the French sea captains refused to sail within range of the British guns and the whole group returned to their home port.

1921

The first Labour Day workers' procession was held, with 2,000 dockers and general workers taking part. At 2 o'clock, watched by a large crowd, the march left Museum Street en route to West Park. A band led the way and upon their arrival hymns were sung and speeches made. The Dean was present throughout, not intending to speak but simply to rejoice with the workers on Labour Day.

1951

A plan to construct fountains in the Parade Gardens to commemorate the Festival of Britain was defeated in the States, the project being rejected as being a waste of money.

1952

It was Muratti day and for the first time Jersey's team were all locally born. The football match, held at Springfield, was enthusiastically supported, with Guernsey's fans invading the pitch when their team scored the first goal. Three more followed, one for Jersey and two for the visitors. Although of obvious interest to Islanders, the match was also considered important enough that a commentary of the game by John Arlott was broadcast by the BBC on the west of England home service.

02 May

1848

The iron paddle steamer *Dispatch* made her maiden voyage to Jersey on this day. She was a sister ship to the *Courier*, which had begun service to the islands the previous November. The *Dispatch*'s home port was Poole, then a newly built packet station, and she travelled on from Jersey to St Malo before returning to England. Harbour facilities in St Helier were being improved all the time but in August of the same year, due to a low tide, the *Dispatch*'s passengers disembarked by being carried piggyback to shore.

1851

The States passed a law which decreed that 'it shall be forbidden to leave the vehicles called omnibuses standing in King Street or Queen Street or in any other street where two vehicles cannot easily pass side by side'. Traffic and noise pollution were sufficient cause for concern at the time for a petition to be circulated 'praying for the suppression of the omnibus horns' which, it claimed, disturbed the peace even on Sundays and 'inflicted torture upon the sick and dying'. The buses were, of course, horse-drawn vehicles.

1987

The Duke and Duchess of York arrived for an official weekend visit. A crowd of 30,000 people had been predicted but only a fraction turned up to see them at the airport. The royal visit coincided with Jersey's international air race, which this year included a Concorde flypast and the Red Arrows doing an air display. The crowds were thin and dignitaries knee deep, with those who had wanted to see Sarah and Andrew having a long, cold wait.

1989

Plans to spend £25 million developing the reclaimed area to the west of Albert Pier were announced. A multi-storey car park, with three floors below ground, four floors above and 1,500 spaces, was just one of the features. An extensive re-routing of existing roads and the laying of new ones was planned to allow access to the newly created land and to smooth the flow of traffic around the waterfront.

03 May

1865

The Constable of St Helier reminded parishioners of the new public health law, passed on 13 December 1864, which prohibited the keeping of pigs in the area between Fort Regent and Gallow's Hill[14]. Residents were reminded that a £10 fine would be levied on persistent offenders, their pigs would be confiscated and if the fine was not paid, the animals would be sold to recover the money.

1938

A bungalow called Hillside in St Peter's Valley was destroyed by fire. Mr E Gilley of Tesson Mill had called the fire brigade when he saw flames coming from the chimney, but by the time they arrived the property had already burned to the ground. Mr P Mollet, who owned the bungalow, rushed home on hearing of the fire but neighbours had already salvaged what they could from the blaze. Although insured, Mollet lost his home, chicken houses, most of his furniture and £12 in cash that he had had in his bungalow.

1941

Islanders were warned that they had until the end of the week to put their gardens to good use. If not, neglected areas would be taken over and no compensation would be paid. The German forces had been occupying the Island for less than a year but it was becoming apparent that the war was going to continue for some time. Food shortages were already a fact of life and the local authorities realised that the Island would need to be as self-sufficient as possible.

1945

The German Occupation of the Island was drawing to a close and despite the ban on radios, Islanders knew it. The German authorities were concerned that growing unrest within the population could cause problems, so they issued a proclamation stating that there were to be 'no public marches, assemblies or demonstrations' and that 'those who transgressed this order will be severely dealt with'.

---

[14] Known today as Westmount.

04 May

1889

Ferdinand Le Quesne's actions on this day won him the Victoria Cross. Born on Christmas Day, 1863, in St Helier, Le Quesne attended local schools before going to King's College Hospital, London, to train and work. Having joined the army medical corps, he was sent to Burma, where the empire was having problems with the 'Chins'. On the day in question Captain Le Quesne had attended to wounded soldiers under fire. With the enemy stockade only five yards away, Le Quesne had dressed Second-Lieutenant Michel's injuries and was proceeding to assist another officer when Le Quesne himself was severely wounded. He recovered and lived to the ripe old age of 86.

1950

Guernsey won the Muratti 2-1, watched by a record crowd. Nearly 10,500 people attended the inter-island football match at Springfield. Hard though it may be to believe, the visiting green and whites completely outplayed the home team. The only solace the locals could have had was that Guernsey had not won since 1938.

1969

A local man crossed to France on a home built hovercraft. It took Mr Gooch one hour and five minutes to travel from Gorey to Carteret. The machine was powered by two motorcycle engines and evolved from the four craft Gooch had built previously.

1974

Mrs Touzel successfully raised the Clameur de Haro in a St Ouen field in order to stop a man digging potatoes which he had mistakenly planted in her mother's cotîl. On coming to court, it was found that the Clameur had been raised correctly and the man, Herbert Petit, was fined £1, with costs of £5, the small sum recognising that it had been a genuine mistake. And Mrs Touzel got to keep the potatoes.

05 May

1828

The Theatre Royal, The Crescent, Don Road, opened its doors to the public. This new theatre was an ambitious endeavour, particularly as this form of entertainment had always been spurned by Islanders in the past. Touring companies were brought over but the locals stayed true to form and the theatre always ran at a loss. When it burned down in 1863, its replacement got a far better attendance, as a church was built on the site.

1848

One of Jersey's rare natural phenomena occurred on this day. When certain weather conditions prevail, mirages have been known to appear off Jersey's south-east coast. This time, between one and two o'clock in the afternoon, distant boats and rocks, some actually seven or eight miles away, appeared to be only a few hundred yards from shore. Men onboard the vessels could clearly be seen, some in several places at the same time, as their reflection bounced around the atmosphere. The distortion was maintained until a light breeze came up, whereupon the mirage disappeared.

One notable case of this bizarre natural occurrence was when Le Mont St Michel appeared off the coast, visible in every detail. These happenings are infrequent and only tend to manifest themselves on hot, calm days, sometimes with a slight haze.

1976

The Jersey New Waterworks Company announced its intention to flood Queen's Valley. Having looked at various areas around the Island, including Le Mourier Valley, Queen's Valley was considered to be the best option to cater for the Island's ever-growing demands for water. In announcing their intentions, the cost was said to be £3½ million and it was hoped that work on the project would begin the following year, with water on tap by 1980. The company's intentions proved wildly optimistic[15] and the campaign to save the valley got underway.

---

[15] See 29th November for further details.

06 May

1847

Eight months after Queen Victoria's visit to the Island, it was finally decided to build Victoria College to commemorate the event. In fact a college had been destined for that site over 200 years earlier but the States had got no further than levelling the land.

1848

Three men went to launch a small boat at Bel Royal. However, when two of the three crew saw the state of the craft they decided to stay on dry land. Mr Dubois, a shoemaker from St Peter, was not put off and he set off in the leaky boat. At this time few people could swim and when the boat later sank, Dubois was drowned.

1897

On this day the Jersey vessel *Cicelia* was towed into Yarmouth, having been found abandoned off the Wash. Her valuable cargo of olive oil was intact, unlike her crew, who had all disappeared.

The boat was owned and registered to Messieurs P Le Masurier and Co, and she was commanded by Captain Cordy. News came later that all her crew were safe, having abandoned ship by taking to a small boat.

1966

Nearly 140 planes had arrived at Jersey Airport to participate in the Channel Islands Aero Club 12th International Air Rally. Said to be the largest air rally in Europe to date, the principal awards went to German pilots.

There were a few problems, particularly when 20 aircraft gate crashed the event. The extra planes confused officials as they were unsure who was and who was not an official competitor.

07 May

1860

A telegraphic service was opened between Jersey and France, allowing the same type of communications with Europe that had existed between the Island and England for the past eighteen months.

1906

The parish of St Clement had two notices published, both offering rewards for information about recent crimes. £5 was offered for information about the person or people who had thrown stones through windows, breaking about 90 panes of glass, a couple of days earlier.

A further £2 was available to those who helped to find the person who had placed a wire across the entrance to John Pallot's property, La Becquetterie. Informants were to contact T P Marett, St Clement's Chef de Police.

1949

The arrival of Jersey's Liberation penny was announced. The Royal Mint had broken precedent by producing the coin to commemorate the historic event. The crowned head of King George VI was depicted on one side, with the Jersey crest and the words 'Liberated 1945' on the other. The Education Committee proposed giving each child in school one of these pennies as a souvenir, noting that already 9th May 1945 was of no particular significance to some school children.

1970

The Island's newly built desalination plant began testing its operational capacity. The plant, which had cost £1,250,000, had been built to convert sea water into drinking water at a rate of 1½ million gallons a day. It was envisaged that the system would be run in August and September each year, to boost the Island's water reserves. Running costs were said to be £500 per day, but that was before the oil on which it ran became scarce and expensive during the oil crisis just a few years later.

08 May

1368

Although the Lempriere family had lived in Jersey for four generations, they were still regarded as foreigners by some. They had acquired property in the Island but this was prohibited to aliens. However, having paid a £70 fine to the King they were pardoned on this day and permission to own property was granted. It is curious that some form of housing qualifications have been in force in Jersey for over six hundred years. One law that no longer exists is the one that almost cost the Lempriere's their home. Norman law of the time said that if a man sold his property, any of his heirs could buy it back for the price paid.

1945

Germany officially surrendered on this day and two British destroyers, the *Bulldog* and *Beagle*, arrived in the Island's waters to complete 'Operation Nest Egg', the liberation of the Channel Islands. The British forces rendezvoused with a German vessel off Guernsey to discuss the German surrender. Upon boarding the *Bulldog*, Lieutenant-Commander Zimmermann gave the Nazi salute, an action which instantly put a chill in the air. And when Zimmermann then relayed Admiral Hüffmeier's threat to open fire on the British ships if they did not withdraw, the British were completely outraged. Brigadier Snow's response was to inform Zimmermann that if the British ships were fired upon, the German Admiral would be 'hanged tomorrow'.

1947

The Island's weeks of anticipation were rewarded in what the newspaper proclaimed as 'Jersey's greatest sporting event'. Jersey's first International Road Race saw racing cars hurtling along Victoria Avenue and down the Inner Road. Teams from all over Europe took part, thrilling the crowds as they thundered past. Prince Bira, one of the most popular drivers of his day, failed to complete the course, breaking down at Bel Royal. However, having borrowed an old bike, the crowds were able to cheer him home as he slowly cycled back to the pits.

09 May

1870

Henry William Vardon was born in Grouville on this day. Until the age of 20 he showed little interest in golf, working as a doctor's pageboy and then a gardener. When, in about 1890, Vardon's brother won £20 in a tournament in England, the idea of golf as a profession became appealing.

Vardon became a greenkeeper on Lord Ripon's estate and in 1896 won the British Open, a feat he repeated five times. He went on to tour America in 1900, winning their Open too.

The Great War put a stop to golf tournaments and ended Vardon's championship days. But he remained in the sport, coaching and writing a number of successful books on the game.

In 1937 he died, but the 'Vardon grip' lives on.

1911

The parish of St Helier unanimously voted to accept Jurat Le Gros' generous offer of land at First Tower. The 22 vergées were being given on condition that a park would be created on the site, which it was. A church was also to be built for the District of St Andrew's.

1945

Jersey's wartime Bailiff, Alexander Coutanche, escorted General Wolfe, the German commander, out to *HMS Beagle*, the British destroyer, to surrender the German forces. Germany as a whole had surrendered the day before and on this day Islanders gathered in town, awaiting the arrival of British troops.

Having lived under the German occupation for nearly five years, the sight of the first British forces was greeted with wild enthusiasm. The Union Jack was raised at the Pomme D'Or Hotel, to enormous cheers, and everyone celebrated the freedom that had been stolen from them five years earlier.

The 9th May was later declared a national holiday.[16]

---

[16] See 28th February for further details.

10 May

1800

The States decided that the site once called the Market Place and now named the Royal Square was no longer suitable as a market place and chose to move the market to its present site.

1841

Edouard Durell, the rector of St Saviour, was suspended for five years after admitting his conduct had caused a scandal. Back in 1836 two of his leading parishioners had accused him of sodomy, the penalty for which was death. Durell had denied the charge and law suits flew in all directions. The controversy raged for five years, after which the rector reluctantly retired into private life.

1959

A light aircraft returning to the mainland after an air rally crashed into the sea to the east of Gorey Castle. Divers later went down, recovering three bodies, and the plane's wreckage was dragged to the harbour by the States tug. An eye witness reported: 'It was like watching a leaf fall from the sky. I saw the aircraft spiral downwards and then go into a vertical dive. It hit the water at tremendous speed and vanished immediately.'

1994

The States agreed in principle to legalise abortion. Termination of a foetus was to be allowed up to 24 weeks gestation, provided two doctors agreed that there was a substantial risk of grave foetal abnormality and if at any time the mother's life was at risk.

Ever since abortion had been legalised in England, local women had travelled to the mainland for the procedure. The Public Health President told the House that over 1,800 women had gone to the UK between 1987 and 1992 to have abortions.

When it came to the vote, it was passed by 32 votes to 18. Although it was stated that it would not be abortion on demand, those opposed to the measures viewed its introduction very bleakly.

11 May

1814

The foundation stone of St Helier's new quay was laid. It was being built in the area in front of Commercial Buildings and was funded by the merchants. But even so the harbour was still inadequate. When, in 1817, the King's nephew arrived, he was forced to scramble ashore on all fours over seaweed covered rocks.

1897

A parish assembly in St Martin's voted to build a new public school. A committee had been set up earlier in the year and it now recommended the construction of a school. It was proposed that a site of about three vergées close to the public hall be acquired, with £153 per vergée being paid. The discussion was said to be 'animated' but when put to the vote, the proposal was carried by 34 votes to 16.

1960

Work at St Helier Harbour came to a halt when local dockers went on strike. At a mass meeting held at Church House on this day, union leaders warned their members that such action would be unconstitutional and therefore unofficial. Despite this the dockworkers withdrew their labour, demanding piecework rates and incentive bonuses when handling local produce for export. Two days later the men returned to work while negotiations took place.

1989

The Defence Committee approved plans to convert the Royal Engineers' Yard at Mount Bingham into the headquarters of the Jersey Territorial Army Squadron. The £2 million plans included offices, a garage block, a rifle range, kitchens and a caretaker's flat. Perhaps the most contentious aspect of the scheme were the three bars that were to be furnished at public expense. But it was pointed out that these were quite necessary, as despite being a small unit with few officers, it was out of the question for different ranks to drink and socialise together.

12 May

1838

Major-General Sir Archibald Campbell, the Lieutenant Governor, died. It was said that his death came about as the result of a chill he had caught at the Gorey oyster riots.[17] Campbell was buried in the Town Church.

1870

Jeremy and Philip Cabot went before the court, having spent the previous few days in prison, charged with entering an unoccupied house and causing damage. When asked if they had enjoyed their first taste of jail, the two, weeping, said they had not. Mrs Cabot, the brothers' mother, offered to pay for the damage, which was accepted by the court. The two boys, the younger of whom was 10 years old, were warned that if they reoffended they would be taken to prison and flogged.

1928

Andrew Driscoll appeared before the Police Court, charged with cruelty to a dog by hitting it with a bottle. Driscoll claimed that the dog had gone for him and he had tapped it on the head with the bottle which he happened to be carrying. However, a string of witnesses claimed he had kicked the dog, which had been sleeping on the pavement, and then hit it on the head. Found guilty, Driscoll was given the choice of paying a 10 shilling fine or spending a day in prison. He paid the fine.

1970

A new system of parking control came into effect on this day. The town's on-road parking had been divided up into zones and a parking disc, costing 2s 6d, allowed drivers to park for a specified period of time. In a yellow zone you could stay for only 30 minutes, in a red zone for 1 hour, in a green zone for 2 hours and in a white zone for 3 hours. The further from the town centre the zone was, the longer the length of time you were allowed to stay.

---

[17] See 7th April for further details.

13 May

1901

The inquest into the death of Jean Wallace Cabot was held on this day. His body had been discovered in a field in Victoria Village by Jean Cadiou on the previous day. Alongside the body had been an empty beer bottle and the inquest heard from two witnesses that they had each sold Cabot beer the day before he was found.

There were no signs of violence on the body but it was stated that some months earlier Cabot had been involved in a carriage accident, but had deemed treatment unnecessary. One witness told of hearing snoring coming from the field and of finding Jean Cabot apparently drunk, so he had left him where he slept.

However, the post-mortem found that death had been due to a fractured skull. Further investigations revealed that during a drinking bout with a man named Ernest Bechec, accusations of being on parochial relief had been thrown around, leading to Bechec throwing Cabot to the ground. Bechec was later charged with assault.

1921

For the second time in 20 years the Opera House was destroyed by fire. After the first incident, the theatre had been rebuilt using as much non-flammable material as possible, in an effort to avoid history repeating itself. However, the precautions proved ineffective when, at about midnight, following the evening's performance, flame had crept through the gallery and soon the fire had spread through the building. The Fire Brigade quickly had it under control but not before the roof had caved in. By 4 o'clock the fire was out but the Opera House was a complete ruin. An initial estimate of the damage put the cost of repairs at £8,000.

1974

The appeal to raise funds for a new lifeboat was officially closed, having reached the sum of £100,000. Jurat Bailhache, chairman of the Jersey branch of the Royal National Lifeboat Institution, thanked Islanders for their generosity but reminded those who had yet to give that running costs of £12,000 were incurred each year and that donations were always welcome.

14 May

1603

Along with new strict religious edicts came new laws and on this day an ordinance proclaimed that all games were prohibited on Sundays and all taverns were to stay closed. The law makers were keen to protect the souls and bodies of Islanders, so much so that eight years earlier they had nobly ordered no tavern to sell wine unless it had been sampled by the Bailiff or Jurats. The beer was to be tasted by the Constables or Centeniers.

1834

The first horticultural show was held by the Royal Jersey Agricultural and Horticultural Society in the cattle market. Since that date, the venue has changed, as have the growing techniques. Guano was introduced to the Island in 1844, reducing the reliance on the traditional vraic, and in 1880 Mr de la Haye first propagated what is commonly known as the Jersey Royal Potato, on which the Island's agricultural economy had relied until recent times.

1850

HMS Cuckoo, previously named the *Cinderella*, was a 234 ton vessel which had begun serving the Island as a mail steamer in 1839. In 1845 she was taken off the cross Channel run and began work as a fisheries protection vessel, based at Gorey. However, on this day, she was being used to ferry men to and from a troop ship which was anchored in St Aubin's Bay. The unfortunate *Cuckoo* struck the Oyster Rock and, taking on water, just made it back to the harbour before she sank. The crew and troops on board were rescued without loss of life. Despite being almost completely submerged, she was later refloated. The following year she was replaced by *HMS Dasher*.

1925

The public were notified that sweepstakes were illegal in the Island and that the police intended to prosecute anyone caught participating in one. Hotels and clubs often ran a sweepstake, particularly on football or horse racing results.

15 May

1648

On this day a duel took place on the outskirts of the town. Michael Duhamel, an 18-year old Jerseyman, and James Biggs, a young man of English origin, had been friends. However, a dispute had arisen and a duel was arranged. About an hour before sunset, with each having drunk a pint of Spanish wine beforehand, they met. The two fought bitterly with their swords. Duhamel suffered a wound to his thigh before running his opponent through.

News of the fight had spread and the duel was broken up, with both parties wounded but alive. Michael Duhamel left the Island that night, before he could be arrested. James Biggs was less fortunate, as the sword wound that had gone right through his chest killed him three weeks later.

1857

Miriam Evans arrived in Jersey on a ten week visit and stayed at Rose Cottage in Gorey Village. Miriam Evans was an author, better known as George Eliot.

1871

A meeting was held to hear landowners' objections to the proposed route of the Eastern Railway. About a dozen people attended, the majority being content to receive compensation for their loss, only a few having strong objections. The States decreed that the construction of the railway must be finished within three years and that at any time they thought fit, the States had the right to purchase the railway, paying the company the cost of construction plus 33 1/3 percent.

1982

Jersey's Public Health Committee announced their intention to ban smoking on buses. Anyone found doing so would be fined. The proposal met with almost universal support and was said to be long overdue.

16 May

1893

The steam ship *Dora* struck rocks on this day. The mailboat, owned by the London and South Western Railway Company, had begun serving the Island four years earlier and was a 820 ton twin masted steamer whose single screw engine could push her through the water at 16 knots. On this particular day, having left St Helier, she caught a rock off Guernsey. The disabled ship was towed to St Peter Port by another steamer, the *Lynx*, where her passengers and the mail were landed safely. She had been under the command of Captain Nutbeam, who was severely censured for his error.

1904

One of Jersey's first motor crashes was reported in the *Jersey Evening Post*. It was rumoured that motor cars and motor bikes had been racing in the early hours but that it was definite that one had crashed at Beaumont. Having hit the pavement, the machine had careered into Mrs Olsen's shop. It was stated that 'the motor car was more damaged than the shop'. After approximately half an hour's repairs, the vehicle limped back to St Helier.

1974

The Jersey New Waterworks Company assured Islanders that the dam at Val de la Mare was safe. A three-year study of the concrete structure had been undertaken after parts of it appeared to be degrading. The softening of the concrete was put down to a combination of factors, including a chemical reaction between the cement and aggregates, as well as the water. It was estimated that the repairs would cost £50,000 but the dam, less than 15 years old, was in no danger of collapse.

1989

Jacqui Huet made history by becoming the Island's first woman Centenier. She was elected unopposed, having failed in an attempt at the office in the St Helier Honorary Police 18 months earlier. Mrs Huet was already serving as a Constable's Officer and hope was expressed that other women would follow her example.

17 May

1468

Mont Orgueil Castle was again under siege. However, this time its inhabitants were loyal to France and it was the English who surrounded the walls. The siege lasted until October, when the garrison surrendered and were allowed to return to Normandy. A great deal of food must have been stored within the Castle, but extra supplies had been brought across from France. Towards the end, though, the desperate men built a craft within the battlements, hoping to escape under cover of night. But they could not.

1830

Jersey's first lifeboat was launched at Rozel, where she had been built by Mr Lillington. After coming under considerable pressure to purchase two lifeboats, the States had voted £150 for the acquisition of one boat with a cart, boat house and other equipment. Once in the water she was tested. Twenty-four men did their best to sink or capsize her and failed. The drain plugs were removed and after 25 minutes the boat, still with 24 passengers aboard, was full of water but did not sink. All aboard then vacated the vessel and after an hour or so, she had emptied herself of water and once again floated.

1847

While men's wages remained pegged at two shillings a day, the price of bread rose weekly, and matters finally came to a head on this day. A large group of men working on the road construction at La Haule downed tools and marched to town. Along the way they were joined by shipyard workers and masons building the Albert Pier, among others. Officials tried to reason with the crowd in the Royal Square but failed. The mob then proceeded to the town mill at Grands Vaux, broke down the doors and loaded up wagons with stolen flour. Order was eventually restored but the shaken authorities agreed to sell bread to the poor at a below cost price and the Island's wealthy donated £715 to a relief fund.

18 May

1938

A parish assembly voted in favour of building public toilets at Rozel. Proposed by Trinity's Rector, who informed those gathered that the Tourism Committee were encouraging Parish Constables to build lavatories at popular bays, he claimed the facility would pay for itself, pointing out that the toilets in the town market easily brought in £80 per quarter. There were some dissenting voices, but the motion was passed on the Rozel toilet.

1948

The feud in St Ouen between the Carré and A'Court families is legendary. On this day it was fact. Edward A'Court was in the Police Court, charged with committing an unprovoked assault on Francis Carré. Carré told how his hands had been in his pockets when A'Court had hit him in the face. Carré had kept them there as he had previously been warned by the Magistrate that prison awaited him if he appeared in court again. A'Court claimed that he had thought that Carré was about to hit him, so he had got in first. Before fining A'Court £5, the Magistrate heard that their feud dated back to the Occupation and a dispute over 28 lbs of wheat.

1954

A one legged man whose trousers exploded when he fell off his bike was recovering from second degree burns in hospital on this day. Mr Le Breuilly had a container of weed killer in his pocket as he cycled down the road. When his wheel caught on an obstruction, he fell, his artificial leg creating sparks as it scraped the road, thus igniting the weed killer. His clothes burst into flames, which were doused by onlookers, but not before Le Breuilly had been badly burned.

1983

It was announced that the children's home, Haut de la Garenne, was to close. A report had been prepared two years earlier on all aspects of Island child care and it was felt that the institutional style building was no longer acceptable.

19 May

1845

Local mariner Henry Le Vesconte set sail as part of an expedition to find a northern passage from the Atlantic to the Pacific Ocean. The first summer was unsuccessful. Having overwintered they tried again, making good progress, until becoming iced in. Again they overwintered but in the summer the ice didn't melt and the ship remained stuck. A third winter was endured until April 1848, when the surviving crew decided to march out. It was 1,200 miles to the nearest help but they set off dragging sledges. The route they took was later traced by the skeletons as they all gradually died. Le Vesconte's remains were discovered 150 miles from the ship and now lie in Greenwich.

1917

Ada Barette was before the Royal Court, charged with criminally forsaking her children. As it was the time of the First World War, her husband was serving at the Front. Mrs Barette received 31 shillings a week, yet despite this she had moved in with another man and abandoned her children with her father-in-law. The couple then travelled to London, where she was later arrested and brought back to the Island. Having heard the facts, the Bailiff accused her of heartless neglect and of cohabiting with men while her husband was doing his duty. She was sentenced to six months hard labour.

1923

Clement Gallichan tried to have his mother and father evicted. The Royal Court heard that Gallichan's parents lived in rooms in their son's house but had been trying to find new accommodation, without success. The Bailiff seemed astonished that a son would take legal action to evict his parents, the father being crippled, leaving them homeless. However, as they were classed as lodgers, not tenants, the law under which the proceedings had been brought did not apply and the case had to be withdrawn.

20 May

1542

Having returned from his pilgrimage to Jerusalem, Dean Mabon set about creating a Jersey version of the Holy Sepulchre. On his land stood the mound at La Hougue Bie and on top of that was a ruined chapel. The Dean added a new chapel and restored the old one, his intention being to create a place of pilgrimage.

It is alleged that Dean Mabon also used to supplement his income by performing fake miracles. Visions were said to appear and candles suspended on wires convinced many that they were burning in mid air. This ecclesiastical man of alleged dubious ethics was appointed Dean seven times during his life, the last occasion being on this day.

1874

It was announced that the new lighthouse at Corbière was to be lit. The notice informed mariners that in clear weather the white light would be visible for 17 miles. Red lights would be visible marking dangerous areas. The light was said to be 119 feet above the high water of a spring tide. In fog a bell was to be rung 'three times in quick succession at intervals of thirty seconds'.

1880

The London and South Western Railway steamer *Alliance* came on to the Jersey route. She was not a young ship at the time but maintained a service for sixteen fairly uneventful years.

1938

A notice appeared in the *Jersey Evening Post*, informing it's readers that 'itinerant photographers' would no longer be able to trade on Sundays. The Constable of St Helier, who was responsible for issuing licences, made it known that they were only valid on weekdays. The photographers were less than happy about the enforcement of the Sunday Trading Laws, as Sundays were their busiest days.

21 May

1900

The relief of Mafeking during the Boer War must have seemed a million miles from Jersey but the ripples caused by the military action reached our Island on this day. Upon hearing the news Islanders celebrated spontaneously with a parade about the town and bands playing. France had opposed the war and as the celebrations died down, trouble developed in Jersey's French quarter. The riot that ensued raged around the Hilgrove area, with countless windows being smashed and gas lamps being damaged. Eventually the troops stationed at Fort Regent were brought in to restore order.

1919

Permission was sought from the States for fares on the Jersey Eastern Railway to be increased. Originally charges had been limited to 1½d per mile first class and 1d for second, but in the intervening 47 years, costs had risen. A new maximum rate of 2½d per mile first class and 1½d per mile second class was now sanctioned.

1923

In a ceremony attended by States Members, military personnel and prominent Islanders, Elizabeth Castle was handed over to the States. It had been purchased for £1,500 and was to be maintained as an historical monument. The ceremony ended with the grand battery firing a 21-gun salute, the last time they ever did so.

1949

Munitions left behind by the German occupying forces had been removed. However, there remained a quantity of explosives that lay lost and hidden. On this day, while working a field on Noirmont Farm, a horse was badly wounded when it stood on a hand grenade. Mr A Overs was behind the horse when it's hooves triggered the explosion. The wounded animal bolted, taking the machinery it pulled with it. Mr Overs was hit in the eye by flying shrapnel, while the horse suffered severe shrapnel wounds to its stomach. Throughout the rest of the century, remnants of the war have been discovered from time to time, fortunately with few casualties.

22 May

1563

The Reformation was in full swing in Jersey at this time, with most officials being fervently anti-Catholic. A great number of wayside crosses, which had watched over the Island's thoroughfares for generations, were smashed and it was ordered that on this day all Catholic religious books were to be taken to St Helier and there burned in the Market Place.

1651

On this day Captain Collings accidentally killed a boy aged four or five. Diarist Jean Chevalier relates how the Captain had toured the taverns to gather his crew, as his frigate was ready to sail. One of his men was drunk and refused to leave the inn.

The Captain then went into the garden, where skittles were being played, followed by the drunken crew member. As the man jibed his captain, Collings threw a skittle at him. The man ducked and it is recorded that 'the boy was struck on the crown, smashing his skull so that the brains gushed forth'.

Captain Collings gave himself over to the law and 'threw himself on the mercy of the Governor'. The Governor, however, had no choice but to imprison him in Gorey Castle.

1803

Yet again France and Britain resumed hostilities and, as so often before, Jersey readied itself for attack. The signal stations which gave warning of an approaching fleet were re-established and Jersey waited.

General Gordon, the Lieutenant Governor, proposed placing the Island under martial law. Members of the States were so surprised by the plan that they adjourned for 24 hours and for the first time to date reconvened on a Sunday. The proposal was rejected by 26 votes to 10.

But the ten who voted for the proposal were not forgiven by Islanders who, among other things, burnt them in effigy.

23 May

1822

A British gunboat arrived at Gorey, its purpose being to protect the British fishing boats working the Channel oyster beds. The French had never objected to local boats occasionally fishing in their waters, but the huge English fishing fleet that now worked from Gorey was destroying the French stocks. As we know from modern times, the French are quite prepared to take direct action and so the gunboat was intended to protect the illegal activities of the English.

1835

It is recorded that three Jews were placed in the pillory in the Royal Square, having been accused of forgery.

1848

Isambard Kingdom Brunel paid Jersey an official visit. With St Catherine's breakwater under construction and a number of engineering works recently completed, he came over to inspect government works.

1892

This day saw the opening of a biological station and aquarium at Havre des Pas. This popular attraction displayed marine life for study and entertainment. The enterprise was successful at first but similar establishments in England, subsidised by the government, forced it to close.

1945

The Occupation had caused chaos to the Island's monetary system. On this day German currency ceased to be legal tender. The Germans had flooded the Island with marks and pfennigs. They were worth nothing but local money had soon disappeared and so they were used. Goods were still priced in sterling but paid for in marks. In the confused financial system, notes to the value of £55,000 had been printed but with the end of the war Jersey's economy was getting back to normal.

24 May

1850

Over three years after the decision to build Victoria College was made, its foundation stone was laid. The site for the school had been levelled 200 years earlier, but sometimes things move slowly in Jersey.

1913

The States agreed that all types of aircraft in the Island could be requisitioned in times of war. The first plane to land in Jersey had done so less than a year earlier, but the States were aware of aircrafts' capabilities during a conflict. Incidentally, there were no aircraft in Jersey at this time.

1947

Jersey was honoured by the visit of Viscount Montgomery (Monty). He received a tremendous welcome from Islanders, who treated him like royalty. The walkabouts, speeches and parades were well attended by enthusiastic crowds. A patriotic feeling was still very much to the fore and when Monty said that he would return and next time bring Churchill with him, Islanders were delighted.

1952

The Paid Police Force came into operation, with the St Helier Paid Police being absorbed into this Island-wide force. They also had a new headquarters at Rouge Bouillon. The 48 men were to be joined by a further 25 officers when at full strength. The new force could respond to incidents anywhere in Jersey and the public were informed to dial Central 999.

1999

It was announced that De Gruchy's Department Store in King Street was to be sold for £45 million. The Merchant Retail Group, who already had a large shareholding in the company, offered 300p per share in the declared take-over. Islanders were assured that no jobs would go and that the character of one of the Island's longest serving stores would remain unchanged.

25 May

1644

Sir George de Carteret launched an abortive attack on Sark during the Civil War, with four boats to be used to capture the island for the Royalist forces.

During the crossing, the vessels became separated. Captain Lane, who commanded over 70 men, upon approaching Sark, was challenged by three sentries. When asked where they came from, the invading force claimed to be from Guernsey. The suspicious Sarkese discharged a couple of muskets and then ran off. Believing that the initiative was lost, the Jersey boats then returned to their home port.

However the other group, led by Captain Chamberlain, had disembarked at a different point and continued with the attack. The 32-strong team of Royalists quickly captured Sark's Governor and most of the locals.

But in the morning, when the Sark women realised the weakness of the Jersey force, the tables were soon turned. A beacon and a few cannon shots soon brought a large rescue party from Guernsey. Chamberlain's boats did not come to his rescue, leaving the Captain and his men with no choice but to surrender to the greater force.

Captain Chamberlain and his soldiers were then taken to Guernsey in irons and imprisoned.

1891

The Jersey Eastern Railway extension was opened. Until that time the line had finished at Gorey Village, which was proving very inconvenient to passengers with a through-ticket to Paris. They needed to catch the steamer from Gorey Pier and so the extra half a mile of track was laid between the newly built coast road and the sea wall.

The cost of the ticket from Snow Hill to Gorey Pier was 1s second class and an extra 3d to travel first class, with it taking 24 minutes to travel the distance.

26 May

1917

The mystery of a headless body found at the Devil's Hole was solved. Some time before a decomposed, headless corpse had been found in the sea. The inquest decided that the unknown man had drowned and coins in his pocket suggested he may have been Norwegian. Inquiries led to the *Navarra*, a Norwegian ship which had sunk with all hands in the Channel.

1940

With the war in Europe getting closer every day, the authorities in Jersey needed to decide what to do about foreigners. Having considered the problem, the Lieutenant Governor ordered the internment of male enemy aliens in a camp in Grouville.

1949

The proposition to compulsorily purchase slum properties in Pier Road and Le Geyt Road was approved by the States. A total of £50,000 was wanted to acquire the land so that Jersey's housing shortage could be solved, it being said that 400 new homes were needed. The area in Le Geyt Street, known as the Piggeries, contained 40 houses, 38 of which were said to be unfit for reconditioning. Concern was expressed for the current residents who, it was said, were 'paying eight or more shillings per week at the moment and would never find houses anywhere else for under £1 a week'.

Red Houses had been suggested as an area for development but this was rejected because people would have difficulty travelling to their work in town. Some houses were being built in the area but it was said of St Brelade that it was turning into a 'big sewage farm', as the buildings had no drains.

1952

Jersey's first policewoman took up her post. Mrs Campbell-Devlin, née Clements, although not Jersey-born, had been educated at Zelzah House School at First Tower and had then gone to college in England. She had worked in the English civil service and was now a stenographer at the new Paid Police Headquarters in Rouge Bouillon.

27 May

1952

Sir Alexander Coutanche officially opened Jersey Airport's new 1,450 yard tarmac runway. The party took off from the grass runway at the airport in 3 BEA Rapides. Having seen the Island from the air they then made the first landing on Jersey's new facility. Included in the party were a number of Public Works employees who had been engaged on the project, many of whom had never flown before. The first scheduled landing was made by the same pilot who had opened the beach service in 1933.

1962

Two boys were killed in abandoned German tunnels off St Peter's Valley. They were in a small party who had found their way into the previously sealed chamber. It appears that a fire was lit within the tunnel and the boys died from carbon monoxide poisoning. A rescue team entered and searched the tunnels once the alarm had been raised, with the other boys in the group very lucky to get out alive.

1971

The swimming pool at Fort Regent was officially opened. Although the public were allowed in to view the facilities, the first swimming session was at 10 am the following day. The advert that accompanied the opening gave out the prices: 15p for adults, 8p for juniors and 5p for spectators.

1980

The Island Development Committee announced plans to buy land between Bath Street and Oxford Road for £1.2 million. The land belonged to the Gas Company, who were being encouraged to move their operation out of town to La Collette. Although nothing specific was planned for the site, a multi-storey car park was considered desirable, as well as housing. The main reason stated for the land's acquisition was that it was 'the last big area of land which will ever become available in the town'.

28 May

1870

During the construction of the railway it was recognised that the ancient law of the Clameur de Haro could easily disrupt its progress. To stop delays in the building work the States passed a bill in effect making the railway company immune to the injunction. It was therefore quite ironic that it was a Member of the States who halted the building work by raising the Clameur on this day.

Jurat de Quetteville stopped the work when the builders appeared intent on demolishing the slaughterhouse on the Esplanade, the problem being that the States had sanctioned the railway work unaware that so much of the abattoir lay in the way. The following month the States allowed the railway's construction to continue as long as butchers were still allowed into the parts of the abattoir that were not being demolished.

1940

Walter George Payne came before the court on a charge of fortune telling. Mrs Griffin and Mrs Williams had each paid Payne 2 shillings to have their fortune told. The accused was fined £2 for the offence.

1946

Peter Edwin Larbalestier, an assistant keeper at La Corbière Lighthouse, was killed while attempting to rescue a visitor who had become cut off by the tide. Irene and Stanley Belsey had been sitting on a rock and failed to notice the rising tide.

Once surrounded by the sea, Mr Belsey managed to wade to safety but Mrs Belsey refused to move. Seeing her plight, Larbalestier went to her aid, but they were both washed away by the strong tide and drowned.

A memorial stone at the entrance to the causeway now acts as a warning to those ignorant of the treacherous Island tides, as well as commemorating a brave and selfless act.

29 May

1824

The *Ariadne*, a 3 masted, copper bottomed paddle steamer, arrived in Jersey to begin the steam era for inter-island and cross Channel shipping.[18] Thirteen days later a rival vessel, the *Lord Beresford*, arrived with the same intentions. And so the sailing cutters' day had come and gone. With crossings now taking only 8 hours instead of at least 16 and wind and weather less of a problem, the old sail driven boats were doomed.

1841

A new fish market opened in Cattle Street, having been transferred from Halkett Place. The building was renovated 30 years later and is now the site of Jersey Telecoms' offices.

1918

Lieutenant Sidney Burgess arrived in Jersey, landing his plane at Grève de Lecq. On finding one of his elevators was bent, he had decided to make a forced landing at this unlikely spot, touching down in the bay. His damaged sea plane became more damaged as it was later towed back to Cherbourg for repair.

1951

Jersey was again under threat of invasion, this time by the Colorado beetle. Several hundred had been washed up on the north-east shore. None were alive but inspectors were keeping a close watch and farmers were warned to spray their potatoes.

1954

The Fire Brigade moved into new premises on this day. They joined the States Police at the site in Rouge Bouillon. Previously the fire service had been stationed in Nelson Street behind the Odeon. Among the features new to the men was a sliding pole to negate the use of stairs. The new station was on the site of the old town arsenal and incorporated many of the original buildings.

---

[18] See 9th June for further details.

30 May

1850

Harriet Benest put a stop to work on laying a pavement by raising the Clameur de Haro. Miss Benest was concerned to find that the new pavement being laid by the Drains Committee meant that her property in Charles Street would end up well below the level of the road. The Clameur acts as an injunction and work was halted until the court could rule on the matter. Three years later the judgement went in Miss Benest's favour and she was awarded compensation for the loss of value on her house and three years lost rent, totalling £60.

1925

The Defence Committee asked the States for £2,000 to buy Red Houses. The area was already leased by the States on a one year tenancy and the owner had expressed a willingness to sell. The area was used as a camping ground for the militia and already public money had been spent erecting kitchens and digging wells. The train made troop movements easy and as well as the land, the Red Houses would be an additional asset. In the debate, Jurat Le Boutillier showed remarkable foresight when he pointed out that the land might later be used as an aerodrome. Although concern was expressed about where the money would come from, the States only having £1,300 in reserve, the purchase was sanctioned with only three votes against.

1941

The Royal Court approved the act increasing the school leaving age for boys, thus making it law. As well as making it compulsory for boys to remain in education until the age of 15, it was now permitted that they live half a mile further from the school.

1975

The Queen Mother made her third official visit to Jersey. As always the crowds turned out to welcome her and although she went through the usual rituals of greetings on the docks, a speech in the States, guard of honour, etc, the Queen Mother managed to meet a few more ordinary Islanders and the whole event had less formality.

31 May

1901

Mr Laurens offered a reward for information about one of his vehicles which had been tampered with. The night before a lynch pin had been removed from one of his carts' wheels. The cart was later sent for a load of gravel and on reaching Hill Street the wheel came off. The sudden shift of weight caused the horse to fall, the animal sustaining serious cuts, while the driver narrowly escaped injury as the load was strewn across the road. The reward offered by Laurens for information leading to the conviction of the offender or offenders was £1.

1917

And to prove that pointless vandalism is not a modern phenomena, on this day a reward of £1 was offered for information about the cutting of ropes at Bouley Bay. A number of boats had had their mooring ropes deliberately cut, much to the annoyance of their owners.

1935

This day saw the inauguration of a new telegram service. From now on Islanders could send nine words to England for 6 pence. The first recipient of this service was the Prince of Wales, to whom Mrs Martelli addressed her message, stating 'I have the honour to address to your Royal Highness the first telegram from Jersey at the new rate of nine words for six pence'. Fifteen minutes later the Prince replied 'Inaugress, Jersey, much appreciate Jersey's inaugural telegram'.

1981

With the end of the month came the news that weatherwise this had been the worst May on record. It had rained on 28 of the 31 days and almost beat the record of over 5 inches of rainfall for the month. It was also the dullest May, with the poorest sunshine figures since records began.

01 June

1323

Having held the title Lord of the Isles for nearly 50 years, Otho de Grandison left his Swiss castle and visited the Island for the first time. The 90-year old knight was on no sightseeing tour, however, but was more concerned with the collection of taxes. Island officials had begun to line their own pockets rather than his. A nephew previously sent to Guernsey had been thrown in prison. Otho was not imprisoned but a petition did call for him to be expelled from the Isles. Otho returned to Switzerland.

1648

Marie Esnouf was hanged, then her body burned, having been found guilty of witchcraft. After her arrest 60 informants had testified against her. Surgeons shaved her head looking for the mark of the devil. In her mouth they noticed a black mark and when it was lanced she did not cry out and so she was executed. One reason for so many accusers was the fear of being accused yourself of a charge almost impossible to disprove, especially as you were presumed guilty.

1937

The Jersey-England airmail service was inaugurated. The usual ceremonies and speeches took place before the cargo of eight mail sacks were taken to St Helier for delivery. The new service took advantage of the recently completed airport facilities. Included in the first airmail were letters of congratulation and good wishes from the Home Secretary, the Post Office Director and the Mayor of Southampton.

1970

The cable car service to Fort Regent was inaugurated on this day. After the official party, members of the public were allowed on. It cost adults 1 shilling and children 6d. Although the cable cars now took people to the Fort, its redevelopment as a leisure complex had only just begun.

02 June

1923

Towards the end of May 1923 Mrs Ethel Ford went to leave her flat in La Motte Street only to find the doorway being walled up. Mr Shaw, the house's owner, had agreed that a neighbour could undertake these building works and persuaded another tenant, Mr Cross, to allow Mrs Ford to use his entrance to get to her rooms and the problem was solved. However, on this day, Cross withdrew his permission, leaving Mrs Ford with no way of getting to her accommodation. During an altercation that followed, Cross raised the Clameur de Haro, which meant that everything had to remain unaltered until the case could come to court. It also meant Mrs Ford was now homeless, with only the possessions she wore or carried at the time. When the court looked at the case they fined Cross for frivolously raising the Clameur, as well as having to pay costs. Mrs Ford, it was ruled, had a claim against Shaw and Shaw had a claim against Cross.

1938

Jersey had a potato glut and queues of vans and lorries covered the harbour area. The Pricing Committee had decreed that 12/6 per 100 lbs was to be the minimum sale price. Potatoes were bought from the farmers at the Weighbridge by merchants. Due to some ships being delayed and the enormous quantity of Jersey Royals being dug, the merchants were no longer buying, which left the farmers with no option but to wait down on the docks until the market improved. The authorities tried to help the situation by issuing 'stop digging' orders, a procedure that continued into the 1980s as a way of regulating the potato supply.

1952

The Odeon Cinema opened on this day. It was the first post-war Odeon to be built in the United Kingdom and was said to be one of the most up-to-date cinemas in Europe. The film shown was the world premier of *The Importance of Being Ernest*. Among the stars present were Kay Kendall and Anthony Steel, with the master of ceremonies being Eamon Andrews.

03 June

1792

The brig *Liberté*, captained by Charles Hocquard, set sail for St Lawrence, Newfoundland. She carried with her letters for the many Jerseymen who were involved in the cod fisheries. Pierre Mallet was in charge of the mail and a notice in the *Gazette* advised that letters should be taken to him. At this time Channel Islanders were heavily involved in cod fishing around the Grand Bank off Newfoundland. Ships were built locally and fortunes were made, the cod being salted down then brought back to Europe.

1917

One of Jersey's rare natural phenomenon occurred. When weather conditions are right things far offshore can appear close by. From St Aubin and St Brelade bays the French islands of Chausey could be clearly seen. They appeared to be about a mile offshore and, although quite clear and distinct, were upside down. The weather was hot and still, as is always the case when these mirages appear.

1949

Huelins' warehouse in Anley Street was completely gutted by fire. The blaze broke out at about 3 am and was spotted by George Crocker, who raised the alarm. The Fire Brigade were soon on the scene but as the three storey building was filled with tomato trays and box wood, little could be done except to try and stop the fire spreading. Once extinguished, the Brigade spent the day ensuring that the fire would not re-light. However, there was little left to burn as all that remained was the building's shell and a pile of ashes.

1986

The proposition to broadcast States proceedings was passed by 30 votes to 14. Those opposed, led by Senator John Le Marquand, feared that Members would play to the audience, reading speeches rather than debating issues. The broadcasting of British Parliament was said to be a mockery that brought the place into disrepute. Those in favour pointed out that it was only to be a trial, but everyone knew that once the facility was there, it would be permanent.

04 June

1804

Before the construction of Fort Regent, the Town Hill had a makeshift set of defensive earthworks on its summit. Among these was a powder magazine holding 5,000 barrels of gunpowder. To honour the King's birthday on the day a royal salute was fired and somehow material in the powder store caught alight. Three men burst open the door and extinguished the flames just in time, as afterwards barrels full of gunpowder were found to be very badly charred. A grateful States gave all three gold medals and a sum of money.

1906

It was reported in the *Jersey Evening Post* that the paving of certain town roads had been delayed and that tradesmen from Halkett Place and York Street had approached the Constable of St Helier to clarify the situation. It had been decided to pave some town roads with wooden blocks, a sample block having been approved. However when the full load of paving had arrived, parish officials had deemed them to be substandard and not of the quality of the sample. Mr Laurens, who was to supply the timber, accepted that his wood was not up to the job and so the scheme was delayed until a fresh supply could be obtained. In more recent years areas of wooden paving have been uncovered when service suppliers have excavated town streets, the more modern surfaces having been laid directly on top. The work started eleven days later.

1954

The Jersey Gas Light Company inaugurated its new carbonising plant. The grand ceremony was attended by most local dignitaries, with Lady Coutanche pushing the lever to start the work.

1974

Women's rights were under attack in the States when St Mary Constable Le Cornu wanted to allow only rate payers to vote at parish assemblies. As most property was registered in husbands' names a large proportion of women would not be eligible to have a say in parish affairs. The majority of States Members rejected the proposal.

05 June

1897

A fire broke out at a farm on Mont Cochon tenanted by Mr Tirel and his wife, the owner being Mr Coutanche. The blaze was believed to have been started by a lamp which was upset, and it soon took hold. The Fire Brigade set off for the scene, accompanied by two police officers, arriving around midnight. However, they quickly realised that their journey had been wasted as there was no water supply near to hand and the house was well alight.. The cost of the damage was estimated at £300. No one had been hurt and the cattle had been rescued, but it all must have come as a nasty shock for Mr Tirel on his return to the Island, as he had been away with his manservant at the time.

1904

The Paid Police were issued with a new uniform. White helmets and jackets were worn in the summer months, a practice that continued until 1973. In more recent years a move for their return has been voiced, although more as a tourist attraction than for effective policing.

1917

Mr J Barette of Malta House, St John, had his boat stolen from Bonne Nuit harbour. The *Lydia* had been taken during the night and Barette offered a £2 reward for her recovery. A week later she was found near Carteret on the Normandy peninsula and it became apparent that whoever had taken the boat had done so to avoid both the Jersey and French authorities.

1978

It was announced that the National Trust had bought St Ouen's Pond for £56,100. The pond had originally belonged to St Ouen's Manor but had been sold off to clear debts. The National Trust had been unsure whether to make a bid for the area, however, a donation from the Meaker Trust allowed them to acquire this unique wetland.

06 June

1921

The airship *R36* flew over Jersey on this day, an event worthy of note. But a balloon of a more primitive design had been flown over the Island over 130 years earlier. A local headmaster had taken off from the Hospital courtyard in a hot air balloon in June 1790. Mr Granger enjoyed a second flight a week later, taking off from the Town Hill and landing in the sea forty-five minutes later.

1943

Two RAF sergeants, D C Butlin and A Holden, were buried, having been washed ashore within days of each other. The German forces, fearful of local reaction, had tried to keep the funeral low key, however, Islanders had other ideas. Businesses and individuals made donations to pay for headstones. Following an early morning service at the Hospital chapel the two coffins, covered with the Union Flag, were transported to Mont á l'Abbè cemetery. Hundreds of Islanders lined the route and two lorry loads of flowers, which had been left at the Hospital, were taken to the graves. The Bailiff laid two wreaths, one on behalf of the States of Jersey and one in the name of the King. Only officials were allowed into the cemetery for the burial, but hundreds of locals filed past the graves after.

1944

The Allies' D Day operations on the Normandy beaches meant the German troops in Jersey became very nervous, manning their posts with ambulances ready. Anti-aircraft batteries were kept busy throughout the morning, one position being machine-gunned by an Allied plane. A proclamation was issued ordering Islanders to stay calm and reminding them that hostile acts were punishable by death.

1984

Iris Le Feuvre was elected Constable of St Lawrence, becoming the first woman Constable in the Island. In a three way fight she polled 651 votes, Deputy Hendric Vandervliet 464 and Denis Satchwell 198.

07 June

1813

Colonel Humfrey, who was helping design the Island's new defences, wrote a report on the state of the works and their cost. On fortifying the Town Hill[19], he explained that the cost from 1st February 1806 to 30th April 1813 was £198,786 16s 8d and an estimate for the cost of the finished project was £307,382 0s 5½d. By the time Fort Regent was completed the actual cost was £375,203.

1871

The States granted permission for the building of a railway from St Aubin to La Moye to assist with the transportation of granite from the quarries. Work on the project, however, did not start for over 2 years, partly due to difficulties in acquiring the land. Prices up to £400 per acre were being demanded for land which was 'unproductive rock'.

1921

A shipment of 91 cattle left Jersey for the long journey to New York and eventually Oregon. The world famous Jersey cows had been bred as the result of an act by the States in 1789 to stop the smuggling of cattle. Before that time cows imported from France to England paid a heavy import duty. But cows from Jersey paid nothing. Islanders realised that a great deal of money could be made and soon Jersey was awash with cows which were, in effect, in transit to England. To stop this, the States banned the importation of cattle, with heavy fines being levied on transgressors. With no animals entering Jersey, locals had started to breed cattle more selectively.

1945

Less than a month after the Island's Liberation, King George VI and Queen Elizabeth landed at the harbour at 11 am. The whole Island seemed to have turned out to see them. At the end of the visit the Royal party departed from the airport, their aircraft being escorted by Dakotas, a plane that would in future serve the Island for years.

---

[19] Known today as Fort Regent.

08 June

1454

Just as the 100 Years War was coming to an end, the French once again attacked Jersey. However, for once they were repulsed, with 500 men being killed.

1895

On this day it appeared that fire had broken out on board the schooner *Why Not*, while en route to Jersey with a cargo of straw, lime and Breton farm labourers. As buckets of water were being used to dowse the smoke that came from the hold, the captain and crew jumped into a rowing boat and pushed off, leaving the ship, cargo and Bretons to their fate. On arrival in Erquy, Brittany, the captain told of the fire and how all was lost. Meanwhile, the Bretons had discovered that the smoke was merely a reaction caused by the lime getting wet. The resourceful Bretons then set course for their homeland and ironically arrived in the same harbour that the ship's captain had rowed into the previous day. The captain, who had to have an armed guard to protect him from incensed locals after the news had spread, was arrested and spent six months in prison for his cowardliness.

1918

The Channel Islands Motor and General Engineering Co, of 37 Bath Street, started operating the first successful motorised bus service, using Model T Fords. It ran, on specified days, to St Ouen, Grève de Lecq and St Martin's Church. Mr E Lander, who owned the business, later named his fleet the Blue Bus Service, which eventually became Blue Coach Tours.

1942

The German forces order that all radios were to be handed in was greatly resented. The demand was challenged as the Hague Convention allowed the seizure of transmitters - and radios only received. However, the rule was enforced and over 10,000 wireless sets were handed in. Many were not and in the months that followed more than 700 people were sent to prison.

09 June

1824

The *Ariadne* entered St Helier Harbour on the morning's high tide. This gave her the honour of being the first steamship in service between England and the Channel Islands,[20] providing a once weekly service during the summer months. In 1836 she was replaced on the England run and began a service between Jersey and France. The *Ariadne* was broken up in 1849, having ceased operations to Jersey three years earlier.

1905

The *Evening Post* informed its readers that Lillie Langtry had been offered £600 per week to appear in New York. The performance was to be a monologue enacted twice a day, for which she would receive the enormous sum of £100 daily. The article was, however, doubtful as to whether Lillie's busy schedule would allow her to accept the generous offer.

1953

At a special sitting of the States £150,000 was unanimously voted as a contribution to British defence, it being pointed out during the debate that Jersey had prospered since the Liberation. However the Deputy of St Ouen was in favour of re-establishing the militia instead. He was reported to have said 'If Britain had not thrown up her Asiatic Empire in a most disgraceful way, there would have been no crisis now'.

1974

Police were hunting 24-year old Michael Murphy after he escaped from Newgate Street Prison, where he was being held on remand. Using a piece of metal he had dug a hole through the granite wall, then dropped down an 18 foot high wall. Three days later Murphy gave himself up, telephoning the police and asking them to come and collect him. He was calling from a box in the Parade, only a few hundred yards from the prison from which he had escaped.

---

[20] See 29th May for further details.

10 June

1564

Many of Jersey's Bailiffs have been unpopular but Hostes Nicolle, who was buried on this day, was particularly unpleasant. In his time he burned Catholic books and it was also Nicolle who had the first two witches in Jersey burned. But divine intervention is said to have ended his reign. The Bailiff coveted his neighbour's land and hatched a plot. He sent his servants to slaughter two of his finest sheep, the carcasses of which were then concealed in his neighbour's stable. The man was arrested for sheep stealing and sentenced to death that very day. But as the rope went around his neck he said to the Bailiff: 'I summon you to appear within forty days before the just judge'. Thirty-nine days later Nicolle dropped dead.

1668

An Order in Council was registered in Jersey dealing with the proper administration of justice and also limiting the right to vote to those who paid taxes and were heads of families.

1937

The States voted to accept a generous offer made by Lady Trent. She proposed giving her gardens at Millbrook to the Island. They were to be called Coronation Gardens. The conditions of the gift were that they be kept as an open space where the old could rest and the young could enjoy recreation. No bicyclists or organised games were to be allowed, just rest, refreshment and music. Although basically laid out, some work was still needed and Lady Trent was to pay for this as well.

1943

During the Occupation, the German forces had an extensive rail network constructed for the transportation of building materials. On this day a deaf farmer, on his way to move his cows, failed to hear an approaching tram that ran from Ronez Quarry to La Câtelet and was killed. A later inquiry decided that his death had been accidental.

11 June

1643

It was the time of the English Civil War and Sir Philippe de Carteret, Bailiff of Jersey as well as Lieutenant-Governor, had sought safety from the Parliamentarians and retired to Elizabeth Castle.

On this day he ordered a proclamation from the King to be read in the Market Place. The crowd that gathered to listen caused the soldiers accompanying the reader to become uneasy and draw their weapons. At this the crowd panicked and ran.

On hearing from the soldiers of a riot, Sir Philippe ordered a bombardment of the town. Once completed, 42 soldiers were sent from the Castle, with drums beating and colours flying. Unfortunately for them, a now enraged population had set up a barricade and used a small cannon on the advancing force.

After a number of skirmishes, the battered soldiers withdrew, ironically leaving the locals enforcing a strict blockade of the Castle, whereas before the fortress's inhabitants had had relatively free access.

1823

This day saw the first arrival in Jersey of a paddle steamer. The *Medina* had been built at a cost of about £7,000. Colonel Fitzgerald had hired it to carry his family and furniture to Guernsey. After, it had travelled on to Jersey, where it had caused great excitement. The captain allowed visitors to see over the vessel, for a charge. The *Medina* departed the following day and never returned.

1897

A woman was arrested for stealing bedding. The previous Saturday Miss Huston had noticed that some bedding had gone missing. Six days later one of her servants saw a woman leaving the property with a bundle. They gave chase and caught her. She was arrested by the Centenier and the previously stolen quilts and sheets were recovered from a second hand dealer in Hue Street.

12 June

1872

The schooner *Emma* arrived with a cargo of building equipment, enabling the construction of the Jersey Eastern Railway to proceed at full steam. However, two weeks later the labourers went on strike, demanding an extra 6d per day and that their hours of work be reduced to 10 a day. Top wages had been 3s per day but due to the limited time and penalties for late completion the strikers won.

1939

A group of officials arrived at the Minquiers reef on board the States tug to investigate reports of a French invasion. They found that a French artist, Durand Couppel, had taken a group of workmen to the reef and had them build him a hut. The carefully planned operation had landed 50 builders just after a party of States workers had departed for the weekend. This was yet another attempt by the French to further their claim on the Minquiers. But every international ruling has declared them Jersey's.

1978

Giovanni Riva was murdered at La Collette Gardens. The waiter was stabbed twice, once in the back, once in the chest. An anonymous call alerted the police but Riva was dead when they arrived. Two days later two local youths were charged with the murder. It appears that the two had attacked Giovanni, believing him to be homosexual. However, the unfortunate waiter had merely been going for some fresh air in an area occasionally frequented by gays.

1979

The States voted for a new flag design for the Island. The original red diagonal cross was to be augmented by a Jersey shield with its three leopards and a crown on top. The vote in favour of the alterations was not unanimous, a number of Members thinking there was no need for the change. Senator Bill Morvan explained that on hoisting the existing flag on his boat he had been told it meant 'I am in distress. Senator Shenton then remarked, 'He should bring it with him when he speaks in the House'.

13 June

1813

Charles Bertram's glittering naval career struck rocks, literally. Born in St Helier in 1777, he had spent all his adult life in the navy. He had battled long and hard against the French, led raids on their forts and seized their ships. His career had been put on hold for a few years when he was a prisoner of war but this irrepressible Jerseyman was soon back in the fray. However, as commander of the *Persian* his career looked washed up when on this day she was wrecked off the Leeward Islands. Bertram and his crew eventually reached San Domingo, and he was court-martialled for losing his ship. But his defence won the day when it proved that the Admiralty charts had been inaccurate. Bertram was honourably acquitted.

1946

The bodies of 13 American servicemen killed during the Second World War and buried in Jersey were exhumed from Howard Davis Park cemetery. It had been decided that all United States servicemen buried in Europe would be taken home for reburial. The bodies were to be placed on board an American cruiser that had arrived in local waters for the task.

1987

The Bailiff, Peter Crill, received a Knighthood in the Queen's Birthday Honours list. During the war Sir Peter was one of a small group of individuals who escaped from occupied Jersey. His political career began in 1951 when he was elected Deputy for St Clement. In 1960 he sat in the House as Senator before returning to the law as Solicitor-General, progressing through the ranks until in 1986 he became Bailiff.

1989

The States voted unanimously in favour of banning dogs from the Island's beaches. The law was to come into force from 1st July and dogs were to be excluded from 10 am until 6 pm during the summer months. An amendment to allow some beaches to be excluded was rejected on the casting vote of the Bailiff.

14 June

1906

An article in a local newspaper warned of the danger from eating ice cream. It was reported that a local telegraph boy had come down with typhoid fever, which had been traced to an ice cream he had eaten. It was pointed out that with the warmer weather arriving, ice cream sales would increase and that steps should be taken to 'prevent the sales of deleterious ice creams'.

1928

The FB Playing Fields were opened with the usual pomp on this day. It had been noted by the Lieutenant Governor that the physical condition of militia recruits was poor. Sir Jesse Boot, one of the Island's benefactors, decided to resolve the problem by providing facilities for them. Sir Jesse not only gave the 25 vergées of land but had them laid out and a pavilion built.

1954

The Magistrate, Mr P Cabot, advised Alex Adams to bring a civil action against his neighbour when he dismissed the case against Lee Young. She had been charged with allowing her monkey to cause a public nuisance, as it had been straying onto other properties. Defence Advocate T Sowden argued that this was a private matter and that civil, not public, action was required. Having heard the evidence, the Magistrate concurred. If Adams wanted to pursue the matter, he would have to sue his neighbour.

1983

Plans brought to the States by Deputy Don Filleul for a new traffic scheme at the Robin Hood junction in St Helier were so heavily criticised that he withdrew them. The proposals were described by Members as 'irresponsible' and 'folly'. However, 15 years later the same traffic scheme at the Robin Hood had been built, while traffic lights at the bottom of Wellington Road, which had been approved by the House at the same time, were not.

15 June

1648

Marie Grandin's head had been shaved and a mark had been found. When pierced, it bled on one side but not on the other. That fact, along with 70 or 80 accusers, condemned her, as a witch, to be hanged, strangled, then burnt. This was carried out on this day, only nine days after she was arrested. A co-accused had no such mark and was taken to Mont Orgueil Castle for further questioning. Jersey, being more civilised than her sister island, strangled witches before burning them, whereas in Guernsey witches were burned alive.

1948

The States rejected a proposition to limit the amount candidates could spend on their election campaigns. The idea that less affluent candidates should not be disadvantaged appealed to some Members but Deputy P H Le Quesne said that anyone who spent £150 was 'a mug'. Another told of one Member in the past spending £1,800 in order to get into the House. It was noted that in England such a limit applied but Members of Parliament there were paid. In Jersey, other than the prestige of office, there was nothing to gain by spending large sums of money.

1974

Jersey was suffering from a spate of hooliganism, vandalism and violence. Forty-two people were detained by the police on public order offences over the weekend. The previous night, trouble had flared at Sands, formerly the Tropicana, with windows being smashed and property damaged. It had also recently become a regular occurrence for large numbers of drunken youths to roam the town over the weekends, causing damage and getting into fights.

1989

Aids hit the local headlines when it was announced that for the first time someone had died of the disease in Jersey. Seventeen people were known to be carrying the HIV virus and a number of others had previously left the Island to die. This news confirmed that Aids was not just a world problem, but Jersey's as well.

16 June

1906

There were 16,000 extra pigeons in Jersey's sky on this day when the Island was used as a launch area for racing pigeons. The birds from the Lancashire region, and belonging to members from a number of clubs, had been shipped to the Island. The first batch of about 3,400 pigeons were liberated at 5 o'clock on this fine still morning, the remainder being released shortly after. The prize money was good, with up to £5 for the first bird home.

1919

Cabman Joseph Gosling appeared before the Magistrate, accused of over-charging. Mrs Evelyn Edwards had wanted to go for a drive. When she enquired of Mr Gosling as to how much two hours hire would be, she was told 10 shillings. At this she reported him to Jurat Crill, who happened to be nearby.

Fares were regulated at 2/6 per hour, so Gosling was intending to charge double the legal rate. In his defence it was noted that forage for the horse had doubled in price since before the war, a plea the Magistrate obviously had sympathy with. He pointed out that while prices had risen during the war, the States had not allowed an increase in fares. Fining the cabby 5 shillings, the Magistrate suggested that cabmen should form a union.

1940

A flotilla of boats left Jersey to help evacuate St Malo. The German army was advancing quickly across France and it was decided to remove British troops before it was too late. Cargo boats, private yachts and just about anything that could carry men sailed for St Malo. The 75,000 besieged men were ferried out to larger vessels while work continued destroying anything that might be of use to the invading forces. Fuel dumps were blown up, as were the harbour lock gates. Any armaments and ammunition that could not be removed went the same way.

17 June

1809

The States decided to build a main road from St Helier to La Haule. At the time most of the land in St Aubin's Bay was sand dune, with people travelling across the beach at low tide.

1905

Jersey was hit by a cyclone. At about 6 pm heavy rain clouds came across the Island, dropping their cargo, and a terrific wind suddenly blew up. Shop blinds were torn down and lighter material, including many hats, were sucked into the air. A number of skiffs were sunk in the harbour. But no one appears to have been injured during the brief but violent storm.

1911

Florence Elizabeth Sexton broke new ground in Jersey when on this day she was registered at the Royal Court as a medical practitioner, the first woman doctor to practice in the Island.

1940

For the short time between the outbreak of war and the Island's occupation, Jersey became a valuable staging post for air traffic. On 11 June 36 RAF bombers had refuelled on their way to raid northern Italy. And as the German forces advanced towards the Channel, Jersey Airport was used in the operation to get aircraft and personnel across to England. On this day General de Gaulle joined the hectic cross-Channel traffic when he landed briefly in Jersey.

1957

Farmers from the Trinity area mounted a protest of civil disobedience. The Constable of St Helier had banned lorries carrying potatoes from New Street. Lorries carrying other cargoes, cauliflowers for instance, were allowed, but potatoes had to skirt the town under the new regulations. A convoy of farmers, accompanied by members of the press, now attempted to pass down New Street. Not surprisingly they were stopped by the police, but the protest had been made.

18 June

1923

Advances in engineering brought the Pioneer No 1 to the Island and on this day it made its first run. The Pioneer was a steam railcar and thought at the time to be the transport of the future. It could perhaps be described as a steam powered tram and the Jersey Railways Co bought three of them. They were quick and economical, burning one fifth of the fuel that a locomotive would consume to cover the same distance.

1938

It was announced that the War Office was to open an army training school in Jersey. St Peter's Barracks were to be developed to take apprentice tradesmen and were to be named the Army Technical School (Boys) Jersey. Two hundred and fifty boys were to be trained in trades which the army required. It was said that the boys' parents would be required to pay nothing for the training and the boys would be paid, as well as receiving food, clothing, an education and good housing. It was forecast that the facility would open at the beginning of October.

1954

Richard Marett, Richard Anderson and Desmond Blampied faced the Magistrate, where they admitted to having cut lead from St Aubin's Methodist Chapel to use as ammunition for their catapults. Jurat Cabot took a dim view of the damaging of a church and sentenced each boy to four strokes of the birch.

1970

Work at St Helier Harbour came to a halt when the crane drivers went on strike. All Jersey's sea-borne cargo was craned on and off ships in the days before the advent of car ferries and containerisation. A month earlier the States had carried out a work study at the harbour and the dockers were concerned that redundancies would follow. But work resumed the following day, after assurances that no jobs would be lost.

19 June

1823

An advert appeared in a local paper offering a reward for the capture of smugglers. It informed readers that Humphrey Oxenham, while on duty in the service of Customs on the morning of this day, had seen a smuggling vessel being off-loaded by up to forty men, all armed with bludgeons. Having been knocked to the ground, Oxenham was then severely beaten. The commissioners were therefore offering a £50 reward to anyone with information.

1906

Jersey Royals were fetching a good price and shiploads to Hull, Manchester, Southampton, Weymouth, Newhaven and Fleetwood were due to sail overnight. Over 770 loads of potatoes had been weighed by mid afternoon and farmers were keen to unload quickly, with prices up to 2s 2d per cwt being paid.

1919

The results of a referendum held in St Helier were published. While 101 voted in favour, 538 rejected the parish's proposition to undertake the installation of electric lighting. As with all new inventions, it is difficult to ascertain if they are a fad, gimmick or the shape of things to come. A debate had raged for some time over the various merits and safety implications of both gas and electricity. Although electric lighting had obvious advantages over gas, no one was sure that electricity was here to stay. Parishioners therefore decided to play it safe and stick with the tried and trusted gas lights.

1984

The States were officially informed that the British Government wanted the Island to make a contribution towards defence. A proposition to set up a committee to examine the issue was lodged while States Members considered the implications. After the Falklands War the States had given £5 million, a gift that drew the British Government's attention to Jersey's wealth. Two years earlier, Senator Ralph Vibert claimed that 'we have money coming out of our ears'. Now the British Government wanted some of it.

20 June

1815

Duc d'Aumont, along with a French general, officers and 2,000 French Royalists, arrived in Jersey's waters. It was just two days after the Battle of Waterloo and the force was en route to Arromanches in Normandy, where they intended to make a landing.

1892

George Barter may have had dreams of running away to join the circus but his death on this day meant he never would.

The 20-year old was employed as a coachman and gardener for Mr de Gruchy, of de Gruchy's in King Street, at Glenville, just behind Mont Cantel. A circus was due in town and on this day, probably inspired by the forthcoming attraction, Barter amused himself on a trapeze that he had erected in the garden.

A maid noticed that Barter had fallen and went to his aid, trying to sit him on a chair and revive him with water. However, his broken neck meant this was of little help and medical assistance was summoned.

Dr Thomas Godfrey said at the inquest that he had seen the deceased between 5 and 5.30 pm and had found him lying dead on the lawn. The ground had been soft but the 6 ft drop from the trapeze had accounted for the broken neck.

1973

Plans to build an 18 hole golf course, as well as tennis and squash courts, were rejected. The proposed site was on dairy land at Le Câtelet, St John. The grounds of the rejection were that it 'would be contrary to the provisions of the development plan, and would not be in the best interests of the social and economic needs of the community'.

The proposal was revived some 20 years later, when the same scenario was again played out.

21 June

1764

Rear Admiral Philippe de Carteret set sail in the *Dolphin* on a voyage of discovery, having installed his sister in his property at Trinity Manor. On their way out they annexed the Falkland Islands, which nearly caused a war with Spain. This expedition was only really noted for its lack of discoveries. However, on returning to England in May 1766, de Carteret was promoted to commander.[21]

1806

General Don took office as Lieutenant Governor and immediately began the work required to fortify the Island against the threat that Napoleon now posed. Among the many projects General Don put into effect was the building of a series of major roads down which troops could gallop to provide a rapid response to any coastal landing of enemy forces. It is these routes that now form the major thoroughfares across the Island, where before there were only narrow winding lanes. The road building was paid for by the States, who increased duty by 3d per gallon on wine and spirits to cover the cost.

1810

A general store was opened at St Peter's by Abraham de Gruchy and his wife. They moved to King Street 15 years later, where they opened de Gruchy's.

1876

This day and the next saw horse racing on Gorey Common. So popular was it that 28 trains left St Helier on each of the two days.

1929

After 56 years, the Jersey Eastern Railway closed, a victim of the increased use of buses and private cars. Once the assets had been sold off, creditors received 1s 6d on the pound and ordinary shareholders got nothing. The locomotives and other metal went as scrap to Poland and the Snow Hill station became a bus terminus.

---

[21] See 22nd August for further details.

22 June

1615

On this day, in the middle of Jersey's great knitting boom, Philip Picot was ordered not to knit in the company of girls.

1646

A day of fasting was ordered by the States when they learned of Prince Charles' impending departure from the Island.

1795

Philippe Dumaresq, noting that due to some long forgotten midsummer's ritual crowds traditionally gathered at Bonne Nuit on this day, decided to give them something to do. His first fair in 1792 was rained off but he persevered and by 1795 over 6,000 people attended the event. Fifty stalls selling all sorts of produce were there, as well as horse races, a cattle market, tight rope dances, comedians and a fireworks display. A whole ox was roasted and distributed to the poor. But in 1797 the States put a stop to it as it was 'contrary to good morals'. They also forbid anyone starting a new fair or market.

1901

Marie Josephine Tachet was charged with 'keeping a disorderly house'. The house in question was 18 Belmont Road and the sentence she received was banishment from Jersey for five years. Her husband and children were to be repatriated. Her husband, Mr Masson, claimed he had left his wife and therefore it was not his responsibility. However, he was told he should have stayed to 'maintain order'.

1949

Princess Elizabeth and the Duke of Edinburgh arrived on a Royal Visit. Thousands watched and cheered at every stop on their itinerary. From their arrival at the Albert Pier, massive crowds gathered. The Royal Square was also a mass of bodies when Her Highness appeared to give and receive official addresses. There was much talk of loyalty and the usual receptions, including one in Howard Davis Park.

23 June

1646

Prince Charles, who had arrived in Jersey in April after fleeing the Parliamentarians, was about to board his vessel to travel to France when two enemy warships appeared. A number of boats had already been loaded with baggage and were underway but the danger of the Roundhead warships caused the Prince's departure to be delayed for two days.

1863

A dispute over a piece of Jersey's foreshore erupted on this day, leading to a raising of the Clameur de Haro. Frederick Clarke owned a shipyard on the seafront at West Park and believed he also had title to adjacent reclaimed land. St Helier Constable, Mr Marett, sent his men to remove Clarke's timber from the land, so Clarke raised the Clameur. Despite this injunction, the Constable ordered his men to continue their allotted task. When the case was eventually settled in court, the parish was fined £5 for this contempt. Clarke was also fined for raising the Clameur improperly. One hundred and thirty years later a similar dispute between the States and Les Pas Holdings, concerning the Island's foreshore, cost considerably more to settle.

1966

A 300 lb shell discovered in Trinity was safely destroyed. The explosive had lain in a hedge since the Occupation and was found by French farm workers. A large area of the parish around the Zoo was warned to keep indoors. This proved unnecessary as Mr Walker, Jersey's bomb disposal expert, as always, disarmed the device without incident.

1976

It was reported that a hoard of Bronze Age implements had been discovered in St Lawrence. While digging a swimming pool, a pot containing a number of Bronze Age axes and spear heads was unearthed. Thought to date from 800 BC the artefacts were in excellent condition. The work was stopped while archaeologists excavated the find.

24 June

1915

A system whereby it was necessary to get four tickets in order to be admitted to the Infirmary was abolished. At a special general meeting of friends and supporters of the Jersey General Dispensary it was acknowledged that change was necessary. The service relied on donations and it was said that 'the charitable were not sufficiently charitable'. Money was short and it was accepted that if the sick did not pay, the doors would have to close. After some debate it was agreed that a charge of half a guinea, 10s 6d, per week would be levied on patients.

1924

The Jersey Labour Party decided to put up its first candidate for the States. Mr S P Channon was to stand as Deputy in the forthcoming election. The Labour Party had been in Jersey for some years, however, they had never before put up a candidate. The fight turned out to be just two way, with Mr Renouf getting 748 votes and Channon 143. The Labour Party said they were 'encouraged'.

1941

The German forces altered the rules of the road from driving on the left to driving on the right. This had less effect than might be thought as the lack of fuel had lessened motor vehicle activity greatly. Some buses still ran and others were adapted to be powered by charcoal or to be pulled by horses. The new rules did, however, create one problem for the buses, as passengers were now picked up and put down in the middle of the road.

1952

Vivienne Gruchy, the proprietor of a local newsagent, was accused of selling postcards on a Sunday. Centenier Laurie told the court that it had been brought to his attention that some small shops and cafes were selling cigarettes, films and postcards on Sundays, which was against the Sunday Trading Law. Mrs Gruchy admitted the offence, saying that she found it difficult to refuse people. She was fined £2.

25 June

1911

Religious sensibilities were ruffled on this day. The Breton mission had been conducting an open air service in Jersey's French district when a number of Roman Catholic followers arrived. Members of La Jeunesse Catholique, led by Albert Durand, began distributing tracts which the Breton mission objected to. Things became quite heated and both parties were ordered to attend the Town Hall. Having had their say, the Breton mission were ordered not to conduct services in the French quarter in future.

1935

Jersey was in the middle of a heat wave. Both men and women were said to be dressing lightly, however, the hot weather did not suit everyone, as two people died from the heat.

1969

The case of Maria Batista opened Jersey up to international criticism and ridicule. Batista was a Portuguese girl, aged 21. She was also an unmarried mother. States policy was to return alien mothers to their country of origin, but Batista's family lived in Jersey. A petition was raised asking for clemency, however, on this day, the States voted to expel her. After 2½ hours of debate 33 States Members backed the Defence Committee's decision. Offers of marriage came in, which would have allowed her to stay, but she departed in July.

1983

One of Jersey's worst road crashes occurred at the top of Mont à la Brune, St Brelade. A Volkswagen Beetle with five on board failed to make a corner and ran head on into a granite wall. Two of the passengers died soon afterwards and a third died later.

1985

The States approved £15 million for the building of a new harbour to the west of Albert Pier to provide deep water berths for the larger vessels which were expected on Island routes in the future.

26 June

1650

During the English Civil War many Jersey ships indulged in privateering. On this day the *Patrice*, having captured an English cargo ship, was heading for St Helier with her prize. However she was attacked by an English frigate. For five hours the cannons roared, the Jersey vessel out gunned and slower in the water. As the splinters flew and cannons crashed the *Patrice*'s captain threatened to run through anyone suggesting surrender. Eventually the English frigate broke off and ran for Guernsey, with the *Patrice* firing as she fled. During the fire fight the *Patrice* had discharged 234 cannon balls at her foe. Four of her crew were killed and others wounded. On reaching St Helier the ship was fairly intact but had seven or eight holes in her hull, one below the water line.

1857

On this day local man, Captain George Henry Ingouville, was among the first to receive the Victoria Cross,[22] which the Queen presented in a ceremony in Hyde Park. Ingouville went on to build a number of houses locally, hence Georgetown and Ingouville Place.

1873

A newly arrived carriage belonging to the Jersey Eastern Rail made an unscheduled journey. During the lunch hour, the unattended carriage, weighing four to five tons, rolled away from the Green Street area, picking up speed as it travelled down the steep incline past Roseville Street, demolishing a pair of crossing gates in the process. Fortunately no one had been hurt when the carriage finally came to a stop at Grève d'Azette.

1945

The massive programme to remove German land mines was officially completed. Troops from the occupying forces had been retained to assist with the dangerous task. However, over 50 years on, these reminders of the past still make regular appearances.

---

[22] See 13th July for further details.

27 June

1562

Queen Elizabeth I granted a charter directing that Islanders shall not henceforth be 'cited by any form of legal process to appear before the English courts'. She also restated the Channel Islands' neutral status in times of war.

1884

The first mailboat, named the *Caesarea*, met her end on this day. The London and South Western Railway Company had ordered her to be built in 1867. She was a 282 ton steam ship driven by propeller and for 17 years she had served the Island well. However, while en route to St Malo she collided with the *SS Strathesk* in thick fog and was wrecked. The ship may have been lost but the historic name was given to two subsequent mailboats, including the last one to ply Channel Island waters.

1931

A small JMT bus travelling down Mont Felard, St Lawrence, lost control and overturned at the bottom. Several passengers were fatally injured. During the period 1930/31 a bus war had broken out among rival businesses, particularly on the route to Gorey. The tactics involved drastic fare reductions, buses detailed to run just ahead of a scheduled service, thus stealing its passengers, and generally racing one another to stops, all of which reduced safety standards. So there was little surprise when the accident occurred. The firm's manager was arrested and also resigned from his position.

1978

Queen Elizabeth II and Prince Philip arrived on a brief visit. Thousands of locals and visitors lined the Royal Party's route from their arrival at the Albert Quay and on throughout the day. The first stop was, as always, the States Chambers, but protocol dealt with, it was on to Grainville which was filled with children. After lunch at the Hotel L'Horizon, Her Majesty called in on a cattle show. The final item on the itinerary was a walk in the Howard Davis Park.

28 June

1641

Maximilien Messervy was given the King's pardon. Although from one of the best families in the Island, Messervy had financial problems. He had resolved them by making money, literally. When arrested he claimed that a Norman had given him the forged coins in payment for a horse. However a search of his house revealed a melting pot and all the necessary equipment for forgery. After spending eight months in prison influential friends secured his release. His skill as a forger was quite impressive. When shown to gold smiths in the City of London, they declared Messervy's work the best they had ever seen. His time in jail had not reformed him and he was continually in trouble until his eventual execution.

1883

One of the town's most distinctive buildings was opened to the public on this day. De Gruchy's arcade was lit by electric light at a time when gas was the norm.

1907

Mont Orgueil Castle was handed over to the States by the British Government. With all the pomp and ceremony that usually accompanies such occasions, States Members and other dignitaries assembled and, at noon, to the accompaniment of guns, the Jersey flag was raised.

1940

Just after 6 pm, six Heinkel bombers over flew the Island, discharging their payload at La Rocque and St Helier, killing eleven civilians and wounding many more. The machine guns and explosives caused damage to a number of buildings, the harbour area being particularly badly hit. None of this was unexpected and a programme of evacuation and demilitarisation had been in progress for some time. Later that same evening the BBC officially declared the Channel Islands a demilitarised zone.

29 June

1897

An inquiry into the death of a new-born baby girl was held on this day. The child's body had been found by John Le Cornu in a field of his at La Pointe, St Ouen and the inquiry was held at Le Cornu's house. His wife testified to seeing one of her Breton servants trampling something underfoot and then covering it with earth, the object being buried being unidentifiable at the time. However, Mr Le Cornu had discovered the body on the same spot shortly afterwards.

Medical evidence was given that the cause of death was 'inflicted violence' and with this information the jury's verdict was that the child had met its death at the hands of its mother. The woman, Anne Bla, had been arrested once the body had been discovered and, found to be in need of medical help, had been immediately sent to hospital.

1923

Dr Hays was sued by an architect for £72 17s 9d. Hays had commissioned the architect to design him a house costing no more than £1,000 to build. Having seen the plans, Hays queried if the house could indeed be built for the sum specified and was informed 'I am an architect and ought to know'.

However, the lowest tender for the work was £2,300. The plans were revised, the lowest tender this time being £1,250, at which point Hays looked elsewhere for another architect. Of the £72 demanded in fees by the architect, Hays was willing to pay only £10.

Once in court the Bailiff sent the two men out to discuss the matter. They returned, with the architect demanding £60 and Hays only willing to pay £50. The Bailiff split the difference, warning that if the case went any further the expenses would be greater than the sum in dispute.

While the action had been underway, Hays' new house was being built without the aid of an architect, the design having been taken from *The Daily Mail Bungalow Book*.

30 June

1847

The tranquillity of St Catherine's was shattered and would remain so for nine years, as the building of St Catherine's breakwater got underway, with its eight hundred workmen imported from England. The civil engineering contractor Jackson and Bean also moved in, opening quarries needed to construct the new harbour.

For many years the need for a deep water port had been discussed. The plan was to build the breakwater at St Catherine's, then create an enormous pier projecting from Archirondel. The massive harbour this would create could house a large English fleet that would protect the Island from French attack.

But although the first, smaller arm was run out from St Catherine's, the second, and far greater, arm was barely started before the project was abandoned. Whether due to rising costs, changing technology, or, as was said, France's protests at having a potential enemy fleet within sight of their coast, the reasons for the abandonment remain unclear.

1890

Today saw the first publication of the *Evening Post*. The newspaper was printed on pink paper and consisted of one sheet. The price was a half penny and unlike many publications of the time, it was in English.

1944

On this night, despite Royal Navy activity, a German convoy left St Helier Harbour. Among those on board were Louis Gold, Harold Le Druillenec and Berthe Pitolet. All three were being deported for sheltering and helping escaped Russian slaveworkers. Pitolet soon escaped captivity. However, Le Druillenec and Gold were less fortunate. Mrs Gold was eventually taken to Ravensbrück Concentration Camp and in 1945, with her health broken, ended her days in the gas chamber. Le Druillenec was taken to Belsen Concentration Camp, which was liberated in time to save him from starvation. Le Druillenec survived and after prolonged treatment, went on to give evidence at the Nuremberg war crime trials.

01 July

1897

The *Roebuck* made her maiden voyage to Jersey on this day. She is best remembered for being beached in St Brelade's Bay after striking the Kaines Rocks in 1911.[23] Prior to that she had caught fire twice. She continued to work until she was sold in 1914 to the British Government. Under her new name, *Roedean*, she broke her moorings, ramming a battleship and sinking on 13th January 1915

1931

The new West Park Pavilion opened, replacing the 'tin house' which, 40 years earlier, had been built to house a circus. The new pavilion was of South African Dutch design. The main hall was 109 feet long, 59 feet wide and, as well as a sprung wooden floor, there were no pillars to spoil the view. Acoustics had also been considered, with sound proofing applied to the ceiling.

1932

On this day the Jersey Ladies Lifeboat Guild was inaugurated, its purpose being to raise funds to keep the lifeboat service in Jersey. A motorised lifeboat had been stationed in Guernsey since 1929 and the Inspector of Lifeboats was now considering closing the St Helier station, a situation which the women of a seafaring community had no intention of allowing.

1940

German aircraft dropped pouches containing orders for large white crosses to be placed in three key areas to announce Jersey's surrender. And every house was to fly a white flag. As this was happening, a German plane landed at the airport. A 25-year old Oberleutnant, Richard Kern, the vanguard of the occupying force, was rapidly followed by other aircraft and troops. By 5 pm the terms of Jersey's surrender were agreed. British troops had already left, with the realisation that Jersey was impossible to defend. About 10,000 people had already evacuated, leaving a population of 41,000.

---

[23] See 19th July for further details.

02 July

1767

On this day Commander Philippe de Carteret discovered Pitcairn Island and named it after the seaman who had first seen it. The island later came to prominence after Captain Bligh's crew mutinied on the *Bounty*.

1905

Foul play was suspected when a fire destroyed a St Peter's house. The building was untenanted, its owner, Mr J E Martin, having acquired the property for his retirement. In the early hours a neighbour, Walter d'Allain, noticed what appeared to be a lantern moving in an upstairs room. Curious, he checked again and found the house ablaze. He contacted Martin, who lived nearby and was fortunate enough to have a telephone, and the Fire Brigade were called. Animals in an adjoining thatched outbuilding were lead to safety and after only half an hour the Brigade arrived. But their long battle was to no avail as the roof fell in and the house, insured for £600, was gutted. Suspicion as to the cause of the blaze rested on a group of drunken French workers heard in the area at the time.

1940

The newly arrived occupying forces began exercising their powers and a list of orders were issued. All weapons were to be handed in to the Town Hall, a curfew between 11 pm and 5 am was introduced and no spirits were to be supplied or consumed. The airport was out of bounds and no boats were to be used without permission. Banks and shops were to stay open, although no price increases were allowed. Radios were not banned but they were to be tuned to German stations.

1986

Prince Edward arrived in Jersey for the 30th anniversary of the Duke of Edinburgh Award Scheme. He had touched down briefly the day before when bad weather had delayed his visit to Guernsey. His informal style was appreciated as he toured youth organisations and the day ended with a charity banquet at the Grand Hotel.

03 July

1795

It was decided that the thousands of French refugees should form military regiments to help the fight at home. 3,500 enrolled but a problem arose as they all wanted to be officers and none would be privates. In fact most wanted to be colonels. On this day, this army of aristocrats landed in Quiberon Bay and were met by Lazare Hoche, the French Republic's best general. The newly formed force was completely destroyed, with very few escaping with their lives.

1873

On this day, only four months after the Mercantile Union Bank had gone bust,[24] the Joint Stock Bank, a Methodist bank in which most members and chapels kept their money, joined them. Unlike the previous case, fraud was not the cause. The directors were not professional bankers and their inexperience had proved costly. Although arrested, they were acquitted after an auditor's report said 'The directors may be good farmers, but they are not good bankers'.

1939

Jersey Airways took delivery of a state-of-the-art, all metal monoplane built by de Havillands called the Flamingo. Once the airport was opened Jersey Airways had decided to operate more advanced aircraft and this new 18-seater was luxury compared to the more common biplanes.

1947

Although it was two years since the end of the war, some goods were still scarce. On this day 53,081 ration books were issued.

1951

The vessel *John V*, loaded with 398 tons of potatoes, turned turtle and sank just off Elizabeth Castle breakwater. The crew were able to get clear and were rescued by the pilot's boat. The ship, which lay half submerged, was eventually salvaged.

---

[24] See 1st February for further details.

04 July

1737

The foundation stone of Jersey's first public library was laid. The building, in Library Place, was instigated by Philippe Falle, the author of *An Account of Jersey*, one of the Island's first historical tomes.

1899

It was election day in the parish of St Helier. Brass bands played, banners flew and the colours of both candidates for the post of Deputy were being sported by the townsfolk. The *Jersey Evening Post* was supporting Philip Bailhache, while the *Jersey Times* backed Mr Nicolle.

It was a close run thing, with Bailhache winning with 625 to 543 votes. Once the results had been announced, the town was alive with celebrating Bailhache supporters, while Nicolle's were pleased that their candidate had done so well.

The small number of votes did not reflect the large numbers involved in the campaigns, as, although relatively few people had a right to vote, those who did not still followed local politics.

The victorious crowd were addressed by their candidate from a balcony more than once, as the enthusiastic parishioners demanded to see their man.

1952

May West appeared in court, charged with committing an act 'injurious to the public morals, tending to corrupt the mind and destroy the love of decency, morality and good order'. Mrs West had a shop in Colomberie and had on display what were referred to as 'obscene postcards'.

The case was deferred and when it next came to court a number of other shopkeepers had also been charged. After a further hearing, the Magistrate discharged all the accused, ruling that the 'comic' postcards were crude, vulgar and in bad taste, but not obscene.

05 July

1778

The go ahead for 30 towers to be built for coastal defence was given by Lord Weymouth, as it was a time when Jersey was in constant fear of a French invasion. Each one would cost £156, the total bill coming to £4,680. Only 23 were actually built, the last of which was La Rocco in St Ouen's Bay in 1798. Once constructed they were known by number, First Tower being most well-known.

1788

A political confrontation was reported on this day. Thomas Lempriere and Philippe Dumaresq met in what is now the Royal Square. They had argued previously and on this occasion walking sticks came into play. Lempriere was beaten back, a sharp blow knocking his stick to the ground. Dumaresq then, holding one ear, 'thrashed him soundly'. After more heavy blows with his fists, Dumaresq gripped both his opponents ears and rubbed his nose in the mud. The most astonishing thing about this incident is that both parties were pillars of the community.

1954

Red Line Motors' coach drivers went on strike. They were paid £6 for a seven day week and relied on the hat being passed around to make up their wages. But these days the hat returned empty. The drivers wanted to put up a sign in each coach telling tourists that, contrary to belief, they received no money from hotels. The company's owner refused, offering them 5 shillings a week instead, but this was not accepted and a strike was called. But two days later the signs were in the coaches, which were back on the road.

1970

The desalination plant at Corbière produced its first clean water. The £1.25 million building took in sea water and distilled it to make it drinkable. The oil-fired plant pumped the water directly into Val de la Mare reservoir, supplementing the Island's natural springs and rainwater. It was built in an old quarry at a time when oil was cheap and the Island's demands for water were growing.

06 July

1553

Mary, Queen of the Scots, acceded to the throne. An embittered Catholic, she reversed the nation's religious policy, with rebellious Protestants being burnt at the stake in Britain and our sister isles. Jersey, however, merely gave lip service to the change, a policy highlighted when the normally powerful Dean was unable to save his friend from the gallows. Richard Averty delivered his servant's baby, baptised it, then strangled the child, burying the body beneath the hearth. Despite the Dean's threats, Averty was sentenced to be dragged to the gallows, hanged and his body left on the gibbet until it rotted away. The execution took place and the Dean's hope for the return of Catholicism died in disgrace along with Averty.

1905

Marie Turmel was in court, charged with attempted suicide. The 27-year old woman had thrown herself into the sea at Grève de Lecq. Two fishermen had dragged her unconscious form from the water and Dr Symons was summoned. It appears that Mrs Turmel's drunken husband had smashed up their house and in despair she had tried to kill herself. The Magistrate decided that the best thing was to send her back home. This was not as unthinking as it may appear as the next case before the court was that of Mr Turmel for drunkenness. Given the choice between a fine of £2 or 12 days in prison, Mr Turmel chose to go to gaol, allowing his wife time to recover. Mrs Turmel's case later went before the Royal Court and, although sympathetic, the court ruled that she had broken the law and sentenced her to a week in prison with hard labour.

1923

Islanders were informed of two recent archaeological discoveries. The first was that of the 'beehive hut' on the headland between Petit Port and La Pulente. The 5 ft diameter circular stone structure was unlike anything previously found in the Island and it predated other Neolithic constructions. The second discovery was a stone axe-head which had been found while groundwork was being done at Portelet Hotel in readiness for an extension.

07 July

1827

St Helier welcomed Jersey's first mail carried by a steam vessel. The *Watersprite*, later renamed *Wildfire*, was a wooden paddle steamer captained by Frederick White. It cost £8,750 and had a crew of 12. Under local pressure, post office officials had come to Jersey the previous year and made arrangements for the *Watersprite* to operate on the route, thus providing a faster, more reliable service.

1915

While on a picnic at Portelet Bay, eight of a 20 strong party of Jesuit students were drowned. The sea had started to fall and despite a high sea, some of the boys decided to swim while others remained on shore. Powerful waves apparently struck the party, sweeping some onto rocks. Despite the best efforts of the masters, eight boys were drowned.

1923

At 7.15 the mail boat *Caesarea* left St Helier Harbour with 373 passengers on board. Shortly after, in thick fog, she struck rocks off Portelet. The damaged steamer was able to limp back to port, despite water entering the stokehold and engine room. With stern deep in the water and life boats trailing, she almost made it back to the quay. However just outside the harbour she stuck fast. No one was injured and the *Caesarea* was later refloated.

1942

The German forces sentenced two brothers to long terms of imprisonment for distributing leaflets. Acts of sabotage and leaflets insisting that the population not surrender their radios, as had been ordered, had occurred two weeks earlier. Ten residents had been arrested and were to be sent to concentration camps if the perpetrators were not found. A number of places were raided, including the *Jersey Evening Post*, in an attempt to discover where the leaflets had been printed. When the two were finally apprehended they were sentenced to terms of five years and two years, the length of sentence meaning that it had to be served on mainland Europe.

08 July

1676

An order was issued instructing everyone to return to their houses when the curfew bell sounded on Saturday evenings. The dictum was an attempt to combat the trouble caused by drinkers when taverns closed in St Helier.

1929

Monsieur Henri Le Roux, a banker from Paris, provoked a territorial incident on this day. Disputing Jersey's authority over the Minquiers, news reached the Island that he was attempting to build a house on the reef. This was just one of the many unsuccessful attempts throughout the centuries by the French to claim Jersey territory.

1940

British servicemen who found themselves in Jersey when the occupying forces arrived were interned in a camp at Grouville. This same camp had previously held Germans and Italians who had been interned at the outbreak of the war. The British servicemen were only detained in the camp for a few weeks before being transferred to prison camps in France.

1988

A classic boundary dispute came to a head when the Clameur de Haro was raised on this day. Roger de Carteret had concreted a post on what he believed to be his land to try and stop cars eroding it. Former St Peter's Constable Winter Le Marquand also believed he had rights to the land and asked that the post be removed.

On the day in question de Carteret was due to be at a meeting which Le Marquand was also to attend but on seeing wheelbarrows with cement and chippings, de Carteret grew suspicious and did not go. Minutes after the meeting was due to begin a mechanical digger arrived on the disputed land, the driver only stopping when the Clameur had been raised.

After a complicated hearing, the court found for de Carteret and fined Le Marquand £10 and costs.

09 July

1751

The statue of George II was unveiled in the Market Place and the area renamed La Place Royal, the Royal Square.

1873

An official party was taken by train from Green Street to Grouville and back to show the progress of the nearly completed Eastern Railway line. Unfortunately, on returning to Green Street the locomotive overshot the intended stopping place by about 20 yards. This section of the track, although in position, had not yet been secured, causing the engine to come off the rails and gently collide with a newly arrived carriage. Little damage was done and the following day the train carried nearly 700 people involved with army manoeuvres to Grouville Common free of charge.

1899

Guillaume Polless was charged with selling spirits on a Sunday, when it was illegal to supply drink from a bottle. Visitors to the house at 2 Peter Street were found to have been served with both spirits and cider. But Polless' troubles had only just begun when he was charged by the Centenier. In court the following day, Polless was fined £5 for the offence. His wife, however, urged him to take the prison sentence and save the money. But the fine was paid and Polless released, whereupon his wife attacked him for wasting the money and was herself arrested.

1994

A group of 150 French nationals invaded Les Ecréhous. The party, made up of men, women and children, arrived in a flotilla of boats from Carteret. They had brought a priest along with them, who conducted a mass. Unlike other French invasions, this one was well publicised in advance and the threat of up to 1,000 Frenchmen arriving on the reef led Jersey authorities to send a police presence. Everything was very friendly, with the French asserting that Les Ecréhous were theirs, while the Jerseymen knew that the French were mistaken, the Union Jack flying from the flagpole proving the point.

10 July

1502

Sir Hugh Vaughan, a Welshman, was appointed Governor of Jersey. He was described as a strikingly handsome man and a great horseman. He was also noted for wenching. But as time went on his behaviour became so appalling that he was eventually removed from office.

1900

The Opera House opened on this day. Lillie Langtry did the official duties, as well as producing and acting in the opening play 'The Degenerates'. The play itself, branded by some as immoral, proved disappointing to those who attended, ready to be shocked. But the whole event was considered a success.

1918

The inaugural meeting of the Jersey Political Association was held at the Oddfellows Hall. The meeting was well attended by an enthusiastic audience who were keen to see political reform. The sale of seigneural rights and corrupt practices were also attacked.

1943

John Laurens of St Lawrence appeared before the Royal Court, charged with selling rhubarb too dear. The fixed price was 6d per lb and the accused had charged Roger de Leschervy 2s 1½d per lb. In his defence Advocate de la Haye said that his client did not usually sell rhubarb and had only supplied de Leschervy as a favour. But this was discredited when it was heard that a number of similar complaints had been made. Laurens was fined £5, with £1 costs.

1970

The Lieutenant Governor declared a state of emergency. A docks strike on the mainland was exacerbated by a strike of local manual workers. The dispute was over money and, locally, was settled within a few days. However, the state of emergency remained as the national dock strike was threatening local food and fuel supplies, and rationing was not ruled out.

11 July

1903

The Royal Court annulled Julia Westaway's will. Miss Westaway had bequeathed some of her estate to Elizabeth Curwood and her brother Charles Curwood. However, Miss Westaway's lawyers contested the will, claiming that pressure had been brought to bear when she was infirm in body and mind. After a long hearing, the court agreed on a majority decision and annulled the will. But with various appeals, the case ran on for a number of years until, in 1906, the Privy Council decided that the will would stand.

1905

Gunner Edmund Newland of the Royal Artillery drowned at Havre des Pas. He had just been learning to swim and had been advised by his comrades to wait until the tide had retreated. However, Newland dived in and sank almost immediately, it taking almost half an hour to retrieve the body. The inquest heard that soldiers were supposed to swim in a designated area with proper supervision, a rule which had been ignored on this occasion. It was stated that the 21-year old had only managed some 14 strokes after his dive and had then sunk to the bottom. The jury's verdict on this not uncommon tragedy was accidental death.

1967

Sir John Wardlaw-Milne, who had resided in Jersey since his retirement, died, bequeathing £100,000 for the construction of a 'kursaal'. Sir John had laid down the proviso that work must start within 18 months of his death. Although the sum bequeathed was large, it was not large enough to provide the facilities intended.

At the same time the States were drawing up plans for an indoor swimming pool at Fort Regent. After negotiations, the two projects were combined, although the executors of the will insisted that the time limit still stood. This is why the construction of the indoor pool moved considerably faster than most States projects. Pressure from the estate's executors also resulted in the Fort being tidied and landscaped, as well as a children's indoor play area being formed.

12 July

1814

Peace with France was proclaimed in St Helier, the last conflict having gone on for twelve years. In recent times the Island's Martello towers had been built, Fort Regent was well underway and around the Island's less populated spots, various small forts and guardhouses stood. Peace may have been declared but Jersey's fortifications continued to be built for a number of years after.

1919

After years of protest and much delay a new law on suffrage granted women over 30 the right to vote. The revised law stated that 'every male British subject of 20 and over, and every British subject of 30 and over ... shall have the right to vote at public elections'. One provision in the bill was that voters must occupy a house or rooms with an annual rental of at least £10 to qualify to vote. This clause caused the greatest debate when the law was passed, some States Members asserting that the £10 limit was too high and that £6 would be more reasonable, particularly for those in country parishes. This amendment was rejected and the States accepted the law, which was based on English legislation.

1921

George V and Queen Mary's arrival in Jersey was heralded with a 21 gun salute. Thousands of people watched and cheered the party as they disembarked before travelling on to the Royal Square and a ceremony in the States Chamber. The Royals visited Springfield, Victoria College and Mont Orgueil Castle, as well as seeing some of the Island's countryside. The girl guides were inspected and all the handshaking and speechmaking that accompanies these events was indulged in.

1963

A change in the law came into effect in the Royal Court. For the first time a criminal indictment was in English and not in French.

13 July

1648

On this day an ox was killed by a thunderbolt in Gorey. Its owner found it apparently without a mark on it. Once moved, one side of the hide was discovered to be burnt. It was noted at the time that 'the flesh of the ox was saved, the blood being still hot in it'.

1855

George Ingouville's actions on this day were later rewarded with the Victoria Cross.[25] Having served in the Merchant and now Royal Navy, Ingouville had seen action. On this day boats from the *Arrogant* had engaging the enemy. Despite being wounded and under heavy fire, Ingouville had leapt into the water to stop a swamped cutter from drifting under a battery. Ingouville's medal was later sold at auction and acquired by the States.

1905

A child named Frank Hope had a nasty scare on this day. He had been running behind an excursion car near Grouville Railway Station. The driver of the horse-drawn vehicle had attempted to frighten the boy by flicking his whip in young Hope's direction. The lad became entangled in the thong and was dragged along the road for some distance. The driver stopped and released the child but not before Hope had sustained injuries requiring a doctor's attention.

1942

70-year old Joseph Nicolle and his son Reginald faced the Royal Court, charged with stealing a cow. The animal had disappeared from John Godel's field in St Martin. Centenier Journeaux had searched a number of farms and on Nicolle's he had noticed freshly dug soil, under which, four feet down, the cow's remains were discovered. Despite not guilty pleas, the jury's verdict was unanimously guilty. Reginald was sentenced to one year's hard labour, while his father, who the Bailiff said 'had brought disgrace upon his grey hair' received six month's simple imprisonment.

---

[25] See 26th June for further details.

14 July

1645

Chevalier's diary notes that on this day it was forbidden to cut seaweed around Elizabeth Castle. This unusual order had a military purpose. In the event of a siege the seaweed would have been needed as fuel in the Castle. The order lasted for two years, after which time the valuable fertiliser was again available to St Helier farmers.

1905

Jacques Marie Cotrel, a Frenchman, while travelling from Snow Hill to Gorey, had opened the carriage door too soon and either jumped or fallen off the train. The guard, Mr Browning, saw it happen and applied the breaks. However, the unfortunate Frenchman had fallen across the rails. Being in a front carriage, four further carriages went over his leg, leaving it barely attached, and giving his head a deep cut. It was reported that the man 'bore his sufferings with great fortitude' and only lost consciousness for a few moments. His leg was removed at Gorey and a further emergency operation at the Hospital amputated more of his leg.

1958

A woman served on an Assize Jury for the first time, as previously women who had been called to jury service had all been challenged and discharged. The case dealt with a robbery charge and the jury's verdict was guilty. Two of the defendants were sentenced to 12 months imprisonment, a third received two years.

1966

For the first time in 11 years the Royal Court swore in newly qualified solicitors. In the previous 18 years the only new face had been that of Mr Tomes. On this occasion there were two new solicitors and both had to produce their birth certificates to prove that they were British and aged over 21 years. Kenneth Syvret and David Moon were the new boys and took similar paths. Thirty years later the two met again in an election for the post of Deputy of St Ouen and in a closely fought contest, Syvret took the prize.

15 July

1872

The construction of piers at Bonne Nuit and Grève de Lecq was ordered on this day. Once built, the north coast harbours were to give shelter to the Island's fishing fleet. However, the pier at Grève de Lecq, which reached almost half way across the bay, could not withstand the Atlantic storms and was later reduced to rubble.

1906

Jersey was visited by a flotilla of Navy torpedo boats, the six vessels having visited Alderney earlier. There was a certain amount of ceremonial activity and the boats were due to stay in the harbour for a few days, allowing their crews to enjoy the local facilities.

1947

The *Westward*, the yacht owned by T B Davis, was scuttled in accordance with the late philanthropist's wishes. The magnificent vessel, which had entertained many famous and royal people, was taken to the Hurd Deep off Alderney and sunk.

1962

Six people were drowned when the 14 ft, newly built *Jean Rose*, capsized in St Aubin's Bay. A party of seven were motoring between St Aubin's Fort and Noirmont. When the throttle was opened her bow went under, throwing the occupants into the sea. The only survivor was John de Guelle, who lost his wife, daughter and son and a number of friends. De Guelle was rescued by Harry Knowlman after spending an hour in the water, by which time the others had all been lost. A dog who was also thought to have drowned was later pulled from the water in an exhausted state.

1980

A proposition was lodged to allow the States to acquire land under compulsory purchase and argue about the price later. As the law stood, negotiations about compensation for land compulsorily purchased could take years, delaying vital works. This proposition was intended to speed up the whole process.

16 July

555

On this day Helier is said to have died, beheaded by pirates or Vikings. Helier was a Belgian hermit who lived his self imposed life of poverty on an islet in St Aubin's Bay. In the sixth century large numbers of religious people took up a hermit's life as they were disenchanted with the increasingly affluent church. St Helier was credited with a number of miraculous deeds, most of which originate from a thriller style book entitled *The Passion of St Helier*, which was written over 400 years after his death. It features a great number of events originally attributed to various other saints.

1902

The Royal Court annulled the recent election for Constable of St Helier, which Philip Baudain appeared to have won by 151 votes. It came about when Thomas Augustus Scott took legal recourse after he had not been allowed to vote, despite being on the electoral roll. It seems that an electoral list from the previous year had been used. The case was heard by, among others, Jurat Aubin, who had been the returning officer at the election and a debate had ensued as to whether it was constitutionally right for him to sit, although it was stressed that no implication as to Jurat Aubin's impartiality was intended. After much discussion it was decided to call another election and the Constable was fined £5. During the proceedings it was noted that the nomination meeting had been by ticket only.

1942

A new railway was officially opened on this day. It ran from the harbour to Millbrook and had been built by the occupying forces. As with all official openings, whether during a war or not, certain formalities had to be adhered to. So speeches were made, a ribbon was cut, the whistle was blown, a band played and, most importantly, all the officials went on to a big lunch at the Pomme D'Or Hotel. The irony of the situation, when the Germans had announced that they intended laying a railway, was not lost on locals. Only five years earlier Jersey had abandoned railways as uneconomic and had ripped up all the lines, lines the Germans were now intending to re-lay.

17 July

1876

The railway from St Helier to St Aubin ran along a raised wooden platform or viaduct for part of its route near St Aubin. On this day the stilt-like structure had become so unsafe that the section was closed and remained that way for over two months while repairs were carried out, with Le Haule as journey's end for train passengers.

1879

Warring neighbours Thomas Rose and Arthur Jones had previously clashed when Rose had dug a trench across a lane to Portelet, the ownership of which was disputed.[26] This time Rose had a wall built across the lane to which Jones claimed a right of way. Jones ordered his workman to demolish the wall, at which point Rose raised the Clameur de Haro. The case was a long one, so much so that Rose died and his son took over the action. The court looked into the ownership of the lane and decided that Rose did not, as he claimed, own the road, but merely had a right of way. He therefore had no right to build a wall nor to raise the Clameur. The court also decreed that Jones had no right of way, as he claimed, and therefore had no right to use the road nor to knock down illegally built walls.

1921

The first pilgrimage to the Hermitage off Elizabeth Castle was held. St Helier's Day is 16th July, but the tides are not always favourable. The pilgrimage has become an annual event and each year a procession lead by the Dean walks to the Castle for a service.

1952

An air display watched by 30,000 people took place at Jersey airport to celebrate the opening of the tarmac runway. Participants included US Tornado jets, a Sycamore helicopter, Sabre jets and a Vampire. There were displays of formation flying, helicopter pick ups and a parachute jump. Interest was enormous. The JMT transported over 3,000 spectators and 7,000 cars filled the roads.

---

[26] See 24th October for further details.

18 July

1663

Prior to the Reformation, each parish church had a perquage, a path by which criminals who had sought sanctuary in the church could reach a boat and escape. Once the paths were no longer in use, they became overgrown and on this day Charles II gave them to Edouard de Carteret. Most of them he later sold to the owners of adjoining property and these routes to the sea were lost.

1826

There had been a market in St Aubin for many years and on this day a new building opened to house the stall holders. The rents were fixed at 25 livres, about £1.05, per year. The cost of construction had come from four lotteries. Originally the sum of £775 had been considered enough for the project but as with most States projects, even to this day, the cost had increased to £900. As time passed St Helier took over as the centre of commerce and the St Aubin market declined. For a time part of it was used as a fire station, while another area became a temporary jail. But gradually the market building fell into disuse until renovated to become a branch of the National Westminster Bank.

1843

By 1843 the town of St Helier had grown dramatically. On this day the States ordered that all streets should have their names marked and houses should be numbered. Direction sign posts on main and minor roads were also to be erected.

1904

A property in St Brelade that had been struck by lightning was well alight. The fire brigade, being unable to find a water supply, used liquid manure instead. Unfortunately the supply soon ran out and the fire finished its work. In the days before mains water, bore holes and water tankers, liquid manure was often the only fluid available to the firemen and it would appear its use in firefighting was not uncommon.

19 July

1842

On this day St Matthew's Church at Millbrook opened its doors to the public for the first time. Some years later Lady Trent paid for the church's refurbishment.[27]

1911

The *SS Roebuck* became an instant attraction when she hit a reef near St Brelade. She was left high and dry, with her bow in the air, remaining that way until the 28th when she was refloated and beached in St Brelade's Bay. She was later towed to St Helier, then back to England, returning to service on 10th January 1912.

1906

The body of Pierre Le Guen was found in a field at Swan's Farm, St Saviour, lying on his back with his head resting on a hedge, his face covered with blood and his boots missing. Murder was suspected and rumours spread across the Island. Reports that a St Saviour Honorary Policeman had been killed while cornering Le Guen's murderer were untrue but were widely believed. The inquest was adjourned three times before a verdict was announced.[28]

1919

A public holiday was called by the States as a way of thanking all Islanders who had participated in the war. There were celebrations all over the UK and a contingent of locals were in the London parade. £700 was voted by the States to fund the events.

1924

Rosemary Thompson was fined for riding a bike without a licence card or registration number. She explained that she had borrowed the cycle from a friend but the Magistrate fined her £2 for the offence. Up until the 1970s all bicycles had to be registered at the parish hall at the beginning of the year.

---

[27] See 29th September for further details.
[28] See 31st July 1906 for further details.

20 July

1549

On this day the English ambassador was assured by the French that war was unthinkable. The next day they invaded Sark. Ten days later an attack on Guernsey was repulsed, so the fleet sailed for Jersey. Landing at Bouley Bay, the French force were met by the militia near Trinity Church and after a stiff fight the invading men were forced to retreat. Jersey had escaped but Sark remained in French hands for nine years.

1897

Henry Ahier and George Dorey fell foul of a new regulation which had been brought in by the States three months earlier. They were accused of bathing without proper costumes at West Park Beach at 8.30 on a Sunday morning. Ahier told the court that he had bathed in the same place with the same bathing drawers for many years without complaint, and produced his costume as evidence.

Mr Renouf, who had also been bathing in the area and had seen Ahier and Dorey in the sea, was asked if he himself had been wearing a proper costume. Renouf described his as a 'full costume with shoulder straps, reaching below the thighs'.

The problem facing the Magistrate was that the States had not said what a proper costume was. But he decided that Ahier's was not proper and fined both men 10 shillings. He suggested that the costume worn by members of the Bathing Club would be the most suitable for the purpose.

1905

Nathaniel Nicholls was fined for selling beer without a licence. Centenier Luxon said that having received complaints, he had visited the Marina at Havre des Pas and found people 'sitting at lunch, drinking beer'. A number of witnesses were called, including one woman who admitted to having paid 3d for a bottle of stout. Nicholls, who came from Penzance, pleaded ignorance of the law, but to no avail, and was fined £10.

21 July

1728

Josue Pipon was buried in St Brelade on this day. Pipon had been appointed Lieutenant Bailiff in 1715 and was generally liked, despite a dispute with his brother-in-law that had lasted for 14 years. It was under his authority that paper notes had been issued to overcome the lack of coinage in the Island. He had also prohibited pauper children being sold and exported to France by the parishes.

1904

A number of gamblers appeared before the Magistrate on gaming charges. The first accused failed to appear, so his £5 bail was confiscated and his arrest ordered. He had been running a three card trick at the horse races at Grouville. William Walker was charged with running a roulette game. His defence claimed that it was not roulette but a game advertised in the official programme. Found guilty, Walker was fined £10, the maximum, or one month in gaol. John Weston got the same sentence for the same crime. Donald Statt claimed only to play for coppers and said that it was his first time, to which the Magistrate responded 'It is very funny, but it is always the first time'. Statt was fined £5. During the proceedings the Magistrate expressed 'not much sympathy with those who were such simpletons as to play'.

1905

A memorial to the nine former pupils of Victoria College who had died in the South African War was unveiled. The ceremony was attended by the Bailiff, Governor and most Island dignitaries.

1955

An Australian competitor in the International Hill Climb at Bouley Bay was killed when his car hit a bank and turned over. J D 'Bill' Sleeman was driving a 1132 cc supercharged Cooper in one of the meeting's last runs. The spectators helped right the relatively undamaged car but Sleeman had died almost instantly from head injuries. The event had been attended by 7,000 people, including his wife and four-year old daughter.

22 July

1910

The statue of George II, having been removed from its pedestal in the Royal Square, was on this day shipped to England for repairs. The years, and birds, had taken their toll and the King required regilding.

1912

Having previously served in the States as a Deputy, George Crill had stood for the vacant post of Jurat and on this day he was elected unopposed at a Town Hall meeting. However, when he went before the court to be sworn in, the court refused. Ten years earlier Crill, a solicitor, had been taken before the court and fined £30. He had been the 'curator of the property and person of François Mollet', a position he had admitted neglecting. The matter of whether Crill was fit to hold the high office of Jurat went before the Privy Council, where he was exonerated and in 1913 was eventually sworn in as Jurat.

1968

Jersey led the way in the fight against drug abuse when on this day the Island became the first place in the British Isles to ban heroin. The Medical Officer of Health explained that the ban was intended to 'close the stable door before the horse bolts'. Although small amounts of the drug were available to doctors, once this supply was used no more would be imported during a two year trial.

1994

John Le Sueur resigned from his position as Constable of St John. The Constable is also the head of the Parish Honorary Police and as Le Sueur had been convicted of a drink driving offence earlier in the year, his position was considered untenable. From the moment of his conviction public and political opinion had been against his staying in office but this view had been dismissed by the Constable, who was adamant that he would stay put. The Royal Court, however, had other ideas and, having reviewed the case, ordered Le Sueur to resign.

23 July

1868

The ancient law of the Clameur de Haro acts as an instant injunction. On this day the Rector of Trinity, Rev Du Heaume, used it to great effect. Philip Binet had been about to start harvesting his wheat when Du Heaume raised the Clameur against him. He had also raised it against a number of other parishioners. This meant that they could not bring in their grain until the court ruled on the matter and if it took too long the harvest would be lost. Despite the obvious need for haste, it took five weeks to go to court. The Reverend failed to appear to explain his actions, so the court fined him for his frivolous action and the now very ripe wheat could be gathered.

1935

The Prince of Wales arrived in Jersey. The usual formalities were observed and endless speeches made. The newly built Howard Davis Hall at Victoria College was opened and a painting of George V was also unveiled, both of which were gifts to the Island from T B Davis. To celebrate the visit the streets had been decorated and an evening fête with fireworks was held at West Park.

1939

Philip Janvrin Marett died on this day, having improved the health of the Island's population. After the Great War he had been appointed Medical Officer of Health. His new regime, training and methods soon showed results. In 1922 there had been 155 cases of diphtheria. By 1929 there were only 9. Tuberculosis was also a killer. When appointed in 1922 there had been 69 deaths. Fifteen years later it was reduced to 28. A chest clinic was founded in his time and the Overdale Isolation Hospital was opened.

1982

The States fast launch, the *Duchess of Normandy*, caught fire. The *Duke of Normandy*, which had been on an official trip to the Minquiers with a number of dignitaries on board, was quickly on the scene to fight the fire and later took the vessel in tow. However she sank before reaching port.

24 July

1699

A special committee was appointed by the States to find a convenient site on which to build a college. Nothing further happened for 200 years.[29]

1909

Frenchman Fréderic Legolliot died in a bathing machine at the West Park swimming pool. He had bathed with a female companion for a few minutes before they returned to their respective machines. The attendant had heard a thud and discovered the deceased lying dead, dressed only in a vest.

1923

A St Helier Parish Assembly agreed to a private road running from Douro Terrace to Rouge Rue being ceded to the parish. The road belonged to Francis Voisin, who gave the parish £100 as part of the deal, the money being needed to build a supporting wall for the thoroughfare. The question of ownership had been brought up when the parish had sued Mrs Monckton, only to find that the road actually belonged to Voisin. By ceding it to the parish Voisin was absolved of the cost of repairs to land he had not known he owned.

1951

The parish of St Helier voted by 22 votes to 17 to sell land in Bellozanne Valley to the States at a price of £22,500 to build a sewage farm. Some residents at First Tower objected but were assured that no nuisance would be created and the project went ahead.

1974

An appeal was issued, asking for householders with empty bedrooms to take in visitors. Hundreds of tourists were arriving every day without booked accommodation, hotels were full and the Tourism Department were desperate to find extra beds. The situation seemed unlikely to change, with six more weeks of chaos predicted.

---

[29] See 6th May for further details.

25 July

1921

Henry Edward Le Vavasseur dit Durell, having organised much of the King and Queen's itinerary while visiting Jersey, took to his bed after they left and died. Durell had been a popular member of the States for many years. Prior to his political career he was one of the Island's most able lawyers. On one occasion an old master gunner was accused of murdering an eating house proprietor. The man had been arrested, still holding the pistol, but after Durell's three hour speech the jury of 24 people unanimously found him not guilty.

1925

The Florence Boot Cottages at Grève d'Azette were inaugurated on this day, named after Jesse Boot's wife. The Boots, or Lord and Lady Trent, had earned their wealth through their chain of chemist shops and were very generous to Jersey. Florence, a Jersey girl, continued to fund worthwhile projects after her husband's death, in this case low rental housing for working class families.

1946

The last British Liberation soldiers left the Island. For over a year the British troops had been responsible for removing and making safe the German defences.

1957

Queen Elizabeth II and Prince Philip arrived in Jersey. The sun did not shine but Islanders still turned out in great numbers. Arriving at the quay the Royal party were greeted by the usual dignitaries and guard of honour. This was the first time in 98 years that a reigning Queen of England had visited the Island. Her address to the States was described as historic and the Royal Square was packed with people to see her arrive and leave the States Chambers.

Royal visitors' itineraries when visiting Jersey always seem to be the same. The address to the States, a visit to Victoria College, a reception and a visit to Mont Orgueil Castle or the Victoria Cottage Homes. On this occasion the Royal party did all but the Castle visit. Instead they were driven around the Island.

26 July

1848

A presentation made to Constable Peter Le Sueur at the St Helier Arsenal was attended by over 1,200 Islanders. In thanking him for the improvements made during his term of office, notably a town drainage scheme, the assembly of the masses greeted the Constable with such enthusiasm and numbers that any Constable of today would be grateful to receive just a tenth of each.

1923

The horse racing at Don Bridge, St Brelade, proved so popular that 23 trains from St Helier had to be put on, with a fare of 1s 3d for a return ticket. Entry to the course was 1/6, tax included, and the first race started at 12.45. Trains were not the only means of transport, as char-a-bancs and buses were also available.

The crowds could bet on the crown and anchor, as well as the horses, and the more well-to-do made use of the specially built stand to watch proceedings. The first race was a hurdle, with Graceful Mover taking the £50 first prize. The Town Plate, a two mile handicap, was won by Martinique, which gave the owner a prize of £100.

1961

Victoria College's shooting team became the first Channel Islanders to win the Ashburton Shield in a national competition for public schools held at Bisley. The local boys triumphed amid a thousand other competitors, the team captain, 17-year old Terry Marshall, leading by example with remarkably accurate shooting. Guernsey rivals Elisabeth College were beaten by 17 points.

1979

The idea of establishing a transit camp in Jersey for Vietnamese boat people was firmly squashed by Defence Committee President Senator John Riley. A local businessman had offered to accommodate up to 25 refugees, the idea being rejected as impractical by the local authorities.

27 July

1811

A grateful States gave a silver bowl valued at 100 guineas to Major-General Le Couteur, who was Inspector of the Militia and had assisted General Don in his work. In November 1968 the States recovered the bowl from Sothebys as part of Jersey's history, the price having risen to £2,100.

1858

The founder of the Jersey Benevolent and Strangers Friendly Society died on this day. Peter Pequin had spent much of his life helping the Island's poor and had been rewarded with living an impressive 85 years.

1899

On this day in St Saviour's Parish Church Lillie Langtry married Hugo de Bathe. This was the same venue where she had married her first husband, Edward Langtry, 25 years earlier.[30] Nearly 20 years her junior, de Bathe was to become Sir Hugo following his father's death and so Emilie Le Breton became Lady de Bathe. Hugo's father had disapproved of the marriage and had attempted to renounce his son's right to his title, but later relented.

1916

The airship *Astra-Torres* had Islanders looking to the heavens as she flew across the Island. Unlike Germany's sleek zeppelins, this basic airship looked like a clover leaf in section and passengers were suspended from the structure in a gondola.

1964

Jersey's first two zebra crossings were officially inaugurated on this day. They were sited at the Beaumont junction and the long-time campaigner for their introduction, St Peter Constable W P Le Marquand, was first to cross, having first inserted the fuse. The next to cross in safety were six of Le Marquand's grandchildren.

---

[30] See 9th March for further details.

28 July

1865

On this day the foundation stone of a new school situated behind St James' Church was laid. St James' School had been in the planning stage for 15 years and £600 had been raised in that time to buy the site. The building was due to cost £1,400, of which the States would provide £800. So a further £600 had to be raised by subscription.

The school, for boys, was just one of the public buildings being erected at this time. The previous day the foundation stone of St Simon's Church had been put into place and the following day a similar ceremony was to take place for the public lunatic asylum, which was to be built on the site of Queen's Farm, St Saviour.

1904

Elizabeth de Ste Croix and Pierre Le Vaille were facing the Magistrate, where they were told that they were 'poor specimens'. Both had been accused of theft, while assisting during a fire. Mrs Carden's home in Pier Road was ablaze and her belongings had been moved to the couple's neighbouring property for safety. It was while Carden's effects were in their house that the pair had stolen her money, between £8 and £10, and some cloth. Le Vaille had spent the money on a sout'wester for 15s 6d, shoes and clothes.

1947

What appeared to be an earthquake struck Jersey, shaking doors and windows and rattling furniture. The quake theory was confirmed in a BBC news bulletin which claimed that earth tremors had been recorded in Cornwall. Yet no such tremor had been observed at Maison St Louis, despite the effect being felt all over the Island. It turned out that a ship carrying nitrates had caught fire in Brest harbour, on the Brittany coast. It was being towed out to sea when it exploded just opposite a gasometer. The resulting massive shock wave had travelled across the Channel to Cornwall and along to the Channel Islands, where it shook the air but not the seismic equipment.

29 July

1876

Work restarted on the St Aubin to La Moye railway after the original owners were declared en desastre, an event that occurred more than once during its building. The construction of this railway line required considerably more engineering and expense than the run around St Aubin's Bay. A great deal of rock blasting, as well as the steep gradient, building of bridges and demolishing of houses, conspired to slow the work and raise the cost.

1914

The Royal Jersey Militia were mobilised on orders from the Lieutenant Governor. The news was taken quite cheerfully and the following day the relevant units paraded fully equipped before being sent to their respective posts around the Island. The militia force completely encircled the Island and were ordered to keep lookout for enemy activity.

1936

The Petty Debts Court ordered Mrs Avarne to pay Peter Valpy £2 18s. Avarne's dog had killed ten of Valpy's fowl in April and she had agreed to pay him £3 for his loss. Having given 2 shillings on account, no further money was forthcoming. In court Avarne claimed the birds had not been properly fenced in and were not worth the sum demanded. But the court ruled that £3 for ten birds had been reasonable and ordered her to pay.

1954

It is often said that it never rains on the Battle of Flowers. This year it not only rained, it blew a gale as well. Despite the awful weather, the arena between First Tower and West Park was full of spectators determined to enjoy themselves. Anthony Steel accompanied Miss Battle of Flowers, Maureen Hobbs, throughout the parade, which was won by the Jersey Young Farmers with *Fairy Queen Afloat*.

30 July

1806

Lieutenant Governor John Humphrey required more labour to build Fort Regent and informed his Commander-in-Chief that although he had already employed 22 carpenters, 6 sawyers, 5 wheelers, 1 cooper, 62 masons, 26 smiths, 97 miners and 334 labourers, he still needed more.

The construction of the well alone gives an idea of the magnitude of the task, it being sunk between December 1806 and October 1808, with 12 miners working night and day throughout this period. Proceeding at an average of 10 feet per month, 235 feet had been excavated through solid rock until the final blast reached a spring and caused the previously dry chamber to fill instantly with 70 feet of water. The miners still down the shaft were suspended from ropes which fortunately held them clear of the rising water.

Later a force of over 800 men worked each day on the building of Fort Regent.

1905

St Helier's first steam fire engine, the *Lord St Helier*, was christened. Costing £285, the new machine was still horse-drawn but the 20 men who had been required to pump in relays could now be replaced by one engineer.

1926

The shock waves of an earthquake centred in France were felt in the Island. Hitting Jersey at about 2.20 pm, the tremors caused alarm but little damage.

1956

The Agriculture Museum, designed to preserve and display the Island's rapidly disappearing agricultural past, was opened at La Hougue Bie. Many of the old machines and equipment on show had been gathered by Frank Le Maistre who, with remarkable foresight, had preserved many items of the Island's agricultural heritage. The collection remained on display at La Hougue Bie until the mid 1990s when it was transferred to Hamptonne Country Life Museum.

31 July

1890

The London and South Western Railway Company introduced their latest steam ship to Jersey. The *Frederica* and her two sister ships, the *Lydia* and the ill-fated *Stella*, were brought in to serve the Island amid strong competition from the rival Great Western Railway Company. Built this year on the Clyde, the *Frederica*'s 1,000 plus tons were driven through the seas by propellers rather than paddle wheels. A beautifully proportioned vessel capable of over 19 knots, she plied local waters for over 20 years before being sold and then lost during the Great War.

1899

Townspeople were astonished by the activities of established solicitor Peter Falla of St John. The cause of the commotion was the arrival in Jersey of the first motor car, a Benz. Others soon followed and with them the Island's pace of life changed.

1906

Wilful murder was the verdict at Pierre Le Guen's inquest. Le Guen, who had been found dead in a field at Swan's Farm on 19th July, had suffered a fractured skull thought to have been caused by blows to the head with a stone which was found nearby. The jury stated that it was a case of wilful murder by person or persons unknown. And it was thought likely that a drinking companion of Le Guen's had been responsible. A murder hunt was under way.[31]

1936

The Jersey Airways amphibious aircraft *Cloud of Iona*, disappeared. The plane had taken off from Guernsey harbour in poor visibility and never arrived in Jersey. A week later the bodies of the eight passengers and two crew were washed ashore on the French coast. What happened was never discovered although it seems she landed safely somewhere to the south of Jersey before some accident overtook the craft and travellers.

---

[31] See 11th August for further details.

01 August

1922

Norman Stuart Le Brocq was born on this day. The only Communist to ever sit in the States, Le Brocq was respected above all things for his integrity. During the Occupation he had circulated news sheets and aided escaping Russian prisoners, obtaining what food he could for them.

After the war he was a founding member of the Jersey Democratic Movement, standing for election unsuccessfully a number of times. Finally, in 1966, he got into the States, only to loose his seat three years later. Returning to the States in 1972, Le Brocq was mostly concerned with the Island's people and environment and always went with his principles rather than political expediency.

1930

Centenier J P Cabot did his bit in trying to keep up moral standards. In King Street he stopped two female tourists as, in his opinion, they were indecently dressed. He gave the two a choice, either they returned to their lodgings and dressed more appropriately in town or he would take them to the Town Hall and present them before the Constable. The women went to get changed.

1989

The Parish of St Helier failed to elect the required number of Centeniers due to a lack of candidates. In the early decades of the century the honorary positions of a parish were hotly contested, with full campaigns and proper elections. Gradually, the posts became less sought after and elections less frequent.

By the 1980s some parishes were finding it difficult to fill the posts at all. When St Helier Centenier Robert Le Brocq decided to step down, no one came forward to take up the vacant position, which potentially put the parish in contempt of court and facing a fine. When on this day no one could be found, a second assembly was ordered in a desperate attempt to find a volunteer.

02 August

1567

A letter of this date was sent to England regarding Mont Orgueil Castle. It told how work on strengthening the fortress was proceeding. The height of the walls was being increased and new ones were being built but the money was running out. Amias Pawlet, the writer, asks that someone 'speak to the Queen about it, for this castle and Isle are to be preferred to a greater sum than the charge'. Even in 1567 building projects ran over budget, which may reassure the modern reader that in this rapidly changing world some things never change. Incidentally, the Queen's coffers stayed shut.

1923

The States were discussing condensed milk. Recent legislation in Britain had required manufacturers of tinned food to identify the contents. A letter from Nestle, manufacturers of condensed milk, to the Lieutenant-Governor, seeking clarification of the Island's regulations had been forwarded to the States and some Members were concerned that Jersey would become a 'dumping ground', with products that were no longer saleable elsewhere being sent to the Island.

1949

A 60 day drought in Jersey was broken by the heaviest 24-hour rainfall of the year. Just under an inch fell, giving a breathing space to the Waterworks Company, whose reservoirs had been depleted.

1951

This day saw the revival of the Battle of Flowers on Victoria Avenue. Petula Clark lead the procession of floral exhibits and bands. The floats, although not possessing the detail common in more recent times, were displayed in a far less regimental manner than today. The sunshine added to the carnival atmosphere and the day proved so successful that it was announced that a similar event would take place the following year.

03 August

1889

The Great Western Railway's new steamer, the *Antelope*, arrived in Jersey on this day and provided passengers with comfortable crossings until 1903. Four years after her arrival, during a storm, she ran out of coal while crossing to England and had to anchor until a tug arrived with enough fuel for her to complete the journey.

1935

Unlucky is one way to sum up the career of the ship the *Princess Ena*. Two years after being built, on 19th May 1905, she struck the Paternoster rocks off Jersey's north coast. She survived, limping into St Helier Harbour the following day. On 14th August 1923 she again found one of the local reefs, this time the Minquiers, and again she managed to reach a harbour, in this case St Malo. However on this day she caught fire off Corbière. All on board were rescued but the *Princess Ena* continued to burn and then sank.

1939

Visitors to the Battle of Flowers evening fête at Springfield Stadium got more than they expected when Tony Deering and his Motoring Maniacs took to the arena. Things went badly for the stunt drivers from the start when a car felled a lighting pole. Next a motorcyclist failed to negotiate a flaming arch and ended up entangled with it. Finally, in a similar stunt, a car, having crashed through a burning cottage, sped on and crashed into a football stand. Members of the audience and of the Maniacs were treated in hospital.

1979

It was reported that the tradition of nude sunbathing on the rocks at La Collette was now illegal. For over 150 years men had used the area for nude sunbathing. However, reclamation in the area now meant that the once secluded spot was more public. The matter was brought to a head when a couple complained at seeing a naked man on some rocks. The 30-year old was warned by police and cautioned by the Centenier.

04 August

1778

On this day the Jersey privateer the *Lively* was captured by the French. Despite the vessel having 16 guns she was taken by the French captain, Jean Kerby. It is thought that the *Lively* had originally been captured from the French in a previous engagement. The *Lively*'s crew were imprisoned but left their mark by scratching a record of their adventures onto the walls of their cell.

1914

The long predicted war with Germany was declared. The States met, with discussions concerning the supply of food and fuel high on the agenda. It was proposed to stop exports of produce, cattle, coal and general food stuffs.

1931

A Leyland Titan TD double decker bus, the first of its kind in Jersey, pulled up outside the JMT headquarters at the Weighbridge. Its appearance, as well as shocking the public, apparently surprised the company's directors. They weren't even aware that it had been ordered.

The authorities disliked the look of the strange machine as well and refused to allow it to operate. However, once convinced that the Titan was safe, another problem became apparent - low branches.

Eventually, numbered 36, the double decker entered service, the offending branches having been removed at the JMT's expense.

1970

The traffic using Jersey Airport had been continually increasing since it opened in 1937, so it had undergone a redevelopment programme. On this day a new 175 seater restaurant and bar opened, as did a new control tower and an aircraft control radar room.

05 August

1852
Victor Hugo, the poet, dramatist and novelist, arrived in Jersey. Hugo had been critical of Napoleon's regime and had even caused barricades to be erected against the French authorities. Having fled to Brussels with a price on his head, he was subsequently expelled from there and joined fellow political exiles in Jersey. Hugo passed his time writing bitter poems and dabbling in the occult until three years later he was expelled from Jersey too.[32]

1903
Horse racing was held at Les Landes rather than, as was more usual, at Gorey Common. So popular was it that from nine o'clock onwards a string of crowded carriages were heading towards St Ouen. Livery stables abandoned their usual excursions and a cab cost as much as £2 for a day's hire.

1932
The *SS St Patrick* struck rocks en route to St Helier. In thick fog, the steamer, owned by Great Western Railways, came to grief off Corbière. The 314 passengers were safely transferred to another vessel after a wireless SOS was sent. The headland at La Moye soon became packed with anxious relatives and sightseers. The *St Patrick*, although holed, was not badly damaged and was towed to St Aubin's.

1976
Jersey issued a new design of bank note on this day. They were slightly smaller than those issued in 1963, which were then in circulation. Denominations of £1, £5, £10 and £20 were released and it was hoped that the old notes would be removed from use by the end of the month. The Battle of Jersey was on the £1 and Elizabeth Castle on the £5, Victoria College was worth £10 and Mont Orgueil £20. The £1 note was blue and very similar to the English £5, an unfortunate decision that caused problems for visitors who believed they had been given £5 when in fact they had received a £1 note.

---

[32] See 31st October for further details.

06 August

1825

The town of St Helier was growing rapidly. Refugees from the aftermath of the French Revolution and an influx of British military personnel and workmen had created a house building boom. Forty years earlier the town had only consisted of the King Street-Queen Street area but on this day both Halkett Place and Waterloo Street were opened to the public.

1832

An outbreak of cholera raged despite the precautions ordered by the States. It was recorded on this day that 348 people had died in the previous 10 weeks and 806 cases had been notified.

1959

The annual St Brelade's Fête and Water Carnival was described as 'the best yet', with 12,000 people gathering around St Aubin's Harbour. The entertainment ran for nine hours, with a knobbly knees competition and a talent show, as well as a number of beauty contests. A Miss St Brelade, Jersey, was selected, not to be confused with the Miss Jersey who was chosen later. There was also a Queen of the Carnival, a cavalcade with floats and fancy dress.

The event's success reflected that of the parish, who had been the best Island entry in the Battle of Flowers a week earlier. But they hadn't taken first prize, as that had gone to the Italians of St Remo whose float *The Happy Gardeners* had taken the Prix d'Honneur.

1969

The first blue shark recorded in Island waters was caught by Jack Onions. The shark, weighing 80 lbs and measuring 6 ft 10 in long, was hooked off Corbière. Sharks of this kind are apparently not uncommon around Cornwall, where they grow considerably heavier, although Mr Onions was obviously quite satisfied with his catch.

07 August

1873

The Jersey Eastern Railway started regular services from Green Street to Grouville only 16 months after having been given permission to build the line. Twenty days later the track on to Gorey was opened, with all services terminating there instead of at Grouville. The day after the opening of the eastern line, the first derailment occurred at Pontac but services resumed after only four hours. The eastern run took travellers over two iron bridges and a wooden one at Le Hocq.

1897

Philip Le Marquand of La Hougue, New Beaumont Hill, St Peter, shot himself while cleaning his gun. The 20-year old had not checked the chamber of the revolver and it had discharged, the bullet lodging in his left leg. Dr Finlay attended to his wound at the St Peter's Garrison Hospital but failed to remove the bullet. It was later located by Albert Smith, a photographer, using Röntgen rays and Dr Finlay was able to operate, knowing that the projectile was lodged beneath the knee cap.

1906

Mr G G Walker took up his newly created post of sanitary inspector. There had been 21 candidates for the position and the Sanitary Committee had decided to appoint Walker, who came from Glasgow.

1964

Filming for the BBC programme *The Billy Cotton Band Show* came to an abrupt halt when a piano exploded. The sequence was intended to show the piano being towed through Island lanes, with smoke pouring from it, before a smoke bomb went off in the final scene. Unfortunately the wrong charge was used, and the ensuing explosion caused debris to be scattered for 50 yards and put six people in hospital. Billy Cotton, although blown to the ground, was uninjured. However, three extras from the Watersplash Show and a special effects technician were quite badly hurt.

08 August

1649

Under Jersey law women could inherit property, but upon marriage it all became their husbands'. For this reason marriages often took place between cousins, keeping land in the family. For the same reason some women were particularly sought after. Jacques Pipon had died, leaving his young daughter wealthy and highly prized. On this day Thomas Poingdestre claimed that prize. Poingdestre, the Pastor of St Saviour's, married the girl, who was aged 11½. The girl's stepfather had intended that the girl should marry his son, an idea of which her mother disapproved, and he went to the authorities, accusing the Pastor of abduction. Poingdestre fled to France with his young wife, returning later, having installed the girl in a boarding school where she would be brought up and educated.

1689

After 200 years of neutrality, Jersey's privileged position was revoked by William of Orange as he made war on France. However, the war was being fought on such a large scale that Jersey was left out of it. Lead, which cost 2 pence in Jersey, sold for 2s 6d in St Malo. So the ever-enterprising Jerseymen, using Les Ecréhous as a rendezvous, began smuggling enormous amounts of it. When the English authorities became aware of the situation the Lieutenant-Governor was ordered to stop the trade. This he declined to do as he too was involved in the smuggling. When a Major intervened and seized a boat laden with lead, he was ordered to beg the pardon of the Governor on his knees, was called a dog and stripped of his rank.

1994

Roderick Newall was sentenced to life imprisonment for murdering his parents, while his brother Mark was jailed for six years for helping to dispose of the bodies and cover up the crime. Mr and Mrs Newall had been bludgeoned to death in October 1987 and, although suspected, the brothers had removed most of the evidence. Roderick was eventually arrested on a yacht in the Atlantic and taken to Gibraltar, where he delayed extradition for 14 months. Once back in Jersey he confessed and lead police to the bodies.

09 August

1899

Henry Robert Boyce, well known about town as a horse clipper, died, having tried to cure his constipation. It was reported that he was 'of somewhat irregular habits' and it appears that to cure his problem he had swallowed a large quantity of diluted spirits of salts. Doctors were called but could do nothing and 'after passing the night in dreadful agony Mr Boyce expired about 5.30 am'.

1902

The first Battle of Flowers was held as a part of the celebrations of the coronation of Edward VII and Queen Alexandra. The parade of carriages decorated with flowers and greenery was received by a jubilant crowd and soon blooms were showering down on both onlookers and participants. Entertainment was provided by, among others, the White Coon Band, a popular group of musicians who also played that evening in the Triangle Park.

1923

Jersey's first mechanical road sweeper arrived in the Island on this day. Brought in by the Parish of St Helier, the 'international motor road sweeper' had a large brush which cleaned the street, a flap and a water sprinkler to lay any dust. A trial in Commercial Street the following day was viewed by the Constable and other parish officials and proved 'highly satisfactory'.

1984

It was Battle of Flowers day, weatherman Francis Wilson was escorting Miss Battle Sally Vibert around the arena and a good time was had by all. Until, that is, spectators checked their pockets and found their wallets missing. A gang of pickpockets had travelled to the Island to work the crowds that the Battle always attracts. Twelve people reported loosing a total of £2,000 but police believed that a lot more money had been stolen and not yet reported. Visitors were warned to be vigilant but there was little hope of catching the thieves.

10 August

1494

Today was the date set for a trial by combat. Matthew Baker had forged a letter incriminating Philippe de Carteret, allowing a man named Le Boutillier to accuse him of treason. Both men were held in Mont Orgueil Castle. De Carteret was kept in a dark cell, fed only on bread and water, while Le Boutillier was well supplied with food. So that de Carteret could not be aided by the King, his enemies forbid any boats to leave the Island. However de Carteret's wife, despite having just given birth to her 21st child, left her bed and travelled to England, returning to Jersey the day before they were due to fight, with the King's orders to stop the combat.

1911

George Francis des Vaux was found guilty of stealing figs, lettuce and tomatoes. Although he denied the charge, Mrs Le Floch told the court that she had seen des Vaux climb into the fig tree in her garden. Fruit and veg had been taken from a number of Grouville gardens and were traced to the accused. The Magistrate fined des Vaux £1 or eight days imprisonment.

1930

A father and son were drowned when their boat overturned just outside St Helier Harbour. William Noel and his 14-year old son were well-known fishermen. They had rowed out to their nourice, a floating holding tank for fish, adjacent to the Hermitage at Elizabeth Castle, with four other men. As they had adjusted the nourice the boat had tipped and all went into the water. Only two of the party could swim and they saved the other two, but the Noels could not be aided. An appeal was set up and over £200 was given in two weeks.

1976

Seventeen-year old David Sandeman was presented with a silver salver at a Town Hall reception. The young Jerseyman had sailed his yacht *Sea Raider* single-handedly across the Atlantic. The 3,000 mile, 43 day journey had ended in Rhode Island, despite having been in a collision with a Russian tanker in the mid Atlantic.

11 August

1836

A horse race meeting at Grève d'Azette was held under the patronage of William IV and the King's Cup was instituted. Prior to this event the races had been held on St Aubin's beach.

1873

Work finally started on the much delayed railway from St Aubin to La Moye. It was estimated that 50,000 tons of granite would be carried from the La Moye quarry, as well as a large deposit of china clay, facts which gave the project a new impetus.

1906

Thomas Connan and Marie Françoise Connan, the wife of Pierre Le Guen, went before the court, charged with murdering Le Guen. A report of the proceedings described Thomas as 'of a sinister appearance, having a decidedly prominent nasal organ' and of being cross-eyed, while Le Guen's wife was 'somewhat intelligent looking for a person in her station in life'. Thomas pleaded guilty to the charge but claimed his sister Marie had induced him to it, accusing her of striking the first blow, a claim she denied. The pair were remanded in gaol while a report was prepared on the case.[33]

1966

Denize Le Pennec, a 15-year old schoolgirl, became the first person to swim from Jersey to France. The 18 mile crossing, which saw Le Pennec leaving St Catherine's at 6.27 am, was completed when she came ashore below the Carteret lighthouse in the remarkable time of nine hours and 25 minutes.

1999

The skies over Jersey went dark at 11.16 am during a near total eclipse of the sun. Although cloudy, Islanders were still able to see some of event, despite authorities warning against viewing the eclipse live and advising people to watch it on TV instead.

---

[33] See 19th February for further details.

12 August

1796

A painting of George III by Philip Jean was presented to the States. Before being taken into the court, the picture was placed on the steps outside where a march past of military and naval personnel honoured it. Jean was presented with a silver urn in recognition of his gift.

1875

Joseph Philip Le Brun was executed in the town prison for murdering his sister. Le Brun had lived in St Lawrence, sleeping in outbuildings on his brother-in-law, Mr Lauren's, property. When Lauren returned home one day he opened the door and was wounded in the head by a shot fired by Le Brun. Lauren sought aid and when the police arrived, they found his wife sitting on a sofa, her feet in a bucket of water and her head covered with a shawl. On removing the shawl it was discovered that she had been fatally shot. The motive appears to have been robbery, as Le Brun liked to drink and gamble, and £25 was missing from the house. Protesting his innocence to the end, the condemned man was taken to the scaffold in full view of the gathered crowd, where he was hanged.

1911

Emile Jules Bihet appeared before the court, charged with making a false declaration to Mr Labey, the Grouville Parish Registrar. Bihet had cohabited with a widow named Mathurine Morin, who had given birth to a stillborn child. Bihet, when registering the birth and death, claimed to have married Morin the previous year. The reason for the lie was so that the child would not be deemed illegitimate. Having been remanded in gaol for a week, the Prosecutor asked for a sentence of two months imprisonment with hard labour, a fine of £1 and five years banishment. Banishment was objected to as it meant the confiscation of a man's goods and chattels. The court had earlier heard that Bihet was married to a woman who lived with another man and this was the reason he had not married Morin. The court imposed the harsh sentence requested by the prosecution and expelled Bihet's estranged wife with him.

13 August

1859

Islanders were surprised to find the Royal Yacht anchored in St Aubin's Bay. Queen Victoria and Prince Albert had decided to get away from the worrying political situation by taking a sea trip. Island officials were under the impression that no landing would take place. However the Queen decided that she wished to view the college bearing her name. With only half an hour's warning, red carpet was acquired and a carriage made available. With no militiamen to line the route an enthusiastic crowd swamped the carriage with flowers, to the extent that negotiating the street became difficult. Victoria College was taken completely by surprise when the Queen arrived and when the party returned to the pier her yacht was not yet ready. Later, the Queen landed again and may have got more of a feel for the Island, as she was driven quietly up St Peters Valley and across the northern parishes to St Catherine's, where she was picked up again by her yacht.

1896

John Everett Millais died on this day. Although not born in Jersey, his parents had lived here and returned when he was four. He received little schooling, as he was expelled on the second day for biting the master. From then on his mother taught him. Millais' artistic abilities were quickly identified and nurtured. At first he was glad to receive £2 for a portrait but after changing his style he gradually became the most popular painter in England. By 1867 Millais calculated he was making £100 a day painting water-colours. Millais' output was enormous, with only Turner leaving behind more work than him. He painted many of the leading characters of his day, including Lillie Langtry, but of all his paintings, Bubbles, advertising Pears Soap, is probably the most famous.

1938

A Paris-Dinard-Jersey air service was inaugurated by Air France, in direct competition with Jersey Airways who had started a Dinard service a week earlier. The aircraft had a lavatory and room for luggage. But both services were to be short lived, due to the war.

14 August

1923

The *Princess Ena*, having already run aground twice before, did so again. In thick fog, the steamship went ashore on the Minquiers reef. The passengers were transferred to lifeboats, two of which became lost in the fog. As the tide came in the *Princess Ena* refloated relatively undamaged. She then continued, minus the two missing lifeboats, to St Malo. It was 16 hours later, however, before another ship found the missing passengers, the boats having been tied to navigational buoys off the reef.

1906

It was noted in the *Jersey Evening Post* that the painting 'The Death of Major Pierson' was for sale. The report tells how the picture by John Singleton Copley had been ordered by Colonel George Le Boutillier of the Honorary Artillery Company. Le Boutillier, who had been born at La Chasse, St John, had been friends with young Copley and this was the first version of the famous painting that he had completed. It had remained within the family until this day and was now on view at Le Gallais in Bath Street. The asking price was, unfortunately, not recorded.

1947

French priest Henri Lauer was washed ashore at La Rocque, having gone for a little paddle in a boat two days earlier. Lauer had been attending a seminary on the Normandy coast. Dressed only in a swimsuit he had rowed a few hundred yards offshore before losing an oar. The currents had caught hold of the boat and despite trying to attract attention he was swept out to sea.

The following day he had drifted with no land in sight. Searching the rowboat he found only a long dead crab as sustenance, which he ate. During the night he had seen a flashing light and was able to steer towards Jersey's coast.

Despite his ordeal, and in borrowed clothes, the priest recalled his adventure with good humour.

15 August

1904

Mrs Hibbs, charged with obtaining one shilling by false pretences, appeared before the Magistrate. The accused pleaded guilty but said she had wanted milk, as she had six children, and that her husband treated her badly. Hibbs had approached another woman, claiming that a Mrs Lewis was ill and needed the money, which was untrue. It was said in court that Hibbs had 'obtained hundreds of pounds in the same way'. Mrs Peagan, who had given the money, had not wanted to press charges but the Constable had insisted. Hibbs was sentenced to four days hard labour.

1912

Despite the elements, the Battle of Flowers was pronounced a success. The parade around Victoria Avenue had proved very popular, although the antics of an unknown actor appearing at the Opera House were looked on less favourably. Charlie Chaplin was warned for annoying cameramen with his activities and blocking their view of the floats.

1968

Jersey's ancient Clameur de Haro was raised. The dispute was between the owner of a cafe and her tenant. Mrs Bailhache kneeled in the door of her cafe and recited the call to her Prince. The court, however, ruled that she had had no right to do so and fined her £50. When giving its judgement the court had explained the many reasons for her Clameur being invalid, but this useful instruction in the law must have been forgotten as Mrs Bailhache raised the Clameur again four years later, equally invalidly.

1989

A state of emergency was declared. The Lieutenant-Governor, Sir William Pillar, signed the papers allowing the States to impose any restrictions they deemed necessary. The problem was water, or rather the lack of it. As of midnight water restrictions would come into force, stopping some commercial uses. General rationing was not yet introduced but everyone was urged to use less water.

16 August

1645

Thomas Roger, an English soldier, met his end. Having been drinking he discharged a carbine five or six times, until it eventually burst in his hands. Toby Mesner, who owned the weapon, was so angry that he took the broken gun from the uninjured Roger and beat him over the head with its butt 'again and again', the records claim, until 'he smashed his skull into his brain, after which he struck him on the arms and knelt on the pit of his stomach'. Amazingly Roger was able to get up and walk home after the attack. However, he died three days later. His assailant fled the Island.

1869

Jean Nicholas Rene de la Croix died. He can be credited with documenting much of Jersey's history which would otherwise have been lost. The man himself was as interesting as his work. Writing as a journalist, he and his family lived in poverty. It was noted that when one of the countless people de la Croix had libelled arrived at his home intending to break the windows, he failed, because they were already smashed. De la Croix's written attacks on others were incredibly abusive and physical attacks were not unknown. In 1838 he was publicly horse whipped for an article he had written. Four years later he received two black eyes and a bloody nose. By 1846 he had been arrested for receiving stolen property and was also bound over, his whip confiscated, for beating his wife. This 'grubby, disreputable little man' did not complete what would have been a fascinating volume. *The Black Book of Jersey* would have, he promised, 'revealed hideous scandals' about the Island's notables.

1890

A cricket match was held between officers of the South Lancashire Regiment and a ladies' eleven captained by Mrs Lushington. The play at St Peter's Barracks saw the ladies put in to bat first. Fielding officers had their right hands in slings to handicap them, the penalty for its removal being three overs. In their first innings the ladies scored 90. The officers replied with 106. Miss R Le Cornu was the most successful bowler of the day, taking 6 wickets.

17 August

1909

It was announced that the Jersey Airship Fund had received 202 subscriptions, all contributed by women. The sum raised came to £11 3s 9d, money that was forwarded on to the National Airship Fund.

Mrs Edith Wharton had opened a subscription list for Jersey women after the press had noted how many airships Germany possessed and how few Britain had. At this time the Woman's Suffragette Movement was well underway and its effects were even felt in Jersey.

1910

Lady Otway's will was registered in the Royal Court. The doyenne of Jersey society at the time, Lady Otway had no relations and left her wealth to seven of her closest friends. Her jewels, pictures and furniture were to be sold and the money was to be divided between a lawyer and a number of soldiers, as well as a maid and a servant who had been with her for many years.

1936

Jersey's first motor lifeboat came on station and was named the Howard D. She was of the latest design, manned by a crew of seven and if necessary she could carry thirty survivors in rough weather. The Howard D was gift to the Island from T B Davis and named after his son Howard, who had died on the battlefields in the First World War. The new vessel had both sail and motor, its speed was 7¼ knots and it had a range of 100 miles.

1977

David Minty became the youngest person to swim around the Island. The 14-year old also became the fastest, with a time of 10 hours, 54 minutes and 30 seconds.

18 August

1855

On this day the *Jersey Independent* newspaper was founded, joining the already overcrowded local newspaper market. Three years later it became a daily newspaper and later altered its title to *The Jersey Weekly Press and Independent*.

1856

Jurat Charles Le Quesne died, aged 45, on this day. Trained as a lawyer, he was elected Jurat in 1850 and lead the reform movement, but died in the same year that his great book *A Constitutional History of Jersey* was published. When 30 years later the Public Library was built, the names of four outstanding local writers decorated its central dome and Le Quesne's name was one of them.

1947

Frank Le Marquand fell down a newly built, 43 ft deep well. Mr H Blackwell was having a new house built near Grouville Arsenal and needed a water supply. Granite products had carried out the well's construction which, once completed, had dynamite detonated at the bottom to allow it to flood. Le Marquand, who was working on the site, went down to check but the explosive fumes started to overtake him. As he regained the surface, he was in a dazed state and lost his grip, falling the forty feet back to the bottom. Hauled out with a rope, he was taken to hospital where his injuries were treated.

1971

Jersey's new Dean was sworn in at the Royal Court, the Bailiff taking the opportunity to criticise members of the clergy for their 'uninformed comment' on the Common Market. The Very Reverend Thomas Ashworth Goss had previously held the post of Rector of St Saviour and was to become one of the more popular of Jersey's Deans.

19 August

1865

Alfred Le Breton was sent to prison for 48 hours 'with low diet' for ill-treating his wife. The accused was said to have continually referred to his wife as a 'black devil', she having a dark complexion. In his defence Le Breton claimed his wife neglected her household duties. The court suggested the couple seek an act of separation, before handing down the bread and water punishment, which was also the sentence meted out in the following case where a girl had been kicked by her father.

1930

Police were looking for Mathurin Brevost, a 21-year old Frenchman, after he had escaped from Newgate Prison. He had just begun a sentence of two years hard labour and had been put to work white washing. Somehow he managed to scale the walls, having acquired a brown coat and cap, and he made off in his crude disguise. Despite the police being confident of a quick response, it was three days before Brevost gave himself up.

1976

Sir Billy Butlin married for a third time, the ceremony taking place in the Registry Office. The 76-year old's bride was Sheila, his long time companion, and their two children also attended the wedding. The occasion was a private affair with only a few close family members there. It was followed by a reception at the Grouville Bay Hotel, but no honeymoon was said to be planned.

1984

Martin Boizard was killed when the power boat he was racing in crashed. The Inter-Island Challenge Race was taking place in St Aubin's Bay and Boizard and driver David Sheppard were in *That's Right* when it collided with a Guernsey entry, *Liquidator*. The Guernsey boat went over the top of *That's Right*, striking both men. They were taken to hospital but Boizard was found to be dead on arrival.

20 August

1787

John Wesley, the Methodist founder, arrived in Jersey on a ten day visit. A regiment containing some Methodists had been stationed in the Island in 1783 and they had requested a lay preacher. At first Methodism spread slowly in the Island, as the locals spoke French and the preachers English. But once some bilingual residents had been converted and themselves become preachers the movement spread rapidly.

1791

A Royal Commission arrived in the Island to look into the States' proposal for trial by jury. The Commission did not take a favourable view of the proposition and it was not adopted.

1931

Visitors to Jersey rarely comprehend the dangers of the Island's waters. On this day a party of tourists travelled from St Helier to the Château Plaisir area of St Ouen's Bay. Having played cricket and football on the sands, they decided to go for a swim. The party were warned about the tidal conditions and told to avoid the area to the south of the Château. However, they went into the water and some of the bathers soon got into difficulty. A rescue was attempted by forming a human chain to drag the swimmers from the breakers. But there was a strong undertow pulling them out and enormous waves were battering those involved in the rescue. Three people were hauled ashore unconscious, while another was swept out to sea. Mr Le Feuvre, who had earlier warned the group, resuscitated two of the party. But despite his best efforts, the third person died.

1977

A Viscount aircraft with 77 people on board overshot the runway. It came to rest at the very end of the airport's western perimeter with its nose overhanging an arrester just a yard away from falling into St Ouen's Bay. If the incident had occurred a year earlier the consequences would have been far more tragic as the safety overshoot which saved the plane had not yet been built.

21 August

1548

    In July an order had been received in the Island to destroy all superstitious objects and as the Reformation swept across Europe Jersey's wayside crosses were toppled. On this day the States decided to pay for two French Protestant theologians to come to the Island and preach the word of God. They were joined by a Spanish ex-Benedictine monk and all three men later became parish rectors. Jersey, like England, was discarding Catholicism but unlike England, Jersey was taking on a strict French style of Protestantism.

1905

    Agiseribbe Asser, a native of Amsterdam, fell foul of Jersey's hawking laws. The Dutchman was a cutlery salesman and had a permit to trade over the whole of England. However, Asser obviously did not understand Jersey's unusual relationship with England and had thought his permit was valid in the Island. His choice in customers was unfortunate too. He had called on Centenier Le Poivedin's house, who later arrested him. Fining Asser £1, the Magistrate made it clear that the £1 did not enable him to sell goods and told him that a permit had to be acquired from the Town Hall.

1927

    Another earth tremor hit Jersey, the third in a year. The quake was heard in the form of a deep rumble before it struck. The mild movement did no damage in the Island but did cause alarm in Granville where its effects were greater.

1950

    The Duchess of Kent officially opened the new nurses' home. The building work had started some two years earlier, with £170,000 being narrowly voted from the States' coffers, the expenditure being much criticised. However, a wealthy benefactor, Ann Blason-Raynor, had left over £½ million for just such a project. The National Trust for Jersey, the Blind Society, Island schools, the poor and the Hospital were just some of the others who benefited from the same bequest.

22 August

1766

The *Swallow* set sail from England with Commander Philippe de Carteret in charge. While off South America the *Swallow* became separated from the other ship in the expedition. Continuing alone de Carteret discovered the Pitcairn Islands.[34] When he finally returned to his home port on 20th March 1769 de Carteret had sailed around the world, leaving a trail of islands with names like Jersey, Guernsey, Alderney, Sark, New Ireland and Queen Charlotte. Later de Carteret married and returned to his family home, Trinity Manor.

1854

Emigration was often seen as the only hope for the very poor. At a time when Jersey was becoming increasingly populated by the more affluent English, on this day the *Evening Star* left St Helier Harbour with 200 emigrants bound for Australia.

1952

Hollywood film star Rock Hudson was pictured in the *Jersey Evening Post*. He was in the Island to film 'Toilers of the Sea' with co-star Yvonne de Carlo. The production was based on a Victor Hugo story and filming was to take place off Elizabeth Castle, as well as at other Island landmarks. Filming was due to take two weeks and the public were reminded not to walk into shot when the cameras were rolling.

1980

A twin engined light aircraft made a forced landing in St Aubin's Bay. The Navajo was only slightly damaged, despite landing with its undercarriage up. A second light aircraft had become aware of the plane's problems as it made its way from Dinard. When over La Collette the Navajo pilot decided to land on the beach. On hearing this the second craft flew ahead, low to the sand, waggling its wings to clear a path through the beach-goers. No one was hurt and the plane was craned to safety before the tide reached it.

---

[34] See 2nd July for further details.

23 August

1643

Sir Philippe de Carteret, Bailiff, Governor and Royalist, died in Elizabeth Castle. De Carteret had been forced by the Island's Parliamentarians to seek safety in the castle, which he used as a base for Royalist activities while the Civil War raged in England. Once dead, his heart and brain were removed and buried in the old Priory Church. His body was embalmed and remained in the Castle until many months later when Jersey was once again governed in the name of the King. Sir Philippe was finally buried on 20th June 1644 at St Ouen's Parish Church.

1766

After a long naval career filled with battles and adventure, Philip Durell died at sea. This Jerseyman met his end not in a great sea battle but through eating dolphin.

1808

Alexandre Mathieu was buried in St Brelade on this day. Born in 1754, Mathieu was the first man to bring printing to Jersey. Aware of the potential of this new industry, he had left the Island to learn how to master the craft. Returning in 1784, Mathieu set up a six penny monthly, *Le Magasin de l'Ile de Jersey*, printed at St Aubin. The paper was pro-Magot, one of the political parties of the time, and Mathieu's writings got him arrested for libel and accused of inciting people to sedition. His publishing business led to regular visits to court, with cases dragging on for years. In later life he became a moneylender and used the same courts that had frustrated him before to now sue his customers for not repaying their loans on time.

1953

A gold torque on display at the museum in Pier Road was stolen. Due to inclement weather the museum had opened, giving visitors something to do indoors. However, when Mr Clements, the gardien, went to lock up he noticed that the display case had been forced and the torque was gone. Fortunately the item stolen was a reproduction and the real gold torque remained safe in a bank vault.

24 August

1186

Pope Urban III confirmed by papal order various endowments to the Canons of the monastery of St Helier. The abbey stood on the rocky outcrop in St Aubin's Bay where Elizabeth Castle was later built. Its founder was William Fitzhamon but the islet had had religious significance since Helier's time 600 years earlier.

1294

The King ordered compensation to be given to Islanders after he had received a petition from them. It stated that a French attack had killed 1,500 inhabitants, houses and corn had been burnt, chattels carried off and churches sacked.

1836

The *SS Atlanta* made her first voyage to Jersey under the command of Captain Babot. She was to service the islands for many years and underwent a number of overhauls. From April 1847 she carried the Royal Mail to and from Jersey. Later she was lengthened by 22 feet to provide a larger cargo hold. By September 1869 the *Atlanta*'s working days were numbered. She was stripped and used as a coal store for other boats before being sold to Mr Hunt as scrap.

1966

The first modern lottery draw took place on this day. The 20,000 tickets had been sold almost as soon as they had been issued. Shops had taken orders for them in advance, the vast majority being sold to locals. The 10 shilling ticket could be split and sold separately and the jackpot prize was £2,000.

The draw was held at the West Park Pavilion where an audience of 400 watched as a series of girls retrieved balls from a number of rotating drums. The whole procedure took 45 minutes and all the winners declined to be named.

Guernsey had recently decided against a lottery, however, with Jersey's proving extremely successful the latter soon followed suit.

25 August

1786

La Gazette de Jersey was first published and continued to run for fifty years. At the time it was Jersey's only newspaper and was known as the three-sous weekly. The paper was a great supporter of the Magot party and its outrageously biased reporting of events damaged the rival Charlot party. *La Gazette* claimed that every drunkard or thief arrested was a Charlot and it twisted reports to suit its editorial.

1870

Mary Asplet appeared in the Court of Correctional Police, accused of stealing a loaf of bread. She had taken the loaf from a bake-house the day before, her only explanation being that she was drunk. Having heard the evidence, the Magistrate sent her to prison for two weeks with hard labour.

1964

The first motorists to fall foul of the new radar speed traps did so on this day. The States Police had set up their equipment on the Airport Road and two drivers were stopped and warned to attend at the parish hall. From there they were sent to the Police Court, where the Magistrate decided it was necessary to witness the machine in operation. Being satisfied that the equipment worked, the motorists were fined a nominal £1 each.

1976

The introduction of car ferries into Island waters was proving very successful for the shipping company Sealink. However, it was not such good news for hire car firms who, it was reported on this day, wanted the number of English cars coming into the Island restricted. It was claimed that the new roll-on, roll-off ferries would cause redundancies among garage workers and a loss of revenue for the States.

26 August

1865

The Constable of St Lawrence had Adelaide Amy placed in the General Hospital and someone was appointed to look after her affairs. Amy was said to have been of unsound mind for two years. Earlier William Hyde had married her, got access to her money and then left the Island with it, abandoning her. As Amy still had property, the Constable wanted to protect her interests.

1912

Four hydro aeroplanes landed on the sea at West Park during a race from St Malo, the first aircraft to do so in Jersey. The race had been organised by the Automobile Club of France and the Jersey Motor Association. Thousands saw the Sanchez-Besa biplane which touched down first. The amazed crowd's curiosity got the better of them and as the plane was being refuelled onlookers poked, prodded and even scratched their names on the fragile machine. The delay cost Benoist, the pilot, the race because another pilot had landed at Beaumont, refuelled unmolested and headed back to France.

1934

Jersey saw its first aircraft tragedy. A Jersey Airways plane, while taking off from West Park beach, swerved and crashed into the sea wall. A nine-year old boy was killed and another seriously injured as they played on the beach. It was the third incident that had befallen a Jersey Airways plane within 24 hours. However in the previous two instances no one had been hurt. This time the twin propelled craft sustained damage to its nose but was otherwise unscathed. However, the accident shocked the whole Island.

1966

Thirty minutes after taking off from Jersey Airport a Piper Tri-pacer aircraft plunged into the sea, disappearing completely. The light aircraft went down while preparing to land at Alderney airport. The pilot and his two passengers were killed, their bodies being recovered by divers. The plane was raised the following day to allow examination by accident engineers.

27 August

1669

Parliamentarian supporters in the Island spent many years after the Civil War trying to retrieve land which had been confiscated from them and the Island's authorities were finally ordered to return the property in question. In this age, when news travelled slowly and officials had a habit of ignoring British instructions, disputes could drag on for decades.

1846

For some time many English residents had been annoyed that Jersey's laws were not the same as the laws of England. Their spokesman, a local named Abraham Le Cras, challenged the legal authority, claiming that the laws of the British Parliament were valid in Jersey and that local law authorities were entirely bogus.

On 27th April 1846 the British government had appointed a commission to look into the matter. However, when they made their report on this day, the commissioners did not agree with Le Cras' demands for Jersey to become accountable to Parliament. But they did recommend that a paid police force be formed.

1897

The public were warned to beware of pickpockets. A number of complaints had been made by passengers who had arrived in Jersey aboard the *SS Victoria*. Purses and the contents of travellers' pockets had gone missing. It was also noted that a number of bathers, particularly at La Collette, had also fallen victim to pickpockets.

The *Evening Post* hoped that the police would 'not be long in laying hands on the offenders, who should receive an exemplary and salutary punishment at the hands of the Magistrate'. However, a few days later more residents fell victim, one woman having her purse containing £5 (a considerable sum) stolen and another losing 30 shillings in gold, some silver and a gold brooch.

28 August

1911

An inquest was opened after the body of a new-born baby girl was discovered in a water-tank in a conservatory at The Beeches on Wellington Road. The house nursemaid, when questioned, admitted that she had put the child there. Although aware of being pregnant, she told the inquest that she had gone to the lavatory in pain and had unexpectedly given birth to the stillborn girl. The father was a chef at the Royal Hotel and the maid had arranged to go away on holiday before the child was due.

1915

Leswick Forbes appeared before the Royal Court, charged with breaking the blackout laws. Bright lights were forbidden in certain areas and Forbes' wife had failed to draw the curtains at their house one night. When the couple had walked past the lamp in their St Aubin home, it had given onlookers the impression that a signal was being given and the authorities had been alerted. Everyone accepted that it had been an honest mistake and a token fine of £1 was imposed. However, Islanders were warned to obey the regulations, otherwise severe measures would be introduced, as had already been done in Guernsey.

1931

A tremendous thunderstorm struck the Island on this day. A number of houses suffered lightning strikes, roofs were torn off and outbuildings at a property in St Lawrence were gutted by fire after being hit by a bolt of lightning. The Martello tower at Le Hocq was another victim, with lightning smashing wooden steps and doors.

1982

It was announced that the Jersey Island Exquisite Knitting Company was to close. The factory had opened in 1961 and at its peak in the 1970s had employed 225 people. Gradually the business had contracted until only 46 employees remained to lose their jobs when the factory closed.

29 August

1722

The foundation stone of the new harbour at St Helier was laid. At this time cargoes had to be carried across mud flats at low tide, so improved facilities were needed to encourage St Helier's development as the Island's main town.

1730

An announcement in the Market Place that it would now take six liards instead of four to make a sol caused a riot. Different rates of exchange between France and Jersey had caused money to be smuggled across the Channel. This clumsy attempt by the States to correct the imbalance would have meant that the value of people's savings was reduced by one third. People were outraged.

The largest demonstration ever seen in Jersey took place in St Helier and a worried States met and immediately revoked the previous order. However the crowd did not trust them and burst into the chamber. Officials ran for the safety of Elizabeth Castle, while the Dean was forced to hide in a tavern. He left disguised in a borrowed coat and hat.

1810

Captain Thomas was in command of the mail cutter *Queen Charlotte* when he sighted a large cutter off Alderney flying a British flag. As the two vessels drew closer the British flag was replaced with an enemy French pendant. The fire fight that ensued between the two vessels raged for 1½ hours until the 14-gunned French ship finally broke off the attack. Three of the *Queen Charlotte*'s crew were killed and 12 were wounded.

1913

Winston Churchill, then Lord of the Admiralty, arrived in Jersey on the *Enchantress*. A group of suffragettes had gathered on the New North Quay but their protest was foiled when he landed at the Albert Pier. After abandoning the ladies of the party at Springfield to play tennis, the gentlemen toured the eastern parishes, later playing golf at Grouville.

30 August

1884

The first commercial runs on the new railway route from St Aubin to Corbière took place on this day. Permission had originally been given in 1871 and construction started in 1873, but no one could have foreseen that it would take 11 years to complete the line. For although the track to Corbière was passable it took almost a further year of blasting to connect the new line with the existing St Helier-St Aubin track.

1897

On this day workmen began to repair damage done by recent spring tides. Several tons of sea-walling at Millbrook had been swept away and a bank of rubbish was intended to be used to stop erosion while the repair was completed. The estimated cost for the work was £10.

1905

Eyes in the Island were turned heavenwards between 11.50 am and 2.15 pm on this day. The reason for the excitement was a solar eclipse. Locals stood watching the phenomenon through smoked glass as the sun gradually disappeared. By 12.30 approximately one quarter of the sun was obscured and by 1 o'clock only an eighth remained, causing a number of town shops to turn on their gas or electric lighting.

1911

Dr G J Macaura, inventor of the Pulsocon, gave a demonstration of his invention to Islanders at the Oddfellows Hall. Admission was free and it was claimed that Dr Macaura would show how he could make the lame walk and restore life to paralysed limbs. It was also claimed that Dr Macaura's device was able to make the deaf hear. Thousands of people attended and were said to have marvelled at the results.

31 August

1897

A man named Le Cocq received 24 lashes from the cat of nine tails on this day. He had been convicted of indecently assaulting a girl and was sentenced to this corporal punishment, as well as to two months imprisonment. The flogging took place in the prison, the underwarder wielding the weapon. It was reported that Le Cocq 'endured the pain with exemplary fortitude', the only words he uttered being 'Oh, my back'.

It was pointed out that the cat was not the 'instrument of torture of which naval writers in the last century so frequently wrote'. The more modern cat had a short handle with nine lashes of whipcord and it was noted that as it had been washed after previous floggings, the thongs were less stiff than if it had been new.

1933

The skies over Les Quennevais were the setting for Jersey's first aerial pageant. Although 20 planes were due to take part only six actually flew. But the thousands who watched the spectacle were thrilled. Among the craft taking part was a Gypsy Moth, a Flying Boat and an Auto Giro. A parachutist even descended, landing safely. The event was considered a great success but even in 1933 the traffic problems it caused warranted attention.

1986

Five-year old Levan Merritt was on holiday in Jersey with his parents when a incident at the Zoo made him famous world-wide. While watching the gorillas from a wall around the enclosure, he over-balanced and fell into the compound. The boy was knocked unconscious when he landed in the concrete gully and the gorillas whose territory had been invaded soon came to investigate.

The pictures and video footage of Jambo, the male silverback, gently tending to the semiconscious child were seen around the world. The gorillas were taken inside as the ambulance men attended to Merritt, who was then hoisted out of the compound and taken to hospital.

01 September

1866

On this day the opening ceremony of the Imperial Hotel took place. It later became known as Maison St Louis and is now the Hotel de France.

1951

Despite the rain 1,500 people turned out to an open air meeting at West Park concerning the proposed introduction of the insular insurance law, or social security. States Deputy Venables attended the meeting and was assaulted by the angry crowd after he raised his hand to show he was in favour of it. Venables took refuge in the Grand Hotel while the police tried to disperse the angry gathering. Despite the protest social security was brought in.

1962

Channel Television went on-air for the first time. The programming contained twice weekly half hour features on matters of current Island interest, with twice daily weather forecasts and an evening news to be provided. The purpose-built studios and offices could be found near the Robin Hood pub.

1976

A strike by oilmen caused local garages to ration petrol supplies. The sixty men employed by the fuel distribution companies went back to work five days later. During the strike enormous queues had formed outside any garage that still had supplies and once over it was some days before the Island returned to normal.

1992

A human leg was found abandoned at La Hougue Bie Museum. While unlocking the archaeology gallery, site supervisor Richard Henwood noticed something under one of the display cases. It turned out to be a preserved human leg, the tibia and fibia projecting from the intact foot. The police investigated. However, the limb was obviously of considerable age and it was assumed to be a relic which someone wished to dispose of anonymously.

02 September

1846

Queen Victoria and Prince Albert's visit to Jersey on this day may have only lasted three hours but it left its mark. The Queen's yacht had anchored in St Aubin's Bay at sunset and was greeted by a bonfire and fireworks salute. Noirmont was particularly spectacular as the whole headland caught fire. As always with royal visitors the Island went mad. Enormous floral arches were built throughout Jersey in areas the Queen could not possibly visit. On landing at the newly completed South Pier it was instantly renamed the Victoria Pier. The actual visit consisted of an address from the States, a carriage drive to Mont Orgueil and then back to her yacht. Although the visit had been brief it was decided that a permanent structure should commemorate the event. The options short-listed were a tree lined public walk, a lighthouse on the spot she landed or a college. The promenade appealed greatly but after heavy lobbying the college option won.

1891

The authorities discovered a starving family of six living in a greenhouse behind Claremont Terrace. The wife was obviously ill and taken to hospital, as were the four children. The husband, Mr Dwyer, was in work. However, his wife was an alcoholic and had sold everything they owned until, when found, they only had the clothes they stood up in. The family were completely destitute, which was a crime in Jersey.

1906

Hugh de la Haye, a man who changed Jersey agriculture, died on this day. In about 1880 two unusually large potatoes had come into his possession. He cut them up and planted the pieces on a cotîl above Bellozanne Valley. The following spring they produced a heavy crop exceptionally early. Once de la Haye had cultivated enough, he put them on display. A local paper named them the Royal Jersey Flukes and so an industry was born. In 1891 70,000 tons of Jersey Royals were exported, bringing in almost £½ million.

03 September

1890

The statue to commemorate Queen Victoria's jubilee was unveiled on the Weighbridge. The sculptor was M Wallet and his creation was later moved a few yards. For years the statue was sited in gardens surrounded by high railings where the bus station now stands. In 1976 the Queen was moved to the triangular park at West Park. On dismantling the plinth a time capsule was discovered.

1939

The long awaited declaration of war came on this day. At first many Islanders believed it would be much like the First World War. Although a number of the Island's young men had gone to fight in the Great War, the conflict had not affected the Island greatly. Jersey was a back water of no significance - 'why would the war come here' was the naive outlook of some.

1968

The activities of a group of farmers resulted in what must be one of Jersey's most unusual export products. Bulls' semen is now sent all over the world to improve the quality of cattle herds in various countries but in September 1968 the Island's first artificial insemination was being carried out. Looked upon with suspicion initially, the now accepted procedure allows a good quality bull to father many more offspring than would be possible naturally.

1983

Three French visitors were rescued by the lifeboat when their yacht was driven among rocks off the south east coast. In 60 mile per hour winds, the lifeboat picked its way through the reef, eventually taking off the *Cythara*'s crew. A powerful searchlight and flares illuminated their passage in what was a very dangerous rescue. No attempt was made to save the yacht, which was later washed ashore at Le Hocq.

04 September

1870

There was unrest among Jersey's French and Irish communities when news arrived that Marshal MacMahon, who had been expected to lead his French troops to an overwhelming victory over British forces, had been defeated in the Sudan War. Word of the French defeat reached the Island by telegraph and a large crowd of French and Irishmen gathered around the telegraph office, unable to believe their loss. The situation became quite tense, with the police attempting to keep order while telegrams were sent demanding confirmation, which was later received.

1905

Emily Georgina Rowden, aged 27, went before the court, charged with prostitution. The actual charge was 'habitually walking about the streets of the town soliciting prostitution'. Centenier Luxon told the court that he had witnessed the accused accost a man in La Motte Street and had arrested her. It was stated that Rowden was often to be seen soliciting and that neighbours had complained. It was noted that she could be sent home to England, to which the Magistrate agreed, warning Rowden that if he saw her again she would be dealt with severely. Later in the week two other prostitutes each received sentences of a month's hard labour and another was banished from the Island for five years.

1939

The States held an emergency sitting following the outbreak of war. Practicalities had to be dealt with. The law on aliens was altered so that they could not leave the Island without a permit and they also had to notify the authorities of a change of address within 48 hours. Sandbags also needed to be filled. However, sand and shingle could only be taken from well below the high water level and this was proving inconvenient. So it was decided to dispense with this regulation, although sand was also requisitioned from the sand pits at St Ouen.

05 September

1891

If a boat can be accident prone, this was one that was. The *Ibex* was a boat with a very chequered career. Built in 1891 she was a new breed of faster vessel and arrived in Jersey on this day, where she soon broke the speed record.

However in 1897 a hole 10 ft by 2 ft was ripped open in her when the Noirmontaise Rock was struck while she was racing a rival ship. Her passengers were landed in Portelet Bay and she was towed to St Helier.

On 5th January 1900 she again hit rocks and sank with a loss of two lives. Months later the *Ibex* was refloated and went back to work.

In April 1914 she crippled a schooner off Portland and three years later collided with and sank a cargo steamer. The *Ibex* was scrapped in 1926, perhaps making the seaways a little safer.[35]

1911

Rail travellers were appalled to see Mr F Priestley throw himself under the train's wheels at Don Bridge. Having played golf with his father, the two were returning to town. As the train came into the station, young Priestley leapt onto the rails. The slowing engine struck him, but a safety guard swung his body, preventing a decapitation. The wheels went over his left foot, which had to be removed by surgeons that evening. Priestley was an Old Victorian, an undergraduate at Oxford and had been expected to take Holy Orders.

1913

Charles Querée went before the Police Court, charged with being drunk, using abusive language and breaking a beer bottle on the beach. For the first two charges a fine of £2 was imposed, or 15 days hard labour. For breaking the beer bottle a more severe £5 was demanded or 15 days hard labour. Given the choice of paying £7 or going to gaol for a month, Querée chose gaol.

---

[35] See 16th April for further details.

06 September

1826

The sailing packet *Francis Freeling*, which had carried the Island's mail since 1811, ended her career in disaster. In a violent storm while off Portland the vessel was run down by a Swedish brig. Weather conditions made rescue impossible and as a result the seven passengers and nine crew drowned.

1902

Jersey Railways had a fairly good safety record. However at First Tower on this day one train ran into the back of another. The shunt damaged buffers, wheels and windows, but fortunately not passengers. The brake van was derailed but the impact was lessened as the first train had begun to move off. The resulting enquiry reprimanded the guard for failing to put the red tail light in the correct position.

1909

Messieurs Langlois and Poulain entertained Islanders with a new series of electric pictures at St Thomas' Hall. Nearly 10,000 ft of film was shown, with titles such as 'Winter Sports', 'Meskal the Smuggler', 'The Magic Roses', 'The Green Hand' and 'Gratitude', a drama about an escaped convict who is recaptured and on his release shows his gratitude to the humble family who befriended him. A number of other films were shown and with seats costing as little as 6d, locals more than filled the hall.

1959

Mr P Winters had part of his ear bitten off after Eric Williams and Raymond Lucas took exception to the advice he gave them. Winters had followed a car which was driving very erratically en route to town. When the vehicle stopped he approached the driver and suggested he get himself a cup of coffee before driving on. The car's two occupants then followed Winters, attacking him, part of his ear being bitten off before the police arrived. The following day Williams and Lucas were sentenced to two months in prison with the car's driver fined an additional £5 for driving without due care.

07 September

1822

The results of an enquiry into a duel were published. Aaron de Ste Croix had believed that Thomas Le Breton had written a defamatory article about him. When they met in the square de Ste Croix told Le Breton: 'I would spit in your face if you were worth the spittle.' In December 1820 the two had met on Samarès Marsh to settle the matter in a duel. At the second exchange of shots de Ste Croix was badly wounded. He recovered but accused Le Breton of using a rifled pistol. The enquiry held by the Lieutenant Governor however completely exonerated Le Breton.

1826

A new Bailiff was sworn in and the new man, Sir Thomas Le Breton, altered a precedent set over a century earlier by actually living in Jersey. It had become practice for the Lieutenant Bailiff to reside in the Island and carry out official duties while the Bailiff pursued his own interests.

1833

For a subscription of £1 you could join the newly formed Jersey Agriculture and Horticultural Society. Developed after a meeting the previous month when a basic constitution was drafted, the Society's intentions were to encourage agricultural and horticultural improvements as well as the breeding of cattle. Women were allowed to be involved, although they could only vote by proxy.

1858

Jersey's reliance on ships to carry messages to and from the Island was broken on this day when a telegraphic service with England began to operate. The submarine telegraph company had its offices in Church Street.

1977

Fourteen-year old David Minty followed in his sister's wake when he swam the Channel in record time for a Channel Islander, with the crossing taking just over 11½ hours.

08 September

1889

The *Gazelle* saw Jersey waters for the first time. She was one of three steam-powered mailboats run by the Great Western Railway Company at the time, the others being the *Lynx* and the *Antelope*. The three ships had cost the company £35,000 each to build.

The *Gazelle*, with her two funnels and two masts, proved good value for money, first carrying passengers and mail to the Island, then, in 1908, being converted into a cargo ship. She served the Island uneventfully for 36 years before being sold and broken up in 1925.

1948

Just before midday the millionth tray of tomatoes to be exported this year was loaded aboard a cargo boat. But this was nothing compared to the 2½ million trays which had been exported by the same time the year before.

1970

It was the first day of a new term for school children and for some it was at an entirely new school, as Mont Nicolle received its first pupils on this day. The baby boom of the 1960s had meant that more school places were required. St Helier Girls' School was having to use temporary classrooms and those attending Convent FCJ were about to make use of a new £400,000 complex at Grainville.

1981

A scheme to employ out of work young people was announced on this day. £300,000 was to be used to fund the proposals in which employers would be subsidised when they took on apprentices. Unemployment was rising in the Island and the Education Committee was even considering raising the school leaving age in an attempt to stop yet more youngsters entering the job market.

09 September

1087

Twenty-one years after the Battle of Hastings William the Conqueror died. Having in 1066 united Normandy, the Channel Islands and England into one kingdom, his sons now divided up their legacy. The eldest son Robert succeeded to the Dukedom of Normandy, which included the islands, while his brother Rufus became King of England. Thus Jersey's ties with England were severed.

1882

The new covered market, or Central Market as it is often known, opened for business on this day. Its construction had been funded by the States from the proceeds of seven lotteries and it was built on the site of the old open market. The iron and granite structure supported the domed roof, the glass of which weighed 80 tons. In recent years some of the glass has been replaced by a modern lightweight plastic material. However, despite pressures to modernise the opening hours, the Central Market remains closed on Thursday afternoons.

1905

Henry Hake, aged 12, Adolphus Aubert, aged 11, and John Mallet, aged 13, stood trial for stealing a basket of food from the train terminus. The three had also stolen some rings and opera glasses, as well as being responsible for a number of other thefts. The boys' fathers all appeared before the court. Messieurs Hake and Mallet both admitted that their sons were 'trouble', while Mr Aubert said his son had been lead astray by bad company.

After hearing various reports on the children, including all three fathers informing the Bailiff that they would thrash or belt their sons, sentences was passed. Young Aubert was released, while the other two were to be sent to a reformatory in Hampshire where they would learn a trade and be disciplined. Their fathers would have to pay 2 shillings a week for their upkeep.

10 September

1910

A reward of £1 was offered by the owners of Chaumière de l'Orme, Grouville, for information that would lead to a conviction of the thief who had stolen some pears from their garden.

1925

Mr Le Cappelain of St Peter imported a threshing machine into the Island. At this time grain was still quite widely grown and the new machine was horse drawn and powered by a steam engine.

1959

On this day Francis Joseph Huchet was found guilty of murder and sentenced to death. He had been accused of killing John Perree in April, burying the body on the sand dunes. This was the first death sentence to be passed locally for 52 years and was the only option for murder. At 7.30 am on 9th October Huchet was taken from his cell in the Newgate Street prison and hanged within its walls, the last man to be executed in Jersey.

1959

Thousands of people visited Gorey Castle on this evening to view two sets of experimental floodlights and to see which they preferred. The choice was between traditional plain white lights and changing coloured lights illuminating the castle walls. There was a party atmosphere as a pipe band played and the granite walls were bathed in yellows, blues, greens and pinks. Public opinion was mixed but it was generally agreed that the plain white light showed the fortress in more clearly defined detail.

1970

This day saw the first sitting of the Juvenile Court. It was held in a committee room at the Town Hall with Michael Newell, the chairman, assisted by John Vint and Ruth Pilkington. Three cases were dealt with, one of which had been remanded from the Police Court. The first case involved a 15-year old who had committed a number of motoring offences for which he was fined £16.

11 September

1901

Hubert Wood was taken to the Petty Debts Court by the Constable of St Helier for non-payment of rates. Mr Voisin, the solicitor representing Wood, put forward a good defence. He claimed that as the Crown were exempt from local tax and as Wood was serving as an army schoolmaster, he too should be exempt. It was explained that room was short in the barracks so Wood lodged outside, and as those serving within the barracks paid no rates, Wood should not either.

An unsure court deferred their decision for a week before ruling that 'a person need not be resident in the Island to be taxed for property he may hold therein'. The court felt that Wood, therefore, was not only claiming exemption from the paying of rates, but was also claiming he had no obligation to comply with this other law. The court felt this was going 'rather far'. In plain English, Wood had to pay rates.

1920

When a gang of 14 card sharps failed to present themselves before the court their bails were forfeited and their arrests ordered. The gang had been working in the Island for several days, fleecing the unsuspecting populace. The police had posted men in certain areas to try and catch them and when a fight broke out at Westmount the sharps were found to be at its centre. The group of card cheats had been released on £2 bail and had decided to skip town.

1948

Jersey's new lifeboat, the *Elizabeth Rippon*, arrived in the Island, having made a 15-hour crossing from Cowes. The boat, which cost £20,000 and was to take over from the *Howard D*, was 46 ft long, weighed 20 tons and was fitted with a radio. The coxswain Thomas King was one of those who sailed the new lifeboat across the Channel, unaware that one day a new Jersey lifeboat would bear his name.

12 September

1888

The Jersey Ladies' College opened its new building. The college had begun eight years earlier[36] with 41 pupils and since that time the numbers had increased and former students had gone on to receive degrees. The college had been funded by shareholders who received a 5% return on their investment. When His Excellency spoke at the opening ceremony he commended the building's heating apparatus and was pleased that 'chairs had been provided for the pupils'. Among the new facilities were a gymnasium and seven sound-proofed piano practice rooms, as well as lavatories fitted with the latest improvements.

1907

Louis Le Monnier went before the Magistrate, charged with driving a motor car in the streets of town at a dangerous speed. The accused claimed that he never travelled at more than 18 mph in town, had three powerful brakes and did not consider his speed excessive. He also questioned the law under which he had been charged. There was one law for horse-drawn vehicles and another for bicycles and Le Monnier wanted to know under which he had been charged. The Magistrate, disregarding these queries, fined Le Monnier 15 shillings, ruling that 18 mph was in no way a moderate pace.

1960

The steamship *St Helier* left Jersey for the last time. This incredibly long-serving vessel first arrived in St Helier in 1925, the year she was built. She plied the Channel Islands route until 1940 when she was used to evacuate over 10,000 troops from Dunkirk. She crossed the Channel again on 6th June 1944 and this time her passengers were Canadian troops bound for the D-Day landings in Normandy. In 1946 the *St Helier* returned to civilian life, again serving the Channel Islands, where she continued for 14 years until sold for scrap.

---

[36] See 20th September for further details.

13 September

1905

The police were on the trail of a load of stolen seaweed. Mr P Le Cornu had gathered a load of vraic at First Tower but when he returned to collect it on this day it was gone. Centenier F Gallichan was contacted and was told by a road sweeper that the vraic had been taken by one of Mr G Syvret's men, Mr Boschat. Centenier Gallichan went to Syvret's St Lawrence home and arrested Boschat, ordering him to court. However, the matter was settled privately, with Boschat paying Le Cornu for the stolen seaweed.

1949

The St Helier lifeboat *Heart of Oak* set off to search for survivors from a French military aircraft which had gone down off the south-east coast of Jersey. Despite the heavy seas and lashing rain, coxswain Tommy King and his crew remained in the area for over six hours, but found no trace. It was later learned that the plane had ditched and sunk almost immediately, taking six of the nine crew with it. The surviving three were pulled from the water by a Norwegian ship.

Almost out of fuel and badly thrown about, the crew were almost back in harbour when another SOS was received. The lifeboat turned about and set off to rescue a yacht which was drifting among rocks. The crew of the lifeboat, with yacht in tow, fuel gauge reading nil, eventually reached the safety of St Helier Harbour, having been at sea for over nine hours. This feat of bravery won each crew member the RNLI bronze medal and coxswain Thomas James King the gold medal, the first awarded since 1944.

1989

It was announced that the Jersey Electricity Company had abandoned plans to build a coal-fired power station. But they still believed it would have been the best option as oil prices were high and cheap coal was available from Eastern European countries. But as soon as their proposals had been revealed the vision of a soot laden town had concerned locals, who worried that the coal dust and soot would pollute the Island.

14 September

1911

A Board of Trade Enquiry was opened into the stranding of the *SS Roebuck*. The Great Western Railways steamship had run into rocks off St Brelade on 19th July. The key factors being looked into were the speed of 18 knots and the state of the weather. Captain Le Feuvre and the second mate differed in opinion as to the thickness of the fog, the mate stating it to be 'thick as a blanket'. The *Roebuck* herself got a clean bill of health. The captain, however, fared less well, being criticised for failing to navigate properly and for not allowing for tide and weather conditions. The enquiry suspended Captain Le Feuvre's certificate for three months.

1946

Buckingham Palace announced that the Queen was to give a cross and pair of candlesticks to the Town Church in remembrance of the Island's loyalty and as a memento of King George VI's visit.

1948

The States decided to take the long running dispute over the Minquiers and Les Ecrèhous to an international court.[37] For centuries France had claimed the reefs as their own, as they had the Channel Islands. In more recent years inter-governmental discussions had attempted to resolve the matter but the French refused to drop their claim. These avenues now exhausted, Jersey was intent on sorting the matter out once and for all.

1989

Poisoning your guests with salmonella was proving popular this year. A guest at a St Helier hotel had died of food poisoning earlier in the month and two other outbreaks had been reported. On this day it was revealed that 30 people attending a wedding reception in St Martin had become the latest victims. Public Health were concerned about the situation, as were Tourism, who feared that poisoning your visitors might not be the best image to portray.

---

[37] See 17th November for further details.

15 September

1646

Two young English soldiers, having been drinking together, began to quarrel. Each challenged the other to a duel and they soon found themselves in a field on the outskirts of town. Having exchanged several thrusts with their rapiers the matter was quickly settled when one ran his sword through his opponent's chest. The soldier died instantly. The victorious soldier, although slightly wounded, fled. A search was made for him but he was eventually smuggled out of the Island by friends.

1942

An order directly from Hitler regarding the Channel Islands was issued on this day. Possibly as a retaliation for the British bombing of Germany, Hitler had decided that all British people not born in the islands should be deported to Germany. Those under 16 and over 70 were to be spared, as were those employed in essential services. Action was to be taken immediately and those affected were to be shipped out the following day. The deportees were instructed to travel in warm clothing, with a blanket if possible, to take only what they could carry and to have enough food for two days.

1971

The Fort Regent Development Committee went back to the States for more money. £2½ million was wanted so that the job could be finished as quickly as possible.

1994

Edythe 'Dot' Fairbairn died on this day. Born Edythe Amy Macready in 1908, this diminutive Jersey figure had caused a sensation in 1933 with her diving prowess. A keen swimmer and diver, she was often seen plunging from the highest board at the Havre des Pas bathing pool. She was one of three women chosen to represent England in the high diving event at the Empire Games, where, before a crowd of 80,000 at the new Wembley pool in London, Dot won the gold medal. On her return to Jersey she was greeted like a hero, with a band and a reception at the Town Hall.

16 September

1905

Marie Cornec and Josephine David both went before the Royal Court, charged with prostitution. Cornec pleaded guilty and was banished from Jersey for five years (the standard sentence), while David told the court that allegations against her were 'considerably exaggerated'. The Bailiff told her that an Advocate would plead her case, to which she replied that she needed no Advocate as there was nothing to say and she admitted the accusations against her. She too was banished for five years.

1923

French coinage was no longer officially accepted as legal tender in the Island after this day.

1942

This day was one of the saddest during the Island's five year occupation by German forces. Two hundred and eighty English-born Islanders were deported to Germany. The States had protested against this sudden departure but to no avail. A large crowd, held back by armed soldiers, assembled to see them off as they gathered at the Weighbridge. The States provided each deportee with a loaf of bread, a tin or jar of paste, some chocolate and a tin of milk to help see them through their journey. Everyone put on a brave face, patriotic songs were sung and everything was 'very British'. The deportees did not know where they were going or for how long they would be gone and some never came back. And this was just the beginning.

1961

A Dutch cargo ship struck the Paternosters, a reef to the north of Jersey, and sank within minutes. The *Heron* came to grief at night and of the eleven crew only eight survived. A radio message alerted the rescue services and other shipping. Most of the survivors were picked up fairly quickly but the captain and his wife were adrift in a raft for twelve hours before a French tanker found them. It was reported that 'only a trail of tomato trays mark the scene', tomatoes being the *Heron*'s cargo.

17 September

1649

Just over three years after leaving Jersey, Charles II returned to take up residence in Elizabeth Castle. Although three frigates were ready to transport the King and his party, he decided to cross the Channel in a little galley which had been made for him on his previous visit. Propelled by 18 oars, the small boat arrived with its royal cargo at about 4 pm. So many cannon and musket shots were let off to celebrate the return of Charles that the next morning the Parliamentary commander in Guernsey sent two warships and four frigates to investigate the cause of the noise.

1850

On 15th September the steam tug *Polka* had been bound for St Malo with 50 passengers when she began to take on water. With great presence of mind the captain headed for the Minquiers. When almost there everyone was transferred to the lifeboats just as the tug sank. Rescued from the reef the following day, the passengers and crew were taken on to France, where the captain collected his own vessel, the *Superb*, which had been repaired.

On this day the repaired *Superb* sailed for St Helier and the same captain was persuaded to alter course to show passengers where the *Polka* had sunk. Fate being what it is, the boat hit rocks and in the panic both lifeboats capsized, one because of a large lady jumping into it from a deck. Twenty people were drowned, including four who had been saved from the *Polka* two days earlier. Those who remained on board, however, were quite safe as the *Superb* was left high and dry on the rocks.

1945

A new law on voting rights was adopted. It stated that any residentially qualified person over the age of 21 would now be allowed to vote.

1965

Jersey's first parking meter made its appearance in St Helier, on a small area off Snow Hill. It was intended to be an experiment.

18 September

1816

Vice Admiral Philippe d'Auvergne died on this day in the Holmes Hotel, Westminster, possibly by his own hand. D'Auvergne had lived a life of which films are made. He had served against the Americans in their War of Independence. Later he was taken prisoner and incarcerated near the Franco-Belgian frontier during the Napoleonic war, where, strangely, he became heir to a small principality. He sailed all over the world, spied, ran guns, captured enemy shipping and was about as swashbuckling as you can get. Unfortunately d'Auvergne died heavily in debt after embarking on a costly litigation in an attempt to recover his principality.

1897

The water in a pond at Westmount quarry was pumped out. A woman had been seen throwing a bundle into the pond and passers-by had become suspicious. Anxious workmen watched the reducing water levels and recovered a soggy bundle which was taken to the police station. Once opened the package was found to contain nothing but dirty old linen.

1906

A St Helier Parish Assembly voted in favour of widening Bath Street on what was said to be the most dangerous corner in town. Properties number 1 and 3, by the *Evening Post* building, were to be acquired. Alfred Mollet had agreed to sell his property to the parish for £550 while his neighbour Herbert Foard settled at £326. A question was then raised as to the status of the road. If it were a 'grande route' then the Comité de Surveillance could be asked to pay one third of the costs and the assembly, unsurprisingly, decided to try and get a contribution from the comité.

1959

It was announced that Silver City Airways were to begin a new service for Islanders. The company's Bristol freighters would fly cars and passengers to France three days a week. The cost for passengers was £3, while a car not exceeding 11 ft long was £3 10s.

19 September

1831

Jean Lucas, a leading local Methodist, was kidnapped on this day. Feelings were running high in the Island. Service in the Militia was compulsory, as was taking part in the drills which were held on Sundays. But Methodism was spreading and to its followers Sundays were sacred. And the two could not be reconciled. It was the day before an election when Lucas was dragged from his horse and bundled into the hold of the cutter *Le Lion*. The following morning the vessel set sail from L'Etacq in rough weather but conditions were so poor that they were forced to turn back. Before landing the kidnappers got word that the police were going to arrest them, so they sailed on to Plemont and dumped their victim at the foot of the cliffs. Eventually Lucas made his way home but arrived too late to vote in the Jurat's election, the probable reason for the abduction.

1863

The London and South Western Railway Company's new ship arrived in St Helier Harbour. The *Normandy* was a paddle steamer capable of 15½ knots and carried 200 tons of cargo. However, she was not to have a long career.[38]

1905

Yves Ordelet was arrested for 'vagabondage and begging'. It was said that the Frenchman, who had lived in the Island for 20 years, had no home and had been begging. As banishment was the most common way to rid Island society of its unwanted, it appeared that Ordelet would soon be revisiting his homeland.

1925

The States of Jersey met at noon to legislate on time. Summertime had been introduced experimentally during the Great War and now England had made it a permanent event. Concerned that Jersey would be out of step, the States agreed to permanently adopt the same time as the mainland.

---

[38] See 17th March for further details.

20 September

1600

Jersey's most distinguished governor, Sir Walter Raleigh, was sworn in. Credited with bringing tobacco and potatoes to the Island, he in fact spent very little time here. Sir Walter stayed for a month on his first visit and two years later he took up residence for an even shorter time.

One thing he did achieve was the saving of Mont Orgueil Castle and he also named the new castle Fort Isabella Bellissima (Elizabeth the most beautiful) after Queen Elizabeth I.

1859

The *Express* was an iron paddle steamer run by the South Western Steam Packet Company. She was 160 ft long and powered by two boilers which produced a pressure of 15 pounds per square inch to drive the 18 ft paddles.

On this day the *Express* struck rocks off Corbière as she journeyed to Guernsey. The resulting hole in her bow meant she was taking on water fast but she managed to beach on rocks at St Brelade.

The only casualties were two passengers who panicked and jumped overboard, both drowning. The other passengers, who numbered over 100, as well as three race horses, were able to clamber to safety.

1880

This day saw the opening of the Jersey Ladies' College in Roussel Street.[39]

1901

Julia Westaway died at 5.40 am on this day. She had been unwell for over six months, so the death of the octogenarian came as no surprise. Miss Westaway had poured a great deal of money into local charities, founding the Westaway Trust and funding the ragged school.

---

[39] See 12th September for further details.

21 September

1811

The States were informed that a French attack was imminent. It wasn't and they didn't.

1861

The Jersey Constitutional Reform Association was formed. A petition had been raised containing 1,001 signatures of people demanding reform of the constitution. Some Members of the States regarded the signatories as 'denizens of a fools' paradise'. However, the Lieutenant-Governor invited the newly formed Reform Association to Government House and assured them that their petition would be forwarded to the Secretary of State to show the feelings of a 'very large proportion of the educated and independent members of this community'.

1960

Geoff Vowden scored his first hat-trick for Nottingham Forest, so helping the team win their first home match of the season. Twenty-year old Vowden had signed to play for the first division club the previous season. The Jersey lad, who had previously played for First Tower United and had represented the Island in the Junior Muratti, was now making headlines in the sports pages of the national press.

1976

An extra £55,000 was to be spent in an attempt to eradicate Dutch elm disease, which was ravaging the Island's hedgerows. A policy of tree felling had been adopted in the hope that removing infected trees would lessen the chance of the beetles spreading the fungus. The extra money was to pay for the felling of 3,000 trees, stepping up the programme which had begun two years earlier.

But history shows that the strategy did not work. Despite injecting healthy trees with various chemicals and the clearance policy, the disease gradually covered the whole Island and what was once the most common of trees has now almost disappeared.

22 September

1636

A law was passed forbidding men and women from wearing clothes that did not reflect their social position.

1692

Eight victims of the Salem witch trials were hanged on this day. Salem was a smallish town in the north-east of America which had been settled by a large number of Channel Islanders. In 1692 an outbreak of satanic hysteria had overtaken the already superstitious population. By this day at least 21 people had died, eight more were condemned to be hanged and about 250 had been accused of sorcery and were awaiting trial. Among the victims was a church minister and a number of people of Jersey origin.

1897

Dr Rudolph Schiffman announced to Islanders that he could cure asthma. The 'renowned physician', who was based in London, had discovered a remedy which produced 'instant relief' from asthma, hay fever and bronchitis. To prove it worked, Islanders were invited to collect a free sample box from John T Baker's, 27 Halkett Place.

1964

Mr L Holmes of La Fosse, St John, went to inspect the three horses he had tethered in his field, only to find two of them had been shot. They were both still alive when found but were in an obviously distressed state. A vet was called but before he could arrive, both animals collapsed and died. At the abattoir a post-mortem revealed three bullets, which were passed on to the analyst as a police investigation began.

Three days later Ereaut Mason came forward and told the authorities he had been driving Michael East as they went hunting. As they had driven past the horses East had shot at them to test his gun. At their trial both were found guilty, Mason being put on probation for three years and East sent for borstal training.

23 September

1870

The steam ship *Dublin* arrived in St Helier Harbour carrying Jersey's first two locomotives as well as four carriages. Some open carriages had been built locally and were intended for summer use, while the four on board the *Dublin* were covered for winter work. A crowd watched as the rolling stock for the soon-to-be open railway was being unloaded by crane onto the Albert Quay.

1905

Euginie Baud had no visible means of subsistence other than prostitution and to this charge she pleaded guilty. In the Royal Court it was told how Baud, a French national, had been brought to Jersey when aged one year. She had been abandoned as a child and until recently had been of good behaviour. The Attorney-General, prosecuting, said that although banishment would normally be ordered, as Baud knew no one in France he suggested a sentence of one week's imprisonment instead. The court agreed and as Baud had been held in custody her sentence had already been served. Having promised the court that she would reform, Baud was reminded that banishment awaited any further appearances before them.

1935

The steam ship *Lorina* was a war baby. Built in 1918, she spent her first year as a troop ship before taking up her intended role of serving the Channel Islands. The *Lorina* first entered St Helier Harbour on April Fool's Day, 1920. However, it was on leaving the same harbour fifteen years later, on this day, that she hit trouble when the rocks that she struck caused considerable damage below the waterline. But after repairs were made she lasted five more years, when German bombers finished her off at Dunkirk.

1978

The Duke and Duchess of Gloucester officially opened the new sports facilities at Fort Regent during a three-day visit to the islands. They were given full VIP treatment and the *Jersey Evening Post* even produced a special Royal Souvenir.

24 September

1719

The streets of Jersey were so filthy in 1719 that on this day an act of the Cour d'Heritage refers to their disgusting state.

1910

Hundreds of people gathered on the Albert Pier to greet the new triple screw ship, the *Caesarea*, the first turbine steamer of the London and South Western Railway Company.

Her 150 passengers had travelled the last part of their journey from Guernsey in one hour, arriving in St Aubin's Bay at 8.15 am. In the afternoon the gangways were thrown open, allowing the public to view the new vessel.

1922

On this day, being a Sunday, Islanders were taking advantage of a new law that allowed them to fish on the Sabbath. A good number of locals went low water fishing, with Mr Le Cornu and friends landing a 45 lb conger eel.

1923

West Cinema opened in Bath Street, the last film having been shown in their old premises at the old Royal Hall two days earlier. On the morning of the opening everything was ready but for one thing - there were no seats. However, at 2 o'clock the ship carrying them arrived and after four hours frantic work all was ready.

The inaugural picture was a stirring piece called 'Blazing the Airway to India', said to be a true record of British pluck, tenacity and endurance. As well as the official guests, hundreds of people queued to experience Jersey's latest entertainment house.

Showings were thrice daily, with cheap seats costing 6d and, if you could afford to splash out, a box for four could be booked for 10 shillings.

25 September

1666

On this day the States decided that emigration would solve the problem of the poor. Thus it became States' policy to encourage the Island's paupers to leave Jersey, which a great many of them did, taking the opportunity of sailing to New Jersey in the new world.

1895

The West End Bathing Co Ltd held an extraordinary general meeting of its shareholder to discuss building a bathing pool at West Park. It was decided to issue debenture bonds to the value of £2,000, with an interest rate of 4%, to pay for its construction. The company, formed two years earlier, hoped that they would be able to regulate the bathing at the pool to 'prevent the disgusting scenes which daily take place'. And if men wished to bathe with ladies they would be forced to 'abandon that triangular piece of material which they consider a costume for a fully dressed one'.

1901

It was officially announced that the St Helier Fire Brigade had been formed. The estimated cost was £1,725 for equipment and £390 per annum in wages, with the Chief Officer receiving £2.50 per week. The brigade had acquired two manual fire engines, both nearly 40 years old, a wooden escape ladder 50 feet long, a cart to carry the hose, and two horses, Dolly and Fanny. The first fire was at Boobyers Hotel, Grève de Lecq, to which the response time was an impressive 40 minutes. Unfortunately the building was destroyed. In June 1902 it was agreed that a charge would be made, with attendance costing £2 for the first hour and £1.50 per hour after that, while people manning the pumps were valued at 5p per hour.

1969

19-year old Denize Le Pennec became the first person to swim around Jersey, taking just 14 hours to cover the 35 miles. No real problems were reported and she was accompanied by a guard boat all the way. At Green Island Le Pennec swam through the inner passage to the cheers of her supporters.

26 September

1910

Jean Guegon was sent to prison for one month with hard labour for assaulting Eugenie Perchard. Twice he had grabbed her by the throat, threatening to kill her. Perchard told the court that she had lived with Guegon since the potato season and that he had threatened her when she refused to agree to his suggested 'immoral practices'.

1922

Francis Le Feuvre and Francis Le Gresley were fishing from rocks to the west of Grève de Lecq when a wave washed them both into the sea. Their companion, Wilfred Michel, removed his coat and swam out to try and save them. The sea was later said to be the roughest for 20 years, so much so that rescue boats could not be launched. Michel's body was the first to be recovered, however, the sea was less keen to release its first two victims.

1931

The junior library in Dumaresq Street was opened on this day. The intention was to encourage children who had left school to continue with their education. Two thousand books were available for both loan and use in the reading room.

1938

Mrs A M Coutanche launched *HMS Jersey* at Cowes, the new destroyer continuing a tradition. It is recorded that in 1698 another ship named *Jersey* had been built and launched at Cowes. With the Second World War on the horizon, *HMS Jersey* had been sponsored by Mrs Coutanche and other Islanders.

1946

The States agreed to buy the Noirmont peninsula as an Island memorial to the recent war. As usual, a committee had been set up to consider the proposal, which they took back to the House, recommending approval. The site was to cost £9,000 but with a proviso that if funds were not forthcoming from Islanders, the States would make up the shortfall.

27 September

1721

Having died on board ship, Philip Janvrin, a suspected plague victim, was buried on the Ile au Guerdain, the little islet in Portelet Bay. The tomb erected over the site of his grave no longer exists. The building known today as Janvrin's Tomb was not built on the site until 1807 and rather than being a tomb, it was designed to repel French invaders.

1921

The Jersey Labour Party held an inaugural meeting at West Park Pavilion and were addressed by F Roberts, MP, from Labour's national executive. The audience was told that as unionism in Jersey had got such a firm hold and had made such progress, organised labour should have a say in government. It was suggested that any labour candidate for the States should be backed by all the local unions and for that reason union delegates would form a committee to prepare rules for the Jersey Labour Party. The meeting was well attended but the enthusiasm was never translated into political power.

1938

Posters notifying Islanders that Jersey was to be under blackout conditions until further notice surprised many locals. Tension between Britain and Europe was mounting and war was a possibility at any moment. Advertising signs were to be turned off, as were street lights, and motorists were to drive using sidelights or, preferably, no lights at all. Windows had to be covered with curtains or thick brown paper and skylights especially obscured in case of air raids. A few days later tension eased when Mr Chamberlain returned triumphant from Munich, assured that there would be no war.

1977

It was revealed in the *Jersey Evening Post* that Jersey now relied on the finance industry and wealthy immigrants for over half its revenue. Agriculture, once the backbone of the Island's economy, brought in relatively little and Tourism's importance had been declining for a number of years.

28 September

1769

A mob armed with clubs descended on the Market Place and invaded the Royal Court. The reason for the riot was the price of corn. Rents were paid in grain or its equivalent value in money. It was therefore advantageous for the King's Receiver to make grain scarcer and therefore dearer. With this in mind a bill was passed by the States permitting the export of corn. Earlier a group of women had unloaded a ship whose cargo of corn was due for export and, on returning the grain to its owner, had paid for it and departed peacefully with their purchase.

1870

After less than 12 months the first locomotive took to the rails on a test run from St Helier to St Aubin and back. The trip was completed without incident and the next afternoon about 300 guests boarded the train and travelled to St Aubin in four open carriages.

1936

Jersey bulls are notoriously dangerous and on this day John Le Brun of Brook Farm, St John, was lucky to escape with his life. Usually a bull was kept with a ring through its nose and a chain around its horns. However, Le Brun had removed the chain as the animal was getting a sore. As Le Brun crossed his yard he was astonished to see that the bull had broken free from the stable and as he called for assistance the bull charged. The farmer was thrown into the air, the animal then making a series of attempts to gore his owner. Farm hands and a neighbour rushed to the rescue. Sydney Le Gros lured the enraged animal away while Le Brun was removed. Not wishing to risk further injuries, the bull was shot and then butchered.

1981

Houses and businesses were flooded when 2 inches of rain fell in an hour. The fire service and Resource Recovery Board were kept busy pumping out buildings. The Island's drainage system had failed to cope, walls had collapsed and soil from the fields had left a thick layer of mud over many roads.

29 September

1841

The foundation stone of the Victoria Harbour was laid, although at that time its name remained undecided. Thomas Le Gros and Jean Gosfray were contracted for the task.

1852

Victoria College was opened by the Bailiff, Sir Thomas Le Breton. Built by Jean Le Rossignol, the college was to be a permanent record of Queen Victoria's visit to the Island in 1846.

1869

The town's new sewer system was completed. This day saw the inauguration of the waterworks system. Until this point water in town had either come from a private well, collected rainwater or the public street pumps.

1920

A new entertainment was touring the country parishes and on this day it was St John's turn to receive the travelling cinema. While 'The Spark Divine' was showing at West's and Charlie Chaplin could be seen at the Opera House, farm workers and those without transport had little entertainment. The film being offered was 'The Impossible Woman'. The TC, as it was called, proved to be very popular, showing a full programme of films, including a serial to encourage the audience back the following week.

1934

St Matthew's Church at Millbrook, the Glass Church, was reopened, having been extensively renovated. Lady Trent had funded the project in memory of her husband, Sir Jesse Boot. The famous French artist, Renè Lalique, had been employed to provide the church's very unusual glass features. As well as the glass work, a new set of bells were installed. The eight bells, the largest weighing 8 cwt, were claimed to have been made using a process rediscovered after 300 years.

30 September

1643

Another bombardment was launched on the town from Elizabeth Castle as the Civil War raged. Six cannon balls were fired by the Royalists, damaging the churchyard wall, roofs and chimneys. One even shot through a house, smashing the spinning wheel which stood alongside a bed in which four people were sleeping.

1907

Mr N Bougourd, a ships carpenter, began work on the installation of a wireless telegraph at Fort Regent. Three 50 ft poles were erected and would enable communication with England.

1921

A Royal Air Force sea plane arrived, circling above St Helier before landing just outside the pier heads. The aircraft carried a number of passengers who, immediately upon arrival at the quay, drove off in motor cars. This was believed to be the first time passengers had travelled to Jersey by air.

1939

Yet another of T B Davis' generous gifts to the Island was opened to the public. The Howard Davis Park contained a statue of George V, which was also unveiled. Due to the war the ceremony was less elaborate than would otherwise have been the case. Various officials and several hundred members of the public heard Mr Davis ask that all those who visit the park respect his dead son's memory.

1949

The largest fire the Island had seen broke out at Le Gallais' furniture depository in Hilgrove Street. The fire was quickly contained, however, the radiated heat and flying brands continued to be a danger until the fire was completely extinguished a number of days later. Four firemen were slightly injured when a wall collapsed and although arson was a possibility, no evidence was found. Over 500 lots of furniture as well as valuable paintings belonging to the Earl of Jersey were turned to ash in the gutted four storey building.

01 October

1834

English money was declared the sole legal tender. Jerseymen, being reluctant to change, continued to use livres tournois, sous and liards and it was decided that 520 sous should be equivalent to a British sovereign. For many years goods remained priced in livres, so complicated arithmetic was required before payment could be made. Eight years later the States issued their own coins. The half penny and the sous were of the same value and as 520 sous made a pound it followed that 260 pence made a pound. Therefore 13 pennies made a shilling. It was this reasoning that meant that Jersey pennies were marked 1/13th of a shilling where as in England 12 pennies made a shilling.

1921

The previous evening a mass meeting was held to consider the 2d per hour reduction in wages for unskilled labour. Held at Unity Hall, the local headquarters of the Dock, Wharf, Riverside and General Workers Union, the building and allied trades were now on strike.

1969

The States of Jersey took over responsibility for the Island's postal service. After a few hiccups with stamps that didn't stick (the official explanation being that the glue was too hard), the Jersey Post Office has become world renowned for the quality and style of its stamp designs. Prior to this date English stamps were used locally.

1980

A twin engined Cessna light aircraft, piloted by Norman Harvey, crashed into a house near St Peter's Church. The plane exploded as it continued skidding on into outbuildings. The pilot was killed but fortunately no one else was aboard and no one on the ground was injured. At the enquiry the accident was put down to pilot error.

02 October

1819

The States decided to add another storey to the Public Library. Three years earlier the Library, which became known as the Beresford Library, had opened and this now needed additional space reflected the increase in literary and general education standards within Jersey.

1905

A search was begun for a group of fishermen who had set off for the Minquiers the previous day to go ormering and who had failed to return.

The search continued for several days until the *Dervish*, their boat, was washed ashore at Granville and the five men were presumed to have drowned. By the time the first body was found, two weeks later, a fund for their widows and children had risen to over £100.

What happened to the men remained a mystery. At first it was thought that the boat had just drifted away, leaving them to drown when the tide came in. But clothing found in the *Dervish* proved that the men had changed for their return journey, the mishap apparently occurring while en route to Gorey.

1989

Edward Paisnel and Florence Ashcroft-Hawkins were married in the Register Office in the Isle of Wight. The couple, both in their sixties, had known each other for some years, she having given evidence at his trial nearly twenty years before.

Paisnel, known as the Beast of Jersey, was escorted to the ceremony by officers from the Albany Top Security Prison, where he was still serving his 30 year prison sentence for sex offences.

He died in 1994, two years after being released from prison. Despite his wife's wish that his remains be returned to the Island, his sister, who owned the family burial plot in Grouville, and the authorities rejected the proposal.

03 October

1647

Life as a soldier must have been fairly bleak at this time, with fresh food being a luxury. On this night Sir George de Carteret decided to check up on the castle sentries and was surprised to see a guard hauling the body of a sheep over the battlements. Below were a group of men with more suspicious bundles and on seeing this Sir George left unobserved. The following day an unannounced visit to the kitchen found a cauldron full of mutton as well as fresh fruit, cabbages and fowl. All the food was immediately confiscated and distributed among the other troops, while the culprits were strapped to the horse, a common punishment device of the day.

1927

Colomberie and Don Road were turned into one way roads. Policemen were on duty to supervise the vehicles but were considered a nuisance by many drivers. The experiment was intended to aid the movement of the ever increasing amount of traffic in town. However it was not greatly appreciated by the motorists.

1955

Television arrived in Jersey at 3 o'clock in the afternoon. Test transmissions had been made during the previous two weeks but 'Twice Twenty', a women's programme, was the first scheduled show seen. The transmission was relayed via the mast at Les Platons but viewers were warned that the signal might not be perfect as a new transmitter in England was awaiting completion.

1994

Work on repaving the King Street precinct began on this day. The Public Services Department had originally intended to use coloured concrete bricks for the job and had laid out an area for public approval, which was not received. Islanders wanted to know why couldn't granite be used, as it looked good and was long lasting. After further consideration, it was decided to use a volcanic stone from Italy with a row of white marble running the length of the street to aid the partially sighted.

04 October

1736

Marie Godfray went before the authorities accused of dabbling in the forbidden arts and general sorcery. A hundred years earlier she would have been strangled, hanged, and then burned, while all her property would be confiscated. However times had changed and she was released after promising not to do it again.

1786

The States voted in favour of establishing a trial by jury system in criminal cases. Juries were also to sit in civil cases where either party demanded it. Unfortunately when it went before the Privy Council the bill was rejected.

1813

The Jersey National School opened on this day. Sited in Halkett Place, the school survived until 1982.

1853

Frederick C Clarke launched the *Matilda Wallenbach* from his shipyard below Westmount. The *Matilda* was the largest ship ever built in Jersey, at 1,077 tons.

Shipbuilding was a big industry in Jersey at this time, with boat yards along St Aubin's Bay, at Havre des Pas and at Gorey. The sturdy vessels often travelled across the world on trading expeditions, as well as bringing wealth to the Island through the Newfoundland cod fisheries.

1911

Ronez Quarry was sold at auction. The quarry, on the north coast of the Island, included the headland, stone workings, jetty and machinery. They were bought by the Croft Granite Brick and Concrete Company who were based in Leicester. Work at the quarry had ceased temporarily while the sale took place, the price paid being £7,550.

05 October

1646

Between 7 and 8 o'clock in the morning the steeple of Trinity Parish Church was struck by lightning. Although no one was hurt, a quantity of masonry was dislodged. The falling debris caused damage to the roofs below and littered the churchyard.

1812

One of Jersey's better known artists was born. John Le Capelain, who died 36 years later of tuberculosis, had specialised in water-colours. He was commissioned by the States to paint 25 scenes to be presented to Queen Victoria on her visit to Jersey and the pictures were later reproduced in book form.

After his death a fund was set up to found the Le Capelain Gallery. However only £210 was donated and the money was instead used to purchase a number of his works for the Island.

1919

The 'Seaplane Special', a 130 hp auto biplane, brought copies of the newspaper *Lloyds Weekly News* to the Island for the first time.

A sister plane was due to do the same in Guernsey but just off Alderney engine trouble caused the pilot to ditch in the sea. Plane and papers were lost, the pilot was not.

1950

A series of arson attacks on buildings and businesses had occurred between 1948 and 1950. Things had got so bad that some firms employed watchmen to secure their property at night and detectives from Scotland Yard were brought in to investigate.

On this day the firebug was nearly apprehended while preparing to destroy a garage in Halkett Place but he fled after being disturbed by an Honorary Police patrol.

The culprit was never caught.

06 October

1585

Three members of the Le Brocq family were detained in Mont Orgueil Castle 'in order to make inquisition upon them' for seeking a cure from a woman who had long been suspected of sorcery.

1714

Clement Le Couteur died on this day, having caused the ecclesiastical authorities problems for many years. One particularly noteworthy incident occurred in 1706. Le Couteur had decided to alter his pew in St John's Parish Church. However he was ordered to shorten it as it obstructed Josue Ahier's pew. When he refused he was threatened with excommunication. Le Couteur then appealed to the Royal Court, who found in his favour and instructed Ahier not to disturb him. A week later Le Couteur complained that Ahier had indeed disturbed him, at which point Ahier was committed to prison.

1729

The States discussed a generous offer made by Philippe Falle. His proposition was to set up a Public Library and to start it off he was willing to give 2,000 volumes to form its nucleus. He later contributed £300 towards the building costs of the structure being constructed in the area still known as Library Place.

1769

Shocked by the uprising caused by their decision to export grain, the States cancelled the order. Members met at Elizabeth Castle as feelings were running so high that the politicians feared for their safety, the anger of a riot a week earlier still close to the surface.[40]

1848

Developments at the Hospital continued both structurally and surgically. This day saw the opening of the chapel and two months earlier the first operation under chloroform had been performed.

---

[40] See 28th September for further details.

07 October

1406

Fed up with Jersey's privateering activities in the Channel 1,000 French soldiers, under the command of soldier-of-fortune Pero Nino, landed in St Aubin's Bay, watched by 3,000 Jerseymen. After an initial skirmish they took over the abbey where Elizabeth Castle was later built and the following morning took part in one of Jersey's biggest battles.

Nino's force was met by an army of about 1,500 locals. The local force attacked with 200 horsemen, who were cut down by the French archers. In the bloody fight that ensued on the dunes where St Helier now stands hundreds of men were killed. The Islanders retreated to a large earthworks and awaited the next attack.

But because the invading force had learned of the Island's four other castles and believed an English fleet was in the area they settled for a ransom of 10,000 gold crowns, as well as the release of all French prisoners and a tribute of lances, axes, bows and trumpets which was to be paid for the next ten years.

1477

Jean Hue, the Rector of St Saviour, offered to build a house near the Chapel of St Manely for use as a school. Accommodation for a master would be supplied and it was to be entirely free, even for boarders. Permission was given by the Dean but he insisted that 'Masters and scholars must sing Mass in the church on all festivals'.

1643

The market place was as busy as usual on this Saturday when at 2 pm the Royalist forces at Elizabeth Castle sent 20 cannon calls into the bustling heart of St Helier. Some of the terrified inhabitants ran for cover while others threw themselves to the ground. One stranger to the Island remained standing, despite the fact that the local to whom he had been talking fell to the floor. The unfortunate Norman was killed outright when struck by the cannon ball which continued, rebounding off a wall, killing a horse in the process.

08 October

1845

A meeting was held in St Helier about the proposed setting up of a local railway. It was anticipated that trains would run from St Aubin to St Catherine because the Admiralty planned to build a deep water harbour there. It was also suggested that as well as building a tunnel under Fort Regent, that in time extensions to the system would take in both St Ouen's and St Brelade's bays. But nothing came of the proposals.

1850

Following the loss of life when the *Superb* struck rocks[41], the following advert headed '£5 Reward' appeared in the local newspaper *The British Press and Jersey Times*: 'The above reward will be paid to any person finding the body of Mr W D Knott, late of Gorey, who was among the passengers on the *Superb*. He was in height 5 ft 9 in; dark hair and small dark whiskers; wore at the time of the wreck a light coloured coat and light trousers. Apply to Mr P Mauger, Pier, Gorey.'

1924

One of the most severe storms to hit the Island uprooted hundreds of trees and unroofed houses. Storm force 11 winds blew from the west at over 70 miles per hour and the accompanying rain flooded many buildings. Concern was expressed about the *SS Reindeer*, which was en route to the Island, but she appeared in the bay despite the mountainous seas. Her 100 passengers were said to 'not look too bad considering the crossing'.

1963

Senator Venables' proposition to allow remuneration for Members of the States was rejected by 24 votes to 20. The suggested payment of £500 per year was designed to encourage 'wage earners' to come forward but the breaking of the Island tradition of honorary service proved too great a sacrifice for Members.

---

[41] See 17th September for further details.

09 October

1643

During the Civil War, with the Royalists besieged within Elizabeth Castle, news was hard to gather. On this day in Jean Chevalier's diary an unusual code is noted. The Castle's porter sent word to his wife, who lived on the seafront, for news of the king. She was to hang on her washing line three sheets if the news was good, only one if it was bad. If no news was available two sheets with a shirt in between were to be displayed. The porter, using a telescope, would then know what was happening. However one of the porter's notes fell into the wrong hands and the porter's wife fled to France.

1842

Jerseymen, being great travellers, have influenced events all over the world and on this day, with the birth of William Mesny, it was China's turn. At the age of twelve Mesny went to sea. Six years later he jumped ship and headed for Hong Kong.

He soon became involved in the Chinese civil war, recruiting foreign mercenaries. Later, after running salt to the black market and dabbling in the arms trade, Mesny was captured by one of the warring factions. A ransom of $100,000 was not paid and he was rescued by a British gunboat some months later. After that Mesny got involved with the Chinese army, rising to the rank of Lieutenant General.

Some of his other notable activities were that of publisher, writing on all manner of subjects Chinese. He was also famed as a plant collector and was said to be the only European to speak Chinese without an accent.

1945

Edgar Whatley was sentenced to 18 months hard labour for bigamy and 3 months for leaving the Island without a permit. Whatley had married Norah Winters in 1941 but he was already married to a woman in England. When his first wife had written to him via the Red Cross, he claimed to be very ill. A second letter told her he was dead.

10 October

1591

The enquête (jury) in the trial of Symon Vauldin found him guilty of sorcery, so he was sentenced to be strangled, his body burnt until it was reduced to ashes, and his goods and property confiscated by the Crown. Vauldin had confessed to communicating with the Devil, who had appeared in the guise of a cat or sometimes a crow.

1964

Some of the strongest winds ever recorded in Jersey were the backdrop to a tale of survival. Alison Mitchell had been one of five people on board the yacht *Mariecelia* which was found motoring in circles in St Aubin's Bay. The mast, wheelhouse, rails and most of the other fittings had been swept away in the storm, as had all signs of the five people. A great search ensued, with the lifeboat, fire service, RAF, Royal Navy and French helicopter all involved, but nothing was found.

However Mitchell had survived. Along with her companions, she had been swept around the Island. One by one the others had drowned, but on this day, after 18 hours in the water, she eventually struggled ashore on the north coast by Egypt. Her body swollen, and blinded by the salt water, she climbed a steep cliff path and reached a farmhouse and help.

The massive search had centred in the wrong area but who could have known that someone lost in St Aubin's Bay could be swept completely around to the north coast and survive.

1994

Condor's new £20 million Wavepiercer car ferry ran aground before the company had even taken delivery of it. The state of the art vessel had been built in Tasmania and local representatives were aboard when the 78 meter long ferry ran into an offshore reef. The new commission had been due to begin service in local waters the following spring, taking up to 670 passengers and 140 cars across the Channel on each trip. At first the damage was thought to be relatively minor, however, it was soon discovered that repairs were going to cost several million pounds.

11 October

1897

A man died of his injuries, having fallen from a seaweed laden cart. The farm hand, Renè Marie Robert, was riding atop a load of dried seaweed which was being taken up St Brelade Hill. Unaccountably, he fell off, landing just in front of the wheels, which ran over one of his hands. The unconscious man was quickly placed in a horse-drawn van and taken to the General Hospital but he died a few hours later.

1911

Mr G Trachy's attempt at suicide failed, despite shooting himself in the head several times. A visitor discovered the unconscious Trachy in a quarry at Westmount. The police, having been summoned, found that Trachy was able to walk with them to the police station. All six rounds in his gun had been fired and when examined by doctors one bullet was found to have gone through the roof of his mouth and lodged in his brain, while a second had passed by his left eye and gone beneath his scalp. Surgeons said nothing could be done. Trachy later fell into unconsciousness and died two days later.

1966

The first Jewish marriage for over 100 years took place in Jersey. The couple celebrated at the Hotel de France after the formalities at the Registry Office.

1987

In the early hours of this day Roderick Newall beat his parents to death. Aided by his younger brother Mark, the bodies were transported to a meadow in Grève de Lecq Valley and buried. The two brothers continued their activities as if nothing had happened. Despite one of the Island's most extensive and prolonged searches, it wasn't until November 1993, over six years later, that the police recovered the bodies.

12 October

1591

Jean Bichard, having consulted a sorcerer in the hope of curing an injured leg, was condemned to be placed in St Peter's parish stocks on Sunday.

1899

Lady Otway, one of Jersey's leading socialites, received a blackmail note from Jack the Ripper. The letter demanded £1,000 and threatened to assassinate her if the money was not paid.

Lady Otway passed the letter on to the Constable of St Helier, who prepared a box, as had been ordered, and sent it to St Luke's Railway Station. Pc Le Breton kept watch but the package was not collected.

A week later a second letter arrived, again signed Jack the Ripper, containing similar demands. The procedure was repeated, only this time a Frenchman named Ernest Desponts went to retrieve the package from Grève d'Azette Railway Station. Pc Le Breton pounced and despite Desponts initial protests that he was merely collecting the parcel for some else, the blackmailer had indeed been caught.

When the case went to court Desponts' counsel attempted to make light of the affair, describing it as a farce. The Bailiff did not agree and sentenced the Frenchman to a year's hard labour and five years banishment.

1915

The Bailiff called the proprietors of the local cinemas to a meeting and informed them that their opening hours were to change. The Alhambra was ordered to close completely at the end of the month, while West's and the Opera House would be allowed to have only one nightly screening, which had to begin at 8 pm and be finished by 10 pm.

During the month the Alhambra 'cinema deluxe' reduced its performances from twice to once nightly and ended the month with 'Drake's Love Story'.

13 October

1853

Emilie Charlotte Le Breton was born in St Saviour's Rectory on this day, the youngest child of Dean William Corbet Le Breton and Emilie Davis Martin. When aged 14 Lillie, as she was known, received her first marriage proposal. But it was at her brother's wedding that she met the wealthy Belfast widower Edward Langtry, who was later to become her first husband.[42]

1860

The Southwestern Steam Navigation Company's newest vessel docked at St Helier. The *Southampton* was the largest ship to serve the islands at this time. The 232 ft long vessel could carry 460 tons and was powered by steam and driven by paddles. She had twin funnels, as well as two schooner rigged masts. During the 37 years she plied local waters she underwent a number of refits. She was lengthened, had a funnel removed and was finally broken up in 1898, a year after leaving Channel Island seas.

1959

It was agreed in the States to impose an Island-wide speed limit of 40 miles per hour in an attempt to reduce the number of people being killed on the roads. Already during the year 13 people had died in traffic accidents and the new speed limit was viewed as the first measure to try and bring order to the Island's roads. Tractors, towing vehicles and heavy motor cars were to be restricted to 30 mph. Penalties were to be a £20 fine for a first offence and a maximum of £50 for subsequent violations.

1962

An attempt was made to break into the vaults of Barclays Bank in Library Place. Oxy-acetylene torches were used to burn through the strongroom's steel panels. But before the task was done the thieves' gas ran out. Abandoning the safe, the cash desks were forced, all of which were empty, the burglars leaving non the richer.

---

[42] See 9th March for further details.

14 October

1066

It is undocumented whether Jerseymen aided William the Conqueror in his invasion of England but the Battle of Hastings is one of the many reasons that the Channel Islands pledge allegiance to the English crown and not, as would be more geographically logical, the French.

The present Queen is still addressed locally as the Duke of Normandy. However it is the original Duke, Rollo, who Islanders call upon to halt an injustice that is being done them when the Clameur de Haro is raised. This ancient law, which is still in use nearly 1,000 years on, compels all action to cease immediately once an aggrieved party has called on the Duke to aid him.

1528

John Knight, the Gentleman Porter of Mont Orgueil Castle, quarrelled with the Underporter, a man named Louis. The argument soon grew heated and swords were drawn. The two men battled for a considerable time and were still doing so when the Castle's constable saw them.

Attempting to stop the fight, Knight killed the constable and both combatants were arrested. They languished in the dungeons, condemned, for almost a year. In August 1529 Knight was executed, his body hanging from a gallows, his head spiked on the bell tower. Louis was banished from the Island, his goods confiscated and both his ears cut off.

1905

François Marie Landesse began serving his sentence for stealing some lead from a pump. The lead had been taken from a St Lawrence property named Highlands, owned by Alphonse Dallain. Landesse pleaded guilty to the charge. But however much the lead was worth, it cannot have been worth two months hard labour and five years banishment.

Jean Michel, who had appeared before the court just before Landesse, had stolen £1 10s worth of gold and was sentenced to six weeks hard labour and five years banishment.

15 October

1600

Sir Walter Raleigh, the then Governor, wrote to the Chief Secretary of State saying that 'the fortification' would be finished the following spring. He was referring to Elizabeth Castle, work on which had begun in 1594 under the direction of engineer Paul Ivy. Originally the plan had been to demolish Mont Orgueil Castle and reuse the stones but this had been quickly dropped. The Castle cost about £1,100 to build, Queen Elizabeth giving £500 towards the project. The rest was raised by taxes, with each house having to contribute four days labour.

1691

On this day the States decided that within six years all the houses in town should have slate roofs. This was primarily a safety measure as thatched houses burnt too well. And the fire of London, only 25 years earlier, had demonstrated how quickly a fire could spread.

1833

An engineer and cartographer, Elias Le Gros presented the States with a map, a plan of the town of St Helier. So pleased were the States with his efforts that they granted him £200 towards its cost. Le Gros was also the man who erected the sundial in the Royal Square. It shows Jersey time, which is eight minutes different to Greenwich meantime.

1890

The lifeboat *Sarah Brooshoft* was launched for her maiden rescue mission when a French lugger struck the Mangeuse reef. It took the crew of 13 men an hour to row to the scene, only to find the lugger wrecked and its crew aboard the mailboat. Although it had proved an unnecessary trip, it cost the lifeboat service the following: 10 shillings to each of the 13 crew, 2 shillings for each of the 19 people who helped launch the boat and 4 shillings per animal for the hire of six horses to pull the carriage.

16 October

1911

The discovery of a Neolithic tomb was made public. Spreckley Raworth had become curious about a mound on his land and decided to investigate. He began to excavate and uncovered a 12 ft long stone slab acting as a capstone over the tomb. Having made his discovery, he contacted the Sociètè Jersiaise, who then assisted in the excavation. Bone and flint heads were also unearthed.

1936

T B Davis wrote a letter to the States. He wished to commission a bronze statue of George V as a gift to the Island. Francis Doyle Jones was his preferred sculptor and his offer included the cost of a granite base and the statue's erection. The suggested site for it was the Royal Square. When the proposal went before the States it was met with applause, although some voiced the opinion that the new statue should not replace the current one. So it was agreed that the new statue would be placed in Howard Davis Park.

1987

Islanders woke up to some of the greatest damage the Island had ever seen after being battered overnight by hurricane force winds. The roof of the Mayfair Hotel had been ripped off, as had those of flats on Mont Millais and numerous other houses. Cars were crushed, glasshouses flattened and an enormous number of trees were blown over. The wind was funnelled up the Island's valleys, concentrating its destructive force so that in some areas not a tree remained upright.

1994

Police were hunting Kevin O'Brien, a doorman at Buzz night-club, after an assault on Jamie Le Sueur left Le Sueur fighting for his life. In what was said to be an unprovoked attack, Le Sueur had received severe head injuries and remained on a life support machine while police began a massive search for O'Brien. Having remained hidden for several weeks, O'Brien was finally caught when an accomplice tried to smuggle him, in disguise, aboard a private plane. But he was spotted and detained at the last minute.

17 October

1864

Elinor Sutherland, later Elinor Glynn, was born at No 1 St Saviour's Road on this day. A novelist and scriptwriter, she was also the first woman to produce a British 'talkie' film.

1897

An inquest was held into the death of Private William Townsend, who had been shot at Crabbé. Townsend and two others from the 2nd Battalion of the Gloucestershire Regiment had been acting as score markers at the Crabbé shooting range. Thinking that the target practice was over the men emerged. But it wasn't and Sergeant Davis pulled his trigger just as the men came out of their safe area. Private Townsend was hit in the back, the bullet going straight through him and hitting the target. Momentarily he was unaware of being shot but then he complained of chest pains. He was taken to the Hospital, where he died a few days later. The inquest jury found that the death had been caused by an error.

1906

Mr J Campbell sued Mr E Spriggs in the Petty Debts Court for killing his dog. Sprigg and his wife had been at First Tower buying second hand clothing. Mr Sprigg had apparently entered Campbell's property and struck the hound on the head with an umbrella, killing it. Campbell claimed the dog was quiet and worth £10, while Sprigg said it was merely an accident. Opinion as to the Airdales' value varied between £10 and 30 shillings but it mattered not as the judge ruled that it had been self defence and Sprigg was discharged.

1944

An order was issued, with immediate effect, banning everyone from local beaches. Previously swimming had been allowed at Grouville, St Clement and St Aubin's Bay. But it was now forbidden and only limpet and vraic gatherers were permitted on the shore, if they could persuade a German Commander to allow it.

18 October

1806

The States decided that Constables and members of the Honorary Police should have batons bearing the Royal Arms as well as Jersey's. The batons would in effect be a badge of office but might have doubled as a truncheon as well.

1824

The States decided to buy a new site for a market in St Aubin, with the building work to be funded by lotteries. A market at St Aubin is documented back to 1584 but had undoubtedly been established many years earlier.

1933

There were two attacks on women in the St Brelade area, the latest in a series of night-time assaults on women. In the first case, Miss King's progress to her drive was blocked by an abandoned car. When she left hers to investigate, she was grabbed by a man who had been hiding in nearby bushes. Her screams were heard by her mother who, taking a revolver, fired a warning shot, at which point the attacker fled. An hour or so later Mrs Graham was alerted to the fact that she had an intruder in the house by her dog. She climbed out of her bedroom window, intending to go for help, but the man gave chase and they struggled until she was overpowered. Desperately, Mrs Graham offered the man all the money in the house if he would go. He accepted and got away with about £1.

1936

Fire broke out in a butcher's shop in St Aubin and soon spread to four other shops, the Terminus Hotel and the railway station. The fire badly damaged the hotel and destroyed the shops, as well as the station roof and 16 of the latest and best carriages which were housed beneath it. The Jersey Railway and Tramways Company had already been losing money and after this disaster they never reopened. Just over a year later the company was wound up, the track, rolling stock and equipment having been already sold. Finally the States bought the remaining property for £25,000.

19 October

1542

Henry VIII's foreign policy seemed to be heading England towards a war with France. Jersey's defences were poor, with Mont Orgueil Castle still relying on bows and arrows for defence. On this day the States ordered the building of St Aubin's Tower, better known today as St Aubin's Fort.

1646

The English Royal household was short of money due to the Civil War and a rumour now spread that it was intended to sell the Channel Islands to France for 200,000 pistoles (a pistole equalled 18s or 90p). The rumour was plausible as the King had already offered Denmark the Orkney and Shetland Islands. So worried was Sir George de Carteret that he signed a pact with other English knights and even contemplated requesting aid from the Parliamentary forces.

1913

A potentially lethal case of vandalism occurred when a railway carriage in Snow Hill station was uncoupled and pushed until it reached the incline by Green Street. The runaway carriage then smashed through four sets of crossing gates before coming to rest at Grève d'Azette. No one was hurt and the culprit was caught.

1940

A horse-drawn bus service was introduced, as petrol shortages had limited motor bus services. The service was to cover the town suburbs but it did not run for long, due to lack of support.

1982

The tetrapak was replaced by a gable topped milk carton. When introduced, the pyramidal shaped tetrapak had been less than popular. The unusual shape had meant that it did not stack or fit into a refrigerator very well and Jersey's rich milk tended to leave a thick layer of separated cream around the top of the carton. Over the years, the Jersey people's dislike for this ridiculous packaging had not diminished and the new carton was immediately accepted.

20 October

1651

A force of 3,000 Parliamentarians in 84 vessels were anchored in St Ouen's Bay. Sir George de Carteret had 2,000 men at his disposal, made up of the militia, professional soldiers and others pressed into service. This force was spread thinly around possible landing sites, with the bulk encamped on the dunes at St Ouen. The following day a boat was dispatched from the fleet to negotiate a settlement. Sir George ordered it to be attacked and, as the small boat withdrew, the defending force nearly mutinied as they had no wish to fight for the lost Royalist cause.[43]

1680

A Commissioner of Customs was appointed to Jersey after English customs noticed that the Island was importing more tobacco than it could possibly use. The Commissioner seemed to think the whole Island was conspiring against him, as he was unable to get help from either the Jurats or Constables and he was often beaten up.

1925

The Privy Council began talks with Island authorities on the British Treasury's request for an annual contribution of £303,000, plus a lump sum of £870,000, to cover pensions from the Great War. After lengthy discussions, the Island authorities offered a lump sum of £500,000 as a free and final gift. This was unacceptable to the British Government, who reduced their demands to £80,000 annually for 40 years. The meeting ended without agreement.

1938

A full scale air raid exercise, watched by thousands, was held on Victoria Avenue. West Park Pavilion acted as a headquarters, with motor bike dispatch riders relaying messages to where the action was. Simulated bomb, gas and incendiary attacks were dealt with by the volunteers, who had given up their half day holiday to test the Island's readiness for attack.

---

[43] See 23rd October for further details.

21 October

1805

The Battle of Trafalgar had nothing to do with Jersey but as a consequence of the French and Spanish fleets' defeat the fear of French invasion was lifted from the Island.

1905

The Reverend James McCann of All Saints Church stood before the Royal Court, accused of performing a marriage in an unauthorised place, without a licence and of issuing a false marriage certificate. The couple, Mr and Mrs Samson, would also have been in trouble had they known they were being married illegally, which they did not. Their marriage would have been void, but as they were unaware of the offence, it was valid.

The Reverend's Advocate admitted the offence but stated that it had been accidental. McCann was 75 years old, in poor health and his memory was failing. He had only conducted the marriage because the couple were poor and no fee had been charged. The court somewhat reluctantly fined the Reverend £20 and sent him to prison for 48 hours, without hard labour.

1911

The court was told of a raid on No 11 Bond Street and the illegal bookmaking that was undertaken there. The building was used to take bets on horse racing in England and football matches. A number of people had been arrested and now faced the authorities. The betting operation was quite extensive, with betting slips being found in other properties and locally stationed troops frequent visitors to the premises. By the time the court had finished with the gamblers, it had imposed a total of £127 in fines.

1960

Val de la Mare reservoir was officially opened, or rather closed. The dam was not completed but the gates were closed and the reservoir began to fill. This was aided by over an inch of rain that fell the following day.

22 October

1645

On this day Civil War diarist Jean Chevalier records the events surrounding Parliamentary supporter Clement Gallie. When Gallie went before the court charged with treason, he confessed. Kneeling, pleading for mercy and renouncing the Parliamentary cause, Gallie was fined 2,000 ecus. Gallie then set about gathering the money. He sold most of his property and called in his debts. When people refused to pay him he returned to court and obtained an order for payment. Once he had gathered all his wealth, rather than paying off his fine, he escaped to France. Left behind were a furious court, an embarrassed guard and Gallie's wife and children.

1685

On this day the Edict of Nantes was revoked. Ninety years earlier the Huguenots had been granted freedom to worship their religion. With this freedom now removed an enormous exodus from France began. Nearly half a million people fled the State persecution and several thousand set up home in Jersey, many becoming leading citizens in Island life.

1869

The States gave permission for the construction of a railway to run between the two towns of St Aubin and St Helier. An original proposition allowing the Jersey Railway Company to 'take possession of all the seashore below the high-water mark of spring tides' was dropped. It would have involved an enormous area of land as no sea wall existed between West Park and St Aubin's at the time. The States gave the company three months in which to start the work and only 12 months after that to complete the line.

1960

Jersey's eighth road death of the year occurred when a person was riding a light motorcycle up Mont Cochon. The 68 year old man was a learner, only holding a provisional licence, and died from head injuries sustained after hitting a telegraph pole.

23 October

1651

A Parliamentary force of 3,000 men landed in St Ouen's Bay, having spent the previous three days sailing around the Island from bay to bay, gradually wearing down the Jersey army who had to march over land to intercept them. The night before Sir George de Carteret had scouted around the rocks, keeping watch on his enemy, only to find on his return to camp that half his men had vanished. As the game of cat and mouse proceeded an ever increasing number of men had got fed up and gone home. When the landing finally came the battle was short, but bloody. The local forces quickly withdrew, leaving Sir George to head for safety in Elizabeth Castle. St Aubin's Fort had recently been strengthened and orders were given to hold it against the advancing foe, an instruction completely ignored as the garrison mutinied and surrendered almost immediately, leaving the English fleet with a safe harbouring facility.

1911

A fire destroyed farm buildings at La Commune, St Peter, on a dark and stormy night. As the three horses pulling the fire engine galloped along, the firemen could see the glow from as far away as Westmount. Soldiers from St Peter's Barracks also attended with fire buckets but to no avail. The roof of the outbuildings soon fell in and efforts were then concentrated on saving the farm house, which was in danger as the severe wind was carrying the flames towards it.

1962

The 70 year old wreck of the *SS Mera* was blown up. It had been a hazard to small vessels around the Minquiers ever since an earlier salvage attempt had gone wrong and the cargo ship had sunk. Divers placed 250 lbs of gelignite, which solved the problem.

1968

A filter-in-turn roundabout was introduced at Bel Royal. This unique Channel Island traffic system has since worked well in winter months. In the summer months, however, the Island's visitors seem unable to comprehend the idea that you have to take turns.

24 October

1651

A Parliamentary frigate was caught in a sudden storm while at anchor outside St Aubin's Bay. Attempting to get to safety off St Aubin's Fort she struck rocks and was wrecked, with all hands on board perishing. The loss of life was probably about 90 men but some records claim as many as 300 were killed.

1876

A dispute over the ownership of a lane leading to Portelet Bay flared up and the Clameur de Haro was raised. Thomas Rose had ordered that a trench be dug across the lane after his neighbour Arthur Jones left for town. Later in the day Thomas Pincheon, Jones' employee, found the 3 ft deep trench and, worried that it was dangerous, filled it in again. When Rose saw what Pincheon had done, he raised the Clameur. In court Pincheon, who was unfamiliar with the ancient Island law, said that when Rose had fallen to his knees and chanted 'Haro Haro Haro', Pincheon had thought Rose was having a fit. The court, despite describing the case as 'petty' and 'childish', found in Rose's favour and Pincheon and Jones were fined. This, however, was not the end of the matter.[44]

1950

An official notice informed Islanders that cars under three years old could no longer be exported to England. The move was an attempt to try to halt the exodus of good second hand cars that were leaving the Island. The supply of new cars was poor and getting worse and the motor trade were concerned that the lack of vehicles would put garages out of business.

1968

Another Clameur de Haro was raised on this day by Mr Hamel of Jambert Farm, St Clement, when his right of way through a quarry in Grouville was bulldozed away. The court found that the Clameur had been raised correctly and fined those responsible £5.

---

[44] See 17th July for further details.

25 October

1154

Henry II's accession to the throne reunited the kingdoms of England and Normandy and consequently the Channel Islands too. Thus after a split of 67 years Jersey again fell into the same realm as England.

1870

The Jersey Railway Company officially opened the Island's first train service. The fare from St Helier to St Aubin was 6d first class and 4d second class, with a first class return costing 9d. After travelling the 3¾ miles to St Aubin the official party continued by horse and carriage to Noirmont Manor where a meal of 'sumptuous proportion' awaited them. Official events generally have a great many speeches and in this case they went on until 6 o'clock, leaving the train scheduled to return the party to St Helier at 5.30 pm waiting.

1932

In the summer timetable of 1932 the JMT announced that in future the company would only purchase new vehicles. The promise didn't last long as on this day 16 second hand buses were acquired from the West Yorkshire Road Car Co.

1935

The motor traffic law was presented before the States and approved. This replaced the law of 1890 which required the Constable of a parish in which public carriages were kept to inspect them annually before issuing a one shilling licence permitting them to ply for hire. The new law centralised the licensing of buses and other public vehicles and was brought in with motor traffic in mind, something which the law makers of 1890 could not have considered. Among the new regulations it stated that a bus may be used as a coach but a coach may not be used as a bus, and to that end numbered plates with 'char-a-banc' are attached to all coaches so that the difference can be seen.

26 October

1804

Philippe d'Auvergne's flag ship, the *Severn*, was wrecked in a violent storm in Grouville Bay. It was d'Auvergne who had been responsible for stirring up trouble in Brittany which had distracted a potential French invasion fleet. He ran guns to the rebels, spied for the British and engaged in a little privateering.

1861

Walter Matthew Gallichan was born on this day. He regarded himself as a pioneer of sex education and published, among others, the following titles: *The Blight of Respectability, Woman under Polygamy, The Great Unmarried, Modern Woman and How to Manage Her,* and *Youth and Maidenhood, or Sex Knowledge for Young People.*

1899

An advert that regularly appeared in local newspapers did so again on this day. It read: 'Old false teeth bought. Many ladies and gentlemen have them, old or disused false teeth, which might as well be turned into money.' Vendors merely sent their teeth through the post to England, where they were valued and the money returned.

1921

Cyclists who ignored the Constable of St Helier's recent order against leaning bicycles against shops found it to be no idle threat. On this morning a 5 shilling fine was levied on a number of offenders.

1947

Three people were killed and two injured in one of Jersey's worst road crashes of the time. A Hillman Tourer struck a granite pillar while travelling down Trinity Main Road. The car was torn apart as it skidded on, ending up rammed against a wall.

27 October

1862

William McDonald and William Taylor were jailed for theft and assault. Both men were privates in the 18th Regiment, Royal Irish, and had stolen a bottle of sweetmeats and a bowl containing a few coppers from a public house, as well as assaulting and robbing Clement Asselyn and assaulting Jane Hardy. The defence counsel claimed that both accused were of good character and blamed 'the cheapness of drink in this Island'. The Bailiff, before passing a sentence of nine months hard labour, declared the men to be a disgrace to the uniform. However, the following year these two were among a group of seven prisoners, jailed for similar offences, to be given a free pardon on the instructions of Queen Victoria, the authorisation being initialled by the Monarch herself.

1897

A three-year old girl, Eugenie Marie Kerambrun, died after falling 150 ft over a cliff near the Wolf's Caves. François Kerambrun, accompanied by his family, was cutting furze on the cliffs of Frèmont. Mrs Kerambrun, having taken one load of furze back to their cottage, was returning when the little girl ran ahead of her, tripped and fell into a small bay below. The *Jersey Evening Post* report of the accident stated that 'they found the poor little thing dreadfully mangled, its head being battered almost beyond recognition'.

1899

It was decided that Jersey needed a casino and a number of meetings were held to push the project on. The Jersey Commercial Association and the Chamber of Commerce had met to discuss the question of 'much needed attractions'. The increasing number of visitors that the steamers were bringing to Jersey were to be encouraged and the facility of a casino was described as 'vital' if they were to keep coming. It was unanimously agreed that a site to the west of the town would be the most suitable spot for such an amusement and there was even an offer to construct the required building.

28 October

1645

Etienne Maret was killed in a bizarre accident. Two hundred new soldiers were being drilled in the Market Place[45]. Drawn up in ranks they were ordered to fire a volley in salute. However one of the musket balls discharged sideways and shot Maret in the throat. 'The man fell dead in his place without speaking or moving much', diarist Jean Chevalier recalled in his journal of the time.

1805

Daniel Dumaresq died aged 93 on this day, having influenced some of the great historical figures of his time. He was born in Trinity and after impressive achievements in college abandoned academia. He became chaplain in an English factory in St Petersburg and learned to speak Russian, even translating books. Dumaresq became well known in the Russian Court and to Catherine the Great. Later he became Rector of a small English parish, only to be lured back to Russia to establish an education system. Catherine instructed him to set up primary and secondary schools throughout her empire. Dumaresq went on to do the same in Poland before again returning to England. George III held him in high regard, as did Pitt but he turned down high positions in favour of a small rectory.

1831

The States decided to take special precautions to combat cholera. A health office was to be opened and hospitals prepared in each parish.

1944

The German occupying forces took over an empty shop in King Street and filled its display windows with foodstuffs that were in short supply. All the produce had come from a black marketer's store room and signs condemning the thriving black market were placed among the display. At the end of the day the food was taken for use in the public kitchens.

---

[45] Known today as the Royal Square.

29 October

1646

A fight took place between two sailors who had been drinking together as friends. After the quarrel broke out they started throwing things at each other. They then went outside and drew knives.

The smaller man, named Andrew Lawrence, was thrown to the ground and stabbed in the belly 'from which fat and blood poured out, though his bowels were not injured'. The larger man, Janson Garret, then stooped to stab Lawrence again. As Garret bent down, Lawrence knifed him in the chest.

Garret then got up, seemingly uninjured, and returned to the inn. Silently he sat down at a table before suddenly crying 'Oh Lord, I am dead'. At which point he fell backwards stone dead.

The badly wounded Lawrence was cared for and was eventually acquitted by a jury for killing Garret.

1811

The packet *Chesterfield* was attacked off Guernsey by a Cherbourg privateer. One passenger was killed and others were injured when the French ship *L'Epruvier*, boarded the mail-carrying vessel. However, before the privateers had taken the *Chesterfield* the mail and military dispatches had been deliberately sunk, thus preventing them falling into enemy hands.

The Post Office, whose business the *Chesterfield* had been on, paid £1,626 compensation to her owner, Captain Starrwood, the money being used to buy a replacement ship which he also named the *Chesterfield*.

1968

An appeal was launched to raise £17,500 to restore La Rocco tower. The States had backed the proposal to reinstate the Napoleonic fortress and said they would put up half the cost if the public contributed the remainder. The *Jersey Evening Post*, which launched the appeal, started it off with a donation of £100.

30 October

1897

Mr P de Carteret of St John was brutally assaulted outside the Great Eastern Hotel. De Carteret, a blacksmith, had been approached by two brothers while sitting in the hotel bar. The two men, John and Arthur de Gruchy, had tried to pick a fight with de Carteret but were thrown out by the landlord.

Later, as he mounted his bicycle to head home, de Carteret was set upon and severely beaten. The brothers 'who bear a bad character in the neighbourhood' were traced and arrested, while de Carteret was detained in hospital.

1903

The ever-growing city of London required building materials and on this day the first cargo of granite was shipped to London from Ronez quarries.

1947

It was decided to rename Clifton Park Estate. Grasett Estates, as it was now called, a tribute to Jersey's Lieutenant Governor, was the site of a large States housing scheme, the first ones being just about complete. The three bedroom semis had kitchens fitted with modern sinks incorporating hot and cold water. The toilets were outside but close to the house and each home cost the States £1,500.

1962

The Public Works Committee backed down over plans to turn part of the Royal Square into a car park for States Members. Lines had been painted on the granite as an experiment. If successful it was Public Works' intention to remove some of the granite slabs and make a permanent parking area. Islanders were outraged that a public area of historical importance was to be used for parking for a select few and the Committee and its president, Deputy Vernon Tomes, reversed their decision.

31 October

1649

All the Island's militia gathered on St Aubin's beach, where they were inspected by Charles II

1855

On this day Victor Hugo left Jersey to set up home in Guernsey. A weekly paper, *L'Homme*, had published a letter criticising Queen Victoria for meeting the French leader, Napoleon III. The Governor expelled the newspaper's three editors for printing such an outrageous letter. Hugo and 35 other supporters signed a protest against the expulsions and were promptly banished themselves. Jersey may have been famous, or infamous, for its tolerant attitudes but Queen Victoria was held in the highest esteem locally and attacks on her were not welcomed.

1901

Theophile Pierre Le Blancq, aged 19, was sentenced for riding his bicycle at a dangerous speed and for having no lamp or bell. Le Blancq had been cycling near Rozel Lodge when he had knocked down Priscilla Esther Le Huquet, causing her injury. Mr Mallet, who had witnessed the accident, told the court that Le Blancq had been thrown from his machine and when asked where his bell was, the accused had produced it from his pocket. The Magistrate said that Le Blancq had no excuse but he would not be too harsh as he had been injured in his fall. Le Blancq was fined a total of £1 and was also held responsible for the damage caused.

1940

The order to introduce tobacco rationing was given. The Island's population had been well aware that this order was coming and in the previous days long queues had formed outside tobacconists' shops. The weekly allowance for men over 18 years was to be 20 cigarettes or 10 cigarillos or 5 cigars, as well as 2 ozs of tobacco. During the next 4½ years smokers tried just about everything they could think of as a substitute and a lot of tobacco was grown in private gardens.

01 November

1921

The Building and Allied Workers, who had been striking for a month, were joined by the gas company workers. At noon the gas was cut off and as the majority of light was produced by gas this caused a number of businesses to change their hours or close early.

1934

The bus war was hotting up again and on this day the Safety Coach Service (SCS) drastically reduced its fares, with a return ticket to Gorey coming down to 6½d. The rivalry between the JMT and SCS had gone on for some time. However, they had come to an arrangement, dividing the Island into two, with each company only running services on their half. The fly in the ointment was Joe's Bus Service, which had started running buses from Millbrook to Gorey, crossing both companies' territories.

1941

All drapery, clothing and shoe shops were closed on this day and were ordered to stay closed until 4th November when a new rationing system would come into operation. Textile ration books were issued as the authorities tried to ensure that the Island's stocks were shared out fairly. On the same day three Islanders appeared before the Royal Court for infringing the regulations on rationing, one for a food ration book fraud and the other two for trading in rationed goods.

1959

Jersey residents wishing to phone someone could, for the first time, dial direct. Previously callers picked up the handset and asked the operator to connect them to their required number. The central telephone exchange had 5,300 lines and to the amazement of Deputy Venables, who made the first call, it all worked perfectly. One problem did occur with callers who did not understand about dialling and waited with the handset until an engineer investigating what appeared to be a fault came on the line and could explain the new system to them.

02 November

1829

The foundation stone of the Esplanade was laid as Jersey's building boom continued. Already in this year Union Street had been made public, the pier at Bouley Bay had been completed and Rozel harbour built.

1872

A Norwegian ship loaded with 200 tons of timber set off a distress signal after striking rocks around the Ecréhous. Three men set out in the *Mayflower* from Rozel Harbour in response, despite the gale force winds and heavy seas.

At first twelve of the crew were taken off and landed on the Ecréhous, allowing the local men to return to the stricken vessel and take off the remaining six crew, returning with them to Rozel. The following day they returned to the reef and collected the original twelve men rescued.

As a reward for their bravery the RNLI gave Messieurs Blampied, Whitley and Bouchard each a silver medal and £5.

1903

St Lawrence Elementary School opened its doors to pupils for the first time. Costing £3,650 and able to seat 232 scholars, each room had a large grate fire. Of the two playgrounds, one was for boys, the other for girls, and within the yards there were the respective lavatories.

1967

The storms that battered Jersey's south coast caused over £100,000 worth of damage. Granite capping stones littered the Esplanade after the waves breached the sea wall. The sandbag defences were swept away and areas of the town were flooded. Gorey and Le Bourg were also inundated by the tide and its debris.

03 November

1646

A party of English captains were drinking in a tavern in the La Motte area. An Irish captain joined them, having been walking in what was then the countryside. Placing his pistol on the table, the military man enjoyed his beer. Earlier he had tried to shoot a crow but the half cocked gun had failed to go off.

Captain Hopton now joined the gathering, sitting in direct line of the gun. As the Irish Captain's boy gathered his master's belongings on their departure, the pistol discharged. Captain Hopton stood up and cried 'Oh Lord, I am wounded' as the full charge hit him. He died minutes later. Captain Hopton's body was buried in St Helier Church, the ceremony taking place at night because the corpse had been late arriving.

1898

Jack Counter was born in this day. He won the Victoria Cross in the First World War and was later garrisoned in the Island, which became his home in 1919. He swapped his army uniform for that of the Post Office and was so highly regarded within the Island that Jack Counter Close at First Tower bears his name.

1914

It was announced that the appeal to buy a motor ambulance for the Red Cross had well exceeded the target, with two ambulances now being paid for. Over £872 had been raised, which was to pay for the *Duke of Normandy* and the *Jersey*.

1959

It was reported that so far this year 99 people had been deported from the Island at a cost to the tax payer of nearly £300. Sending destitute people back to England cost £3 0s 6d in fares and that did not include the expense of feeding them while they were in custody, nor for their court appearance. By the end of the year, the number had risen to 105 - 71 less than in the previous year.

04 November

1905

With the introduction of compulsory education, parents began being brought to court for their children's non-attendance. Two such cases came up on this day.

Joseph Bequest of St Martin was charged with failing to send his sons Joe and John to school. Bequest claimed his children 'played truant'. Alfred Le Marche of St Ouen faced a similar charge and claimed his son Philip had been ill.

Both fathers were ordered to ensure their sons attended school in future and were fined 2s 6d per child.

1938

Jersey's worst air accident to date occurred just before 11 am on this day when a Jersey Airlines DH86 aeroplane named *St Catherine's Bay* crashed into a St Peter field shortly after takeoff. A farm worker was killed, as were the 13 people on board, when the aircraft exploded in flames.

1939

Food ration books were issued for the first time. Although rationing was not as yet necessary, food shortages were expected by the end of the year. The books were identical to those issued in Britain, with a slip inserted to cover Island peculiarities.

1940

The German authorities issued an order banning meetings of unions, associations and societies. The doors of the Masonic Temple were sealed and the many Island clubs and institutions were suspended indefinitely. The order also outlawed the wearing of 'distinguishing marks' and flags were not to be displayed.

Three months later the Germans ransacked the Masonic Temple and sent their booty to Berlin.

05 November

1585

Jean Mourant confessed at his trial to being acquainted with the Devil and to have indulged in sorcery. He was therefore sentenced to be strangled until he was dead, then his body burnt, and his goods and chattels confiscated.

1802

An area of land in the Royal Square was ceded to the British Government by the States for the construction of a guard house. The guard house remained in use until 1926 and was later sold by the British Government. More recently the site has been occupied by the National Westminster Bank.

1900

Workmen laying a new road at First Tower first received a drenching from Mrs Pinel, then saw Centenier John Pinel on his knees, calling for the assistance of a long dead prince, all in an attempt to halt their work. The road workers had begun digging up the Pinel's garden in order to turn it into a public road. An enraged Mrs Pinel had turned the hosepipe on them, having summoned her husband. But only when the Clameur de Haro was raised did the work stop. In court the Roads Committee admitted changing the planned alignment of the new road, thus taking it through the Pinel's garden. However, despite stating that the Roads Committee had acted improperly, the court fined Centenier Pinel for raising the Clameur inappropriately.

1951

At a bonfire night party put on by the Airport Social Club, 13-year old Patrick Sheehan was killed and Claude Steara fatally injured when an oil drum exploded. Waste oil had been bucketed on to the fire to get it going. At the end of the evening spilled oil caught fire, running to the oil drum, which blew apart the metal container, hitting the two victims. A number of others suffered injuries, either from the blast or from flying debris.

06 November

1772

Field Marshall Henry Seymour Conway was sworn in as Jersey's new Governor. It was Conway who was responsible for the construction of most of the Martello towers, guard houses and small fortresses that can be found around the Island. Once the American War of Independence broke out the French sided with the colonies and declared war on England. Once again Jersey was under threat and it was Conway who intended to stop a Gallic invasion.

1856

Concerned by the recent attempted interference by Britain in the Island's legislature, the States realised reform was necessary if home rule was to survive. On this day a law was passed creating 14 Deputies' seats in the States. Up until then the States had been made up of Jurats, Rectors and Constables. It was not that long ago that States meetings had been held in secret.

1957

The space race was just beginning and Jersey residents got their first sighting of the Russian satellite Sputnik 11. Among those who saw the spacecraft was Brother Francis of de la Salle College, who had watched it cross the face of the moon in the early evening.

1975

Alphonse Le Gastelois, the self styled king of the Ecréhous, was found not guilty of arson. He had been accused of setting fire to one of the cottages on the reef. But he claimed his accuser had done so maliciously, after they had fallen out over the salvage of a dingy. Le Gastelois was 61 and had lived on the Ecréhous for 14 years. The fisherman had been under suspicion of the sex attacks committed by Paisnel and partly to prove his innocence he had set up home on the reef. There he had lived the life of a hermit, viewed with suspicion by some, as eccentric by others. When he came to trial over the fire La Gastelois claimed that he owned the reef, having occupied it for so long, a claim rejected by the court. But Alphonse Le Gastelois had become an Island legend.

07 November

1748

On this day Jean Baptiste was appointed as Jersey's first librarian. Almost exactly a year earlier the States had been informed that the public library was ready for use. The actual building had been completed in April 1742, having been started five years earlier, the whole project having been initiated in 1729.

1806

The foundation stone was laid at Fort Regent by the Lieutenant Governor, General Don. The unusual thing about this foundation stone is that it is located above the central entrance arch and was obviously merely an excuse for a little pomp. Work had actually started on 1st February and by the time of the foundation ceremony construction was well under way.

1972

A change in law, allowing the States Police unrestricted access to all parts of Jersey, was agreed unanimously. Up until this point, the States Police could only operate in a parish if the Constable gave them permission. This meant that police patrolling the Island were technically operating outside the law. This was one of the many proposals that were intended to bring about more efficient policing in the Island without destroying the Honorary system which had served Jersey for centuries.

1989

The Ring of Spiritual Enlightenment, an association of astrologers and clairvoyants, decided to go to the European Court of Human Rights if the law banning payment for their services was not repealed. Although the law had been in existence for a considerable time, it had not been enforced and donations were received by the seers. A year earlier the Association had gathered a 2,000 signature petition asking that astrologers and clairvoyants be allowed to charge for their services which they intended to present to Senator Terry Le Main. But at the last minute he left a message saying he could not attend the meeting, which perhaps the group should have foreseen.

08 November

1904

On this day the *Conqueror* left Newfoundland fully laden with its cargo of cod. Nothing was ever heard of it again.

1964

Jersey was bathed in a cloud of radioactive dust. Well, that was the premise of a civil emergency exercise that finished on this day. Fifty volunteers gave up their weekend to man their posts as part of this NATO simulation encompassing the UK and Europe. The scenario was that various UK cities had been attacked with nuclear bombs and the radioactive cloud was drifting our way. The headquarters was an ex-German bunker, the exercise being to ensure that lines of communication could be maintained in an emergency.

1977

Finance and Economics president Senator Cyril Le Marquand told the States that there would be no £10 Christmas bonus for pensioners this year as it was 'not a proper use of public funds'. This did not please some Members, with Deputy Bob Small bringing a proposition to pay the £10, Senator Jim Scriven amending it to £20 and Deputy Brian Troy wanting it to go to widows and the disabled too. But no bonus was forthcoming. Over 2,000 Islanders held a rally in the Royal Square on 13th December to protest about the decision.

1989

The Public Works Department held a press conference to announce that Government House would have to be demolished. The estimated cost of repairs was £2.4 million, whereas a completely new purpose-built structure would cost just over £2 million. Once the scheme had become publicly known a movement to preserve the historic building gained momentum. Deputy John Le Gallais, the committee's president, wanted the work to take place when the Lieutenant Governors changed over in the spring of 1990, saying that if the work did not go ahead, there would be a delay of five years. This announcement galvanised those campaigning to save the building and several governors later the building remains.

09 November

1939

Mayfair Hotel proprietor Arthur Woodhall appeared before the court, charged with having published a blasphemous libel. Woodhall had given in his passport in order to get a permit to travel to England. While examining the passport two photographs were found to have been left in the back of the document. The first showed a man and a woman in bathing suits, the other showed Woodhall in a swimming costume, lying on his back with his arms outstretched. On the print someone had drawn a cross around the body so that it appeared that the man had been crucified. Woodhall said that one of his guests had embellished the print and that he (Woodhall) did not believe it was blasphemous. He was placed on £100 bail while the wheels of justice ground on. Hearings on whether the court could hear such a case went on into December. The case did not get to trial until January, with the verdict being given on 10th February.

1948

The Island elected its first twelve senators in an atmosphere of apathy. The term of office was nine years with four seats coming up every three years. As this was the start of a new system, the four most popular candidates were in for nine years, the next four for six and the last four for three. This new electoral system threw up at least one surprise when Jurat Le Masurier, before one of the Island's most powerful politicians, came in near the bottom of the poll.

1961

Judgement was given in the Royal Court in the case of Dorey versus Hannam for the death of cyclist Francis Dorey by George Hannam's car. £1,000 was demanded for loss of expectation of life, £66 for funeral expenses and £4,000 for pecuniary loss suffered by the widow. This was the first time that Jersey courts had been asked to put a value on a human life. The funeral expenses were granted and the court ruled that £1,787 should go to the widow for her pecuniary loss. But the value of this human life, the court decided, was £300. Both sides appealed.

10 November

1651

The Parliamentary forces who were besieging Elizabeth Castle had a lucky shot with big bertha, an enormous mortar. The descending bomb hit the Abbey inside the Castle, which had stood for over 500 years, falling straight through the roof, the floor below and ending in the lowest storey. The twelve barrels of gunpowder stored in the Abbey contributed to the massive explosion which not only completely destroyed the Abbey but also the adjoining buildings. The lowest account of the dead is 16 but as many as 50 may have been killed.

The terror that ensued resulted in a number of desertions, five of whom were captured. As a punishment, five pieces of paper were prepared. On two were drawn a gibbet, the other three being left blank. Lots were drawn and an Englishman and a Jerseymen received the unlucky papers. The Englishman was forcibly rescued by his fellow countrymen but no one stood up for the Jerseyman.

The three remaining deserters now drew straws, another local choosing the short one and thus became the executioner. The condemned man was stood on the battlement with a noose around his neck, the other end being secured to a cannon. He was then pushed over by his comrade.

1920

A partial eclipse of the sun was seen in Jersey. Beginning at 1.47 and ending at 5.57, the clear skies enabled Islanders to follow its progress throughout the afternoon, with the phenomena ending as the sun was setting.

1960

D H Lawrence's book *Lady Chatterley's Lover* went on sale in local bookshops, having been cleared of obscenity charges in England the previous week. Booksellers in Jersey had been inundated with orders but some stockists sought advise from the Attorney General before putting it on open sale.

11 November

1918

The declaration of the armistice was initially met with lethargy. However, news soon spread, bunting and flags were hoisted and a carnival atmosphere was created. Jersey's Roll of Honour was 862 killed, 6,292 served and 31 French residents killed. The Island's financial contribution to the First World War had been £500,000.

1923

Five years after the ending of the Great War, a large crowd watched the unveiling of the Cenotaph. Built as a tribute to the Island's 'glorious dead', the last post was sounded and the guns at Fort Regent boomed a salute. In his address, the Lieutenant Governor paid tribute to the thousands of Jerseymen and one hundred Frenchmen who had left the Island to fight a common enemy.

1930

A series of earth tremors shook Jersey on this day. They started at about 6.30 pm and continued until 10.30 pm. None were particularly violent, with their intensity varying throughout the Island.

1977

Radical new proposals to review the States loan scheme were published. Among the suggestions was that property worth up to £30,000 would now qualify for a loan. At the time loans could only be obtained on property worth up to £16,000. It was said that 4,000 new homes were to be built in the next decade and land was to be rezoned. Interest rates were to be fixed and loans were to be made available for long lease flats.

1980

By a vote of 25 to 23, the States decided to flood Queen's Valley. The marathon debate had taken 10 hours, the outcome remaining in doubt until the actual vote. The plan was to increase Jersey's water storage capacity by damming the valley, creating a reservoir able to hold 250 million gallons. Those opposed to the scheme had battled for a number of years and continued to do so.

12 November

1847

The *Courier*, purpose built for the Channel Island route, made her maiden voyage. The paddle steamer regularly visited Jersey during her uneventful life. Her classic lines were captured by the painter Ouless in 1853, with Elizabeth Castle in the background.

1923

On this day the Jersey United Services Club was opened by the Lieutenant Governor and the Bailiff. The ex-servicemen's club was designed to be a 'home from home where kindred spirits could meet and swap again those thousand and one yarns of the Great War' and 'laugh over the glad times spent on the fields of Flanders'.

1924

A ritual cursed by most Islanders was inaugurated on this day. Outside 60 David Place the first paving stone was lifted for the laying of electric cable. The Jersey Electricity Company's activities were accompanied by a party of officials and the inevitable speech-making. The first cable laid in St Helier was the forerunner to the annual winter road digging we all love so much.

1951

Alfred Chapron escaped from Newgate Street Prison while awaiting transfer to England to serve his four year sentence for robbery. The 22-year old got away on a bicycle, having scaled the gaol walls. There were numerous reported sightings during Chapron's week of liberty, but the manhunt ended in Aquila Road. Chapron was found at his home and despite his flight across the roofs of neighbouring houses, he eventually 'came quietly'.

1992

Jersey's £9.5 million underpass took its first traffic, in the shape of a 1957 double decker bus. Rumours claimed that the bridges had been built too low and that large vehicles would get wedged underneath. The double decker, being the tallest vehicle in the Island, took an official party along the road to prove that all was well.

13 November

1750

Charles Lempriere was sworn in as Lieutenant Bailiff. As the Bailiff never visited Jersey, Lempriere was free to use the power of his office as he pleased but his dictatorial attitude made him many enemies during his 31 years in office. In the latter part of Lempriere's tenure a brilliant young Advocate named Jean Dumaresq challenged him, causing Islanders to split into two camps. Lempriere's supporters were the Charlots, Dumaresq's the Magots (cheese mites). Between 1773 and 1781 the two parties battled it out, but with every election Dumaresq's position became stronger until Lempriere eventually resigned his post and left for England. The elections that won the Magots their power were fought ferociously by both sides, it being common practise to bribe, intimidate or kidnap voters. Hauling people from their beds and abandoning them on the Ecréhous for the day to ensure they would not vote, or keeping them drunk, were common occurrences.

1940

The military zones within the Island were extended by the German occupying authorities, further restricting access to parts of the Island. From this day the area containing St Ouen's pond, the airport and Les Brayes slip were out of bounds at certain times. Anyone found in the military zones was liable to arrest, the sentries having orders to shoot at anyone who ignored their challenge.

1950

Homes were flooded after 3½ inches of rain had fallen over the previous four days. The situation was exacerbated by the spring tides, with people at Grève d'Azette, St Luke's Crescent and St Peter's Valley being inundated. Mrs Paxton, who lived in Tesson Mill, having been flooded and the water subsided, lit a fire to dry her home out, only for it to be flooded again the following day.

1972

It was election day for Senators and John Averty topped the poll to become, at age 25, the youngest Senator ever elected.

14 November

1212

A document originating from King John makes the first mention of Mont Orgueil Castle. In the letter John tells how he has appointed Philip d'Aubigny as 'Keeper of the Island within our Castle'. At this time d'Aubigny was paid 40 marks from the Treasurer for the fortifications of Jersey.

1927

The Safety Coach Service first appeared on the Island's roads, providing a bus service from Cheapside to Grève d'Azette. Using a specially fitted out Morris Commercial with 18 seats, all of which faced inwards, the Red Band Bus, as it was called at first, was an immediate success. The enterprise, which added to the already numerous bus companies, was founded by two members of the Salvation Army, which meant no Sunday service. It also lead to the service being nicknamed "The Hallelujahs". When two years later the ever expanding routes demanded a Sunday service, one of the founders withdrew from the firm because of his religious scruples.

1967

The States unanimously rejected joining the EEC when the Common Market Committee reported its findings. In a speech lasting almost 1½ hours, Senator Ralph Vibert, president of the committee, warned of a constitutional crisis if the UK government extended the Treaty of Rome to Jersey. The special report was much praised within the Chamber and was to lead to the position where although Britain is in the Common Market and Jersey is a part of Great Britain, Jersey remains outside the European Community.

1979

It was reported that a local company, part owned by Sir Billy Butlin, had taken over the Miss World competition. Over £1 million had been spent acquiring the title from Grand Metropolitan Hotels, whose subsidiary Mecca had previously run the contest. Sir Billy was said to have become involved because he had started beauty competitions in Butlin Holiday Camps over 30 years earlier.

15 November

1496

Henry VII authorised the founding of a second grammar school in Jersey. Jean Neel and Vincent Tehy, who became mayor of Southampton, put up the funds and built it by an old chapel of St Anastase in a lane off St Peter's Valley.

The school survived until the middle of the 19th century but the endowments are now used for scholarships to Victoria College.

1788

The first public transport service was started by Richard Monk, who operated between St Helier and St Aubin, Saturdays only. The service ran 'tide permitting' because the route taken was directly across the sand, there being no roads to speak of at that time.

1897

Mr F Jeandron of New Street was charged with attempted murder and suicide. Jeandron had recently bought a revolver from Albert Hunt's shop, claiming he wanted the pistol to shoot cats. Hunt loaded the gun as requested but due to Jeandron's strange manner had used blank cartridges.

On this day, having threatened to shoot his wife earlier, Jeandron chased his wife and children, the family finally locking themselves in an upstairs room. Jeandron shot twice through the keyhole at his wife and then shot himself.

Centenier Downer and two police officers attended the scene and found Jeandron threatening to shoot them too. The men regrouped, entering the property through a different entrance, and found the desperado laying with the gun by his side and blood trickling from his ear.

Thanks to Hunt's wise actions, the only person hurt was Jeandron, who was able to walk to the Hospital for treatment. The wound had been caused by firing a blank cartridge close to his ear.

16 November

1891

The *Evening Post* started a delivery service. Unlike today, when newspapers are delivered by racing drivers hurtling through Island lanes, these were delivered by horse and trap. A bugle often announced the paper's arrival.

1930

A low rumble heard in the northern parishes proceeded an earth tremor. The quake, the second in a week, hit at 3.45 pm. It occurred on a Sunday and services were in progress. Although the various congregations became nervous, no harm was done.

1950

Mr J P Le Tourneur had an unusual find while gathering vraic at La Mare slip. He noticed something moving in his load of seaweed and discovered a Hawksbill turtle, alive and well, among the kelp. The animal, about 15 inches long, was taken home, identified by a local naturalist and then offered to the zoological society. The recent stormy conditions that had provided a bumper harvest of vraic were blamed for the turtle's appearance in Island waters, as Hawksbills prefer warmer climes.

1962

At 3.15 pm a man walked into the offices of La Motte Garages and asked for the wages for the Grouville branch. Having been given the £338, he left. It was only when, at 3.50 pm, the genuine worker arrived that the bold deception was discovered. The daring robber appeared in court three days later, charged with the offence.

1976

The *Jersey Evening Post* published a letter from a British government minister, Denzil Davis, confirming Jersey's independent tax status. The letter pointed out that any interference with Island taxation would be unconstitutional, a view always held by local authorities, who were nonetheless pleased to have it confirmed.

17 November

1791

Le Soleil de Jersey, a rival newspaper to *The Gazette* was first published. It supported the Charlot party but mirroring the Charlots decline in popularity, *Le Soleil* lasted less than six years.

1859

Ann Chuquet started minor landscaping work that was to cause her problems for the next 3½ years. She had workmen demolish a culvert in St Martin but Clement Buesnel thought it would restrict his access to a fontaine. Buesnel raised the Clameur de Haro, stopping the work. The case was ruled on by the court in 1863 and Chuquet was found at fault. As well as a fine and damages of £25, she was ordered to pay the legal costs. The Attorney General and Greffier put in their bills, fees Chuquet objected to paying, describing them as exorbitant. The court agreed and reduced them.

1951

The first prosecutions regarding non-compliance with the Insular Insurance Law went before the court. The three farmers were supported by several hundred fellow objectors to this unpopular imposition. The first defendant was fined £1, the second £5, and the third £10. The law had allowed for a £10 fine to be levied for each day of non-payment and a clear warning was issued that the law was going to stay.

1953

The International Court of Justice ruled that sovereignty over the Minquiers and Les Ecréhous belonged to Britain and not France. In the judgement it was stated that Les Ecréhous were treated and considered a part of the fief of the Channel Islands from the early 13th century. Medieval documents, taxes and buildings relating to the reef all related to Jersey's jurisdiction. As regards the Minquiers, the court ruled that as the British had 'exercised state functions' over the reef, it belonged to Jersey. The arguments over the reefs had gone on for many years and this judgement was intended to settle the matter once and for all.

18 November

1667

The last record of James de la Cloche is dated this day, after which he disappears. It is rumoured that he was the illegitimate son of Charles II and Margaret de Carteret. The child was said to have been conceived when Charles was in Jersey and still a Prince. The page in the church records that would have recorded the child's baptism is said to be missing. The infant was allegedly passed on to the de la Cloche family to raise, but after time with the Jesuits as a young adult he vanishes. It is possible that James was the famed Man in the Iron Mask but mystery surrounds his life.

1905

One hundred and twenty eight lives were lost when, in a blizzard, the *Hilda* struck rocks off St Malo. Only one of her crew survived. The iron steamship had been in service around the islands since January 1883, without noteworthy incident. After the wreck, a French company issued a set of postcards showing the remains of the vessel and the captain's body.

1933

Walter Le Cocq and his wife Mabel Le Monnier, of Ben Nevis, Gorey, sued Wilfred Le Seelleur after he sent them a parcel containing seven dead rats. Mrs Le Cocq was said to have suffered severe shock and compensation of £150 was being demanded. The court found in favour of Le Cocq, stating that the matter had been one of wilful wrong.

1960

Any Islander born before the mid 1960s cannot fail to remember the mailboats the *Caesarea* and *Sarnia*, believed to be the Roman names for Jersey and Guernsey. These ships were the result of over 300 years development in the transportation of mail and were also the last mailboats to run between the islands and the mainland. Weighing 4,174 tons, 322 ft long and 51 ft wide, they could carry 1,400 passengers and cost £1,500,000 each. On this day the *Caesarea* first entered St Helier Harbour to begin her career.

19 November

1949

The rescue of the crew of the ketch *Hanna* won second coxswain Silver Le Riche a RNLI bronze medal for his and his crew's bravery and seamanship. The *Hanna*, with its cargo of lime, had struck rocks off L'Etacq. Flares were sighted and at 11.25 pm the *Elizabeth Rippon*, the lifeboat, was launched. Despite the darkness and crashing waves the crew of three were taken off. No attempt was made to save the vessel, which was considered lost. The *Hanna* remained afloat and the following day, at low tide, the grounded craft became quite an attraction for the locals of St Ouen, who crossed the rocks to examine the damage.

1959

The States had appointed a Special Committee to consider the conflicting demands of housing, agriculture and tourism and to recommend an overall policy for the future. On this day the report was published. The conclusions were that tourism generated a lot of money, as did English residents who lived locally, of which there were an estimated 4,000. The report suggested that agriculture could not survive in Jersey just by growing staple crops, but should go in for the luxury market. Among the recommendations was that the tourism industry should be sustained at its current level, but not be increased. One thousand homes for higher income groups should be built, on agricultural land if necessary, and low cost housing should be developed alongside centres of employment to reduce costs for services and transport difficulties.

1964

What were acclaimed as Jersey's first skyscrapers were officially opened. The 14 storey blocks in Green Street offered 'some of the best coastal and inland panoramic views'. The president of the Housing Committee said: 'This is the best possible way to get the numbers of people accommodated and still retain sufficient open space for them.' Rents ranged from £2 5s to £4 7s 6d per week to live in the La Collette Flats.

20 November

1769

As a direct result of bread riots in September of this year five companies of the Royal Scots arrived in the Island. The heavy military presence was intended to restore order.

1905

A daring highway robbery took place in St Lawrence in the early hours of this day. Arthur Tirel was making his way home to First Tower. While travelling down Rue de Bas two men suddenly attacked him. One man carried a gun and shot twice, wounding Tirel in the hand. They stole the 11s 4d he carried, leaving him bleeding in the road. Tirel slowly made his way home and from there was taken to the Hospital. A manhunt was launched but Tirel's description of the assailants - one was short, the other tall - was of little help.

1920

Twenty men charged with illegal vraicing appeared before the court, having gathered drift vraic in St Ouen's Bay before the sea had receded properly. The law said that seaweed could not be gathered until iron pegs driven into the rock had been uncovered by the tide. But this law had been flouted for some time. In court each vraicer claimed that they had only begun work because all the others had. After what was said to be a light-hearted hearing, each man was fined £2, the amount specified by the law for the offence.

1984

The States voted by 40 to nine in favour of abolishing the death penalty. Although no one had been executed in the Island since 1959, the only sentence available for murder was death. This was now always commuted to life imprisonment by the British Home Secretary, but Jersey's lawmakers had still proved reluctant to do away with the anomaly. In 1957 a move to change the law had been soundly defeated but by 1967 and again in 1972, although rejected, revision of the law had only just failed. The situation was said to be a farce, as Jersey was one of the last places in western Europe to retain the measure, which even Guernsey had abandoned in 1965.

21 November

1643

The end of Parliamentary influence in Jersey came on this day. George de Carteret had brought English, Scotch, and Irish troops to the Island and been appointed Governor by the King. St Aubin's Fort was captured and Elizabeth Castle fired its last volley. The underarmed Parliamentary force had no option but to surrender or flee, thus breaking their siege on Mont Orgueil and Elizabeth castles, which had remained the strongholds of the loyal Royalist supporters.

1939

The *Jersey Evening Post* announced that 100,000 cigarettes would shortly be sent to members of the British Expeditionary Force in France. Islanders subscribed to the cigarette fund which supplied the troops with smoking material. A second consignment, which was being arranged, would include pipe tobacco. Each pack had a label informing the recipient that it had been given by the people of Jersey.

1953

Douettin, a farm in Gorey, came up for sale by auction. The granite house consisted of five bedrooms, a kitchen, dairy and two reception rooms. The outbuildings included cowsheds and horse stables, as well as other large sheds, the whole being sited in 36 vergées of land. It was stated that there was a low reserve on the property and a bid of £4,000 began the sale. The highest bid of £5,750 was just below the reserve. The farm, therefore, remained unsold, but the highest bidder was invited to private negotiations.

1978

While debating a proposition in the States to outlaw instant lotteries, the question of bottle stalls at fêtes was raised by Deputy Raoul Lempriere-Robin. In answer, the Solicitor General Mr P Bailhache informed the House that 'the Crown Officers have no official knowledge at all that bottle stalls take place. If they did, then a breach of the licensing law would be involved.' The law was passed and for a while bottle stalls were less numerous. Ironically it was the States themselves who, 20 years later, introduced an instant lottery.

22 November

1909

    The Chalêt Hotel, Pontac, opened its doors to roller skaters who, for an admission price of 3d, or 2d if they came by train, could use the ballroom floor. Since a new rink had opened earlier in the year at West Park Pavilion, the roller skating craze had grown and the Chalêt was offering classes, beginners sessions and in the evening an orchestra to provide the music to skate to.

1952

    Those who complain that Christmas gets earlier every year will be surprised that Father Christmas arrived on this day. The red clad figure clambered down the gangplank of the steamer *Isle of Sark* to be greeted by a crowd of youngsters. A horse-driven landau carried the festive fat man into town, halting outside Briggs in King Street, where he was to set up house for the next five weeks.

1956

    The Lieutenant Governor, Admiral Sir Gresham Nicholson, opened the annual trades exhibition at Springfield. Among those with displays and demonstrations were the Jersey Potteries, both throwing pots and glazing them. The Red Triangle Stores were showing off their small power tools and modelling kits. The latest sewing machine was showing off its ability to do button holes. Food and drink tastings were available, while all sorts of 'useful' gadgets were being demonstrated. But without doubt the star of the show was a model railway with 600 ft of track laid out, as well as stations, signal boxes and more.

1960

    A record 84,000 six ounce tins of Jersey cream were exported by the Jersey Milk Marketing Board on this day. The cream cannery had been set up three years earlier and now supplied Marks and Spencers, among others. The 20 ton shipment was valued at £4,000 and joined new potatoes as the major export of agricultural produce. Over 2 million cans of cream were produced this year, earning over £100,000 for the Island's dairy industry.

23 November

1852

The erection of three cast iron octagonal boxes in David Place, Cheapside and St Clement's Road was to become a historic bench mark. The experimental post boxes were the first not only in Jersey but in the United Kingdom. They were cast by Le Feuvre's foundry in Bath Street and although the design was changed, the idea took off.

1920

George Gellender, the floor manager of the skating rink, wrote to the *Jersey Evening Post* to remind skaters of the correct protocol when skating. Gentlemen should not skate wearing a hat, nor should they smoke, he informed them. They were also reminded that learners needed more room. In a PS he informed the gentleman who hired a pair of 21 shilling skates for the evening at a charge of 6d that if he left them in the lavatory pan again, he would be taken to court.

1967

A special general meeting of La Société Jersiaise was held at the Town Hall. The organisation had acquired the property adjoining the museum in Pier Road and needed to raise funds and reorganise itself. A proposal to increase the cost of membership from £1 to £2 was rejected by 59 votes to 58. It was agreed, however, that a paid curator should be employed to look after the museum.

1984

Some of the worst flooding to hit St Helier occurred when high tides and hurricane force winds combined to push the sea inland as far as the Town Hall. The mighty waves removed a 60 ft section of the wall along Victoria Avenue, the water reaching such a level that cars parked in the lay-bys began to float. Drivers had to abandon vehicles and one parked car was swept into the harbour. Dozens of town shops and homes were under water and the fire brigade were kept busy for several days pumping out basements and low lying properties.

24 November

1810

The States decided to demolish the Island's first prison at Charing Cross and to build a new one in Gloucester Street, in the area where the Hospital extension and Patriotic Street Car Park now stand.

1930

George Robins went before the court, charged with vagabondage. He had gone to the police station the previous evening to ask for shelter, stating that he had no means of support.

However, when his Parish Constable was contacted it transpired that the parish had given Robins 10 shillings the day before, money he admitted spending on whisky and beer.

As Robins had asked for shelter, the Magistrate obliged by sentencing him to a month's imprisonment with hard labour.

1981

Yet another report on the future development of Fort Regent was issued on this day. The leisure complex had running losses of £500,000 a year, as well as £350,000 capital repayments which came from the lottery profits.

Yet the report said: 'Fort Regent is a venture of which the Island can be proud'. It criticised the Tourism and Education committees for not making full use of the facility but did not contain any firm proposals.

1992

It was budget day and Finance and Economics Committee president Senator Pierre Horsfall had bad news for smokers. Cigarettes were to go up 10 p per pack and, similarly on health grounds, leaded petrol would increase by 5p per gallon.

Once all the allowances and expenditures had been calculated, the budget was expected to produce a £64 million surplus for the Island.

25 November

1484

Five Spanish ships were wrecked off Corbière and the cargo washed onto the sand dunes of St Ouen. The Seigneurs, whose fiefs reached St Ouen's Bay had a rich haul, mostly of wine. The Bailiff, acting as Lieutenant Governor, became involved and attempted to keep some of the booty to which he was not entitled. For this he was thrown in a dungeon where he 'at last died, covered with lice and vermin'.

1649

On this Sunday the Town Church was furnished with chairs, cushions and carpet in readiness for the arrival of Charles II and his court. Before their arrival a dwarf, known to the King, entered the church and, positioning himself in front of the altar, began to grimace and clap as well as shout. So he was thrown out. Refused re-entry when the court arrived, the enraged dwarf hurled stones through the church windows, one narrowly missing the King. A furious Governor threw the dwarf into Mont Orgueil Castle, from which he escaped a couple of weeks later. Reappearing at Elizabeth Castle, the king pardoned the dwarf and gave him a new suit of clothes and some silver. The dwarf was a very educated man of French origin who spoke several languages. He had become a part of the King's entourage, despite his sometimes odd behaviour.

1876

Lillian Mary Grandin was born in St Helier on this day. She was the first local woman to qualify as a doctor. Educated at the Jersey Ladies' College she trained in Edinburgh for her medical degree. Once qualified, she went on to study dentistry, midwifery, eyes and tropical diseases. Once her studies were complete she sailed for Shanghai, aiming to do missionary work in China. She went on to provide the only medical service in an area the size of France. This remarkable woman, having started a leper colony, later returned to England during the Great War, before continuing her medical work training the local Chinese. She died on 5th December 1924 in China, a country in which she had worked most of her life.

26 November

1904
　　The St Helier police were investigating the theft of 1½ tons of coal. Mrs Chevalier of Rock Terrace, Trinity Road, had had two tons of coal delivered, enough to last her all winter. But a few days later when she went in to her outhouse most of it was gone. It was believed that the thief had bagged the fuel, then carried it off towards the town mills. But no other information was known about this 'impudent robbery'.

1909
　　Mr Poingdestre of Dicq Road heard noise coming from his hen house in the early hours of this morning. As he approached the run Poingdestre saw a man creeping from it and was able to hit the thief across the back of the head with a crowbar he had picked up en route. The 'bird fancier' was laid out but rapidly recovered and leapt over a wall before the crowbar could be used a second time. The thief got away and an investigation of the hen house found one dead bird, abandoned when the thief had fled.

1943
　　In a simple ceremony the Dean blessed the area of land in Howard Davis Park that was to be used as a war cemetery. A number of bodies of Allied servicemen had already come ashore and had been buried at Mont à l'Abbé. These were now transferred to the new cemetery and future casualties of war, of which there would be many, were to have a well tended resting place.

1978
　　It was announced that the avenue of elms adjacent to St Ouen's Manor were to be felled. The fate of the trees, planted by the present Seigneur's great-grandfather, had been considered for 15 years and now they had come to the end of their natural life. They had been imported from Germany but the unusual variety was no protection from Dutch elm disease. The present Seigneur, Philip Malet de Carteret, intended to replant, his only concern being that the new avenue might be vandalised. When the limes were planted it was.

27 November

1571

The oldest memorial in the Town Church is that of Maxmillian Norreys who died on this day while serving in the army of Henry of Bourbon.

1909

François Auffray returned home, having gone missing while sandeeling at La Hocq. The previous night Auffray and his friend Frederick Lalouet had set off to catch sandeels. The two had become separated and Lalouet returned home unconcerned, as there were a lot of other fishermen working at the low tide. However, when Auffray's wife enquired as to his whereabouts, the authorities were informed.

On this day Auffray walked home, having spent a very uncomfortable night at Icho Tower after being cut off by the tide. The fisherman had had to wait nearly 10 hours while the tide rose and then fell again so he could leave.

1958

It was agreed in the States to create the new post of Schools Dental Officer at a salary of £1,200 in an attempt to improve children's dental health. It was said that 75% of Island school children had bad teeth and although the Public Health Committee employed a dentist to do five sessions a week at the Hospital, it was felt that someone was needed to visit schools to inspect teeth.

1990

Jersey shoppers had a new facility when Besants, the Island's latest supermarket, opened its doors. Built on the site of the Model Laundry at the entrance to Vallée des Vaux, the superstore offered a number of innovations, including an in-house bakery. The supermarket was an immediate success, so much so that only a few years later the British giant in the retail food industry, Safeway, bought Besants out.

28 November

1663

Charles II was now enthroned in England and as a token of his gratitude for the Island's assistance during the Civil War a silver mace was presented to the Bailiff. The mace was ceremonially carried before the Bailiff, a tradition that continues to this day, with the King's gift displayed in pride of place in the Chamber when the States sit.

1797

Mattieu de Gruchy died on this day, aged 36 years. He had lived an adventurous life and met a violent end. Originally he had been destined for religious orders but loved the sea too much. De Gruchy began his seafaring activities as a smuggler, going on to become a privateer. Held prisoner by the French, he escaped, having first been converted to the Church of Rome. Later he dallied in cabinet making before being ordained as a priest. Among his various adventures he was ship wrecked, acted as a spy and tended to stir up trouble wherever he went. Eventually he was arrested at Nantes. On this day de Gruchy stood before a firing squad who deliberately missed him twice, at which point an officer stepped forward and shot him in the head.

1927

T B Davis' generous offer of the property of Parkfield as a gift to the Island was accepted by the States. The house, outbuilding and 40 vergées of land were to be given for the foundation of an experimental farm. Renamed the Howard Davis Farm, the project's objectives were to acquaint young Jerseymen with the science of agriculture and to experiment with agricultural research.

1952

One of the biggest explosions in Jersey's history took place, yielding 100,00 tons of granite. The 12,000 pounds of high explosive were detonated at Ronez Quarry. A tunnel over 150 feet long had been excavated into the cliff to allow the charge to be placed.

29 November

1804

After protracted negotiations which eventually went to a form of independent arbitration, agreement was reached over the Crown's purchase of land for the building of Fort Regent. The sum of £11,280 was awarded to the Vingtaine de la Ville for the sale of Town Hill, the money being invested and used towards the cost of street paving in town. In more recent years it contributed £6,000 towards Green Street multi-storey car park and £1,500 to a playground at Snow Hill. It is important to note that the money went to the Vingtaine, a parish sub-division, and not to the parish.

1956

Jersey motoring took a leap forward with the inauguration of the first sets of traffic lights. Four sets were functioning, with another dozen planned. Motorists were advised where to stop in relation to the lights and that amber was a 'warning signal that the red light is about to come on'.

1977

The States were debating the Island's traffic problems, with Senator John Averty revealing that the plan for a second tunnel under Fort Regent had been abandoned. In the debate, brought by Senator Shenton, the States were asked to restrict vehicle ownership to the current level. It was said that in 1961 there were 25,000 vehicles and the committee responsible had been instructed by the House to prepare a report on vehicle restraint. Little had happened in the intervening years, so on this day the States repeated their instruction of 1961, with exactly the same result.

1990

Ten years after the Waterworks Company had hoped to have completed Queen's Valley reservoir, the scheme was in chaos. The contractors, Shephard Hill, had suddenly gone bust. On this day civil engineering contractor Gleeson were given the task of finishing the job, having unsuccessfully tendered for the original contract, and it was hoped that the work would soon recommence.

30 November

1876

The *Diana*, a special ship in local maritime history, was launched on this day. Her claim to fame was that she was the first screw propelled ship to be built for the mail service. The *Diana* was capable of 14 knots and worked on the Channel route until June 1895. Years later, while en route for Southampton, she grounded on rocks, in fog, off Cap de la Hague. The passengers and mail were taken ashore but *Diana* slipped off the rocks and sank two days later.

1905

Alfred Dauvin stood before the Magistrate, charged with cruelty to his seven-year old son. Dauvin had made his boy walk from Rozel to St Martin's School without shoes. In his defence Dauvin said that none of his children had boots and he took the boy to school, having been told by the authorities to send the boy 'as he was'.

A former employer told the court that Dauvin was lazy and could earn 18 shillings to a pound a week but went drinking instead. Sending him to prison for four days, the Magistrate sympathised with Dauvin's situation.

1917

Allastair McReady-Diarmid lead his men in actions that were to earn him the Victoria Cross. After his education at Victoria College, McReady-Diarmid had not intended a life in the forces. Nevertheless, he was commissioned into the 17th Middlesex Regiment soon after the outbreak of the Great War.

On this day German forces had advanced and penetrated the British lines. Captain McReady-Diarmid and his men drove them back, having gone through a heavy barrage in order to engage the enemy. The counter-attack succeeded, with a number of Germans being taken prisoner. The following day the Germans attacked again and again the Jersey Captain led his men to regain the lost ground.

Later that day McReady-Diarmid was killed in an explosion, so receiving the Victoria Cross posthumously.

01 December

1891

This day saw the first election with voting by secret ballot. There were two positions of St Helier Centenier available, with three candidates standing. The new system seems to have been a little confusing to some voters, with a large number of spoiled papers when some people put two crosses against the same name. The Temperance Party was confident of getting a high number of votes but once in the booth, where electors could vote safe from onlookers, they chose not to support the anti-drink campaign. The new system allowed the electorate to express their preference free from the threat of the verbal or physical abuse which had stopped some people from voting in the past.

1897

The authorities stepped in and stopped a pigeon shooting contest due to be held on this day. At least 20 shooters had arrived at Corbière, the intended site of the competition, only to find that the contest had been banned at the last minute. Undeterred, the shooters made do with clay pigeons instead.

1942

Ernest Le Gresley was killed when he interrupted two men breaking into his hen house. Because of the Occupation, everything was in short supply in the Island and Jersey's crime level had never been higher. Food was scarce so anyone with chickens or rabbits had to be wary if they wished to keep them.

During the night Le Gresley and his sister had gone to investigate a noise and had come upon two men. The Le Gresleys had armed themselves with sticks, however, in the struggle that followed Ernest was fatally stabbed and his sister injured. German forces blamed escaped Russian slave workers.

1953

Today saw the unveiling of a pillar box dedicated to Elizabeth II and commemorating the centenary of the first post box to be erected anywhere in the British Isles.

02 December

1861

A new lifeboat of a self righting design was launched for the first time at West Park. The 30 ft long vessel, complete with carriage, had been paid for by the States, as had her predecessor. The lifeboat's carriage was drawn by four horses and once afloat her crew of nine tested her handling for 1½ hours before entering the harbour where the boat's self righting abilities were checked with the aid of a crane. The new vessel met everyone's approval and went into service.

1875

Henri Luce Manuel died on this day, having spent his latter years writing poetry and studying Jersey's history and culture. His early days, however, had been a little more colourful. Manuel's involvement in the *Jersey Gazette* had caused him a great deal of trouble. Mr de la Croix had violently assaulted him after an article had been published. On another occasion he was sued for libel. Later he became a Constables Officer and accompanied Centenier Le Cronier when he attempted to arrest a brothel-keeper at Gorey. Le Cronier was stabbed to death by the brothel-keeper, who then chased Manuel down the street with the blood stained knife.

1957

Mrs D C Sultowski was fined £5 for wrongly raising the Clameur de Haro. She had raised the cry after neighbours removed part of a hedge and bank in order to build a wall. However the court ruled that the works in no way encroached on her land and she was fined for using the Clameur incorrectly. The Bailiff pointed out that the 1,000 year old law was 'a very sacred institution'.

1968

The manager of the Tropicana night spot was attacked by robbers and left tied up on his bed while his room and the offices were searched. Having found the keys to the safe, £200 was taken, as well as a crossed cheque and other moneys. Once safely away, the thieves anonymously called the police, who released 23-year old former JEP reporter and later Senator John Averty.

03 December

1868

At a St Helier Parish Assembly the subject under review was the poor and the cost of keeping them. The Constable told the assembly that there were at least 14 families relying on St Helier's support who were 'strangers' in the parish. Mr J Brayn said he had proof positive that English people were coming to the Island to live off local charities and that they should be sent straight back, which was greeted with cries of 'hear, hear'. Only the Rector expressed reservations about setting up a 'Poor Law Board', his speech being heard with impatience before the assembly voted in favour of a board to review each claim on the parish's funds.

1904

Alfred George Gosselin, aged 27, was sentenced to eight days hard labour for stealing a chicken. Witness Mr Corbin said that he had seen Gosselin take the chicken from Julien Kerdal's shop in Burrard Street and hide it inside his coat. Corbin had chased the accused and caught him by the cattle market. Gosselin admitted the charge, stating that he had been intoxicated at the time.

1965

A British European Airways helicopter's door fell off while en route from Jersey to Guernsey. Jersey Airport's runway was being resurfaced and so a helicopter had been put into service to allow travel to continue. Despite the door falling into the sea mid-Channel, a spokesman claimed that 'the passengers suffered no inconvenience or discomfort'.

1982

The keys of the £700,000 Cheshire Homes Project were handed over by builders on this day. The building at Rope Walk was intended to house 18 disabled residents, the cost of the project being met by a local benefactor. It was envisaged that people living off the site would use the facility as a day centre. However, the building had major structural faults and in a relatively short time residents were moved out as those involved argued about who was responsible.

04 December

1905

Two husbands were in court, both charged with refusing to maintain their wives.

James Makin had beaten his wife and she had complained to the authorities. Makin said his wife 'constantly aggravated him' but denied being drunk. He was sent to prison for eight days after agreeing to give his wife £3 17s per quarter for herself and the children.

Thomas Bailey told the court that he gave his wife 10 shillings a week to maintain her and their children, a sum Mrs Bailey said she had not received for months. Bailey was released, having promised to give his wife 3 shillings a week.

1964

Carlyle Fox threw himself on the mercy of the Royal Court, having given himself up after jumping bail four years earlier. He and Armand Le Guen had stolen a safe from Grouville Church, been caught and both jumped bail. Le Guen had been rearrested and sentenced to a year's imprisonment.

Fox had, however, left the Island and having now returned, turned himself in. The court, having heard his apology, purged him of his contempt so that he now just faced trial for the original theft. This crime was said to have been due to him having gone through an antisocial stage before having plastic surgery on a nose deformity.

1983

One of the cannons that flank General Don's statue in the Parade was removed and sent to Hartlepool. The 110 lb Armstrong breach loader was needed as a pattern for a series of fibreglass replicas with which the Ship Preservation Trust intended to furnish the restored *HMS Warrior*. Strangely, serial numbers showed that the same cannon had originally been fitted in the *Warrior* before finding its way to Jersey.

05 December

1643

Dean Bandinel and his son, the Rector of St Mary, had sided with the Parliamentarians in the Civil War and as Jersey was again under Royalist control they were arrested on this day.

Later, upon hearing of executions of Parliamentary prisoners, they decided to escape the confines of Mont Orgueil Castle where they had been held for over a year.

Climbing down a home-made rope one night during a gale, Bandinel's son found its length too short and dropped the remaining distance. The Dean followed, dying from his fall, while his seriously injured son escaped, only to be recaptured and later die of his wounds.

1839

Until this day it was not the sender who paid for a letter's carriage but the recipient. The postage charge was levied when the package was collected from the post office. But from now on the system we are familiar with today came into effect.

1900

The *Rossgull* was owned by the Plymouth, Channel Islands and Brittany Steam Ship Company Limited, who covered routes to the islands and St Brieuc, as well as English ports. On this day the captain and eight crew members drowned when the *Rossgull* foundered off St Brelade. However, one of the crew, the fireman, tied himself to a makeshift raft and after nearly two days at sea was rescued by a lighthouse keeper at Carteret in Normandy.

1966

What had been known as Woodford Park in St Brelade was renamed the Sir Winston Churchill Memorial Park. The *Evening Post* had set up a 'penny fund' to pay for a memorial to the wartime leader. This was unveiled by the Bailiff, who expressed the Island's gratitude to the leader of the liberating forces.

06 December

1958

The Inter Island Darts Tournament was broadcast on the BBC's 'Sport in the West' programme. David Monamy was to be Jersey's representative in the three-way match, in which each player had 15 minutes to score as many points as possible. Guernseyman Peter Merrien took the £5 first prize, breaking the record by scoring 5,952, while Jersey could only manage 4,281. This was the sixth such programme broadcast by the BBC, an unusual choice for radio.

1970

The States froze the £1 million requested by the Fort Regent Development Committee while a review into the cost of building a conference centre was undertaken. The rotunda, which was already under construction, was said to be the hub of the parade ground redevelopment. But questions were now being asked about costs and viability, with some Members suggesting that Fort Regent was the wrong place for a conference centre.

1970

The Post Office took over the former tobacco company premises at Mont Millais. It was fitted with 'the latest modern steel fittings' and intended as the main sorting and distribution centre. The move coincided with the issuing of a new uniform for postmen, which was said to be a 'smart new light grey'. The caps, however, had been delayed.

1983

Deputy Hendric Vandervliet, president of the Housing Committee, called for a massive area of land to be reclaimed from the Island's south-east coast. Referring to the area he said: 'At low tide it is a shambles and it needs man to put life into it'. He proposed building a 'satellite town' on the reclaimed area off the St Clement's coast to ease Jersey's housing shortage. Fifteen years later this 'shambles' was proposed as an area worthy of protection for its unique natural habitat and diversity.

07 December

1908

A large crowd was expected at St Thomas' Hall in New Street on this evening. The Island's first cinema or cinemata was to open at 8.30. Bookings were said to be heavy and half of the proceeds were to be given to the French Benevolent Society.

1959

A UFO was seen over St John. The big, luminous, green ball was watched by Miss E Moore as it crossed the sky with sparks coming from its front. The phenomenon was visible for about a minute and at first Miss Moore thought it was a rocket, except that it travelled silently across the early evening sky.

1964

The process of finger printing all Trinity men between the ages of 19 and 60 years began on this day. Approximately 600 men lived in the parish and in an attempt to identify the man who had been sexually attacking children in recent years they were all required to attend the parish hall to give either palm or finger prints. Detective Superintendent James Axon from Scotland Yard had been in the Island for several months to lead the investigation and was to oversee the operation, similar to one that had taken place in St Clement the previous week.

1970

A press conference was held to announce the Jersey Arts Council's plans to buy the Opera House and establish an art centre there. The ambitious plans were to include an art gallery, studios and club rooms, a concert area, tearoom and bar, as well as restoring the theatre.

It was hoped that the project would be well underway within a year, with an arts director and administration manager appointed. But as with so many great plans, it was to be over 25 years before the Opera House was acquired for the Island.

08 December

1874

On this day severe gales caused considerable problems for the ongoing harbour works. The project to construct a larger harbour for St Helier had been under way for over two years but high seas caused £15,000 worth of damage as 200 ft of the La Collette pier were swept away.

1897

An unidentified and decomposed body was washed ashore at Bel Royal. A purse found on the body contained one shilling and a piece of metal inscribed 'George Le Breton 58 King Street'. The inquest heard from the widow of publican Le Breton that such tokens had been given by him and other publicans to customers so they could acquire drinks.

The corpse's unmarked watch had stopped at 9.50 and a metal pencil attached to the watch chain appeared to be French. The lower jaw of the body had been missing when discovered and it came to light that a jaw with teeth and some flesh attached had been found by Mr Hunt. Hunt said that if the body had not yet been buried the jaw and owner might as well be repatriated.

The identity of the corpse was never discovered.

1911

It was agreed to accept Julia Westaway's bequest to fund the building of a home and hospital for poor and abandoned children. She had left Parade House and several thousand pounds to establish the facility. The Westaway Ward would house 10 beds and a trust would fund its future running,

1948

The Island's electoral reform continued with the election of deputies. There was much more interest than there had been in the senatorial election a month earlier. Even the three town districts had a turn out of over 50% for the deputies. The new assembly also had a woman member, with Mrs A Forster being voted in by St Helier District No 2.

09 December

1926

A special sitting of the States was held, as a deficit in the budget meant the possible introduction of income tax. The threat of such drastic measures concentrated minds and £25,000 was pruned off expected public expenditure. This meant that the Island would only have a small shortfall, negating the need for income tax.

1952

An outbreak of foot and mouth disease was confirmed at Captain Perree's farm, La Forêt, St Mary. The herd of six cows and three heifers was destroyed and a standstill order issued throughout the Island. No cattle, sheep, pigs or goats were allowed off their farms and dogs had to be leashed. Offenders' animals were liable to be destroyed and the owners prosecuted. Three outbreaks of this infectious disease earlier in the year had lead to similar restrictions, the policy of containment and destruction the only one available. But three days later a nearby farm was also found to be infected.

1965

St Peter Rector Rev E H Chavasse was overruled by his parishioners when he attempted to halt the tradition of bell ringing on Christmas Day. In 1849 and 1850 ecclesiastical assemblies had ruled against bell ringing on 25th December. However, this had been ignored and, as in other parishes, it was tradition for the bells to be rung, sometimes all day. The St Peter Rector wanted the practice stopped, as it had been except in St Mary and St Ouen, but parishioners disagreed. Bell ringing on Christmas Day declined until by the end of the 20th century only St Ouen continues the tradition.

1980

Jersey's first one pound coins went into circulation. The new coin was easily identified as it was square in shape. This novel and popular design was, however, short lived. Shortly after, the British Government issued their first pound coin, which was smaller, thicker and circular. For practicality's sake Jersey soon produced a similar coin so that slot machines and other equipment could be standardised.

10 December

1952

A St Helier parish assembly decided to turn down a street lighting scheme as it was liable to put 6d on the rates. Two proposals had been put forward. The Jersey Gas Lighting Company could put in the necessary equipment for £49,942, with running costs of £15,734 per annum, while the Electricity Company would charge £33,958 and £4,397 annually.

1954

Fours boys aged 16 and 17 were sent to prison with hard labour for 14 days and a 15-year old was to receive six strokes of the birch for their attempted break in at a beach cafe. The 'teddy boys' had been seen using a piece of wood to force the lock until a wave had come over the sea wall and drenched them. The sanction of the birch seems to have done little to deter them, as three of them had received such a punishment for car borrowing only a week earlier.

1963

The first park and ride scheme was announced. In an effort to ease traffic congestion in the town centre shoppers were able to park at Springfield and catch a free bus into the main shopping area. The scheme ran from 10 am to 6 pm, six days a week. The cost of parking was 6d per session. Buses ran every half hour, on the half hour.

1968

The States rejected proposed drink driving regulations. It was intended that 100 mgs of alcohol per 100 mls in the blood would be the maximum allowable. In what was a fairly one-sided debate, some Members believed the high accident rate in the Island was mostly caused by 'sheer stupidity'. The measure had little chance of success from the outset and was defeated by 35 voted to 15.

1973

The world oil shortage lead the States to issue petrol coupons. Although never actually used, the fuel shortage caused grave concern, with people hoarding petrol.

11 December

1649

In the chapel at Elizabeth Castle Charles II 'touched' eleven people in a ceremony intended to cure the 'King's evil' or scrofula. It involved placing ribbons of white silk around the sufferer's neck, as well as the King touching the victim's throat. Tradition also said that the King gave each sufferer a piece of gold but as Charles was in exile and funds were short, they had to supply their own.

1837

Penal reform took a leap forward on this day when the office of public executioner was abolished. This doesn't mean that people were no longer executed, just that the numbers involved were so low that it could no longer justify someone in a full time post. One hundred years later, murderers in Jersey were still hanged.

1933

The Parish of St Brelade offered a reward of £50 for information on the 'night prowler'. A series of late night attacks and break ins had occurred, leaving parishioners in a state of anxiety.

1952

A St Brelade Parish Assembly rejected the proposal to allow a new inn to be created at Les Quennevais. A A Pitcher Ltd were applying for a licence to convert the property Maison Rouge into a public house to be called The Horse and Hounds. The vote was close, 21 to 19, and despite the parish's rejection, it was not to be long before the facility was established.

1958

Two 13 year old boys were put on a year's probation, having stolen 60 sticks of gelignite and five boxes of detonators from a quarry in Grands Vaux. Some of the explosives and detonators were discovered in one of the boys' bedrooms and had become so dangerous that the authorities had to destroy it. Part of the haul was still missing and the boys admitted to detonating it on the sand dunes and throwing some from Elizabeth Castle breakwater.

12 December

1798

As Methodism took hold in Jersey, a conflict of duty occurred. Sunday drill for the militia was compulsory but Methodists believed Sundays were sacred. On this day an Order of Council in England said that the States were wrong to compel Methodists to drill on Sundays. Previously Methodists had merely paid a small fine for missing drill but when absentees were sent to prison, opposition grew. The authorities then tried to suppress Methodism by expelling all ministers, closing meeting houses and banishing militiamen who refused to drill on Sundays. The ruling from England supporting the Methodists' stand now solved the problem by allowing them to drill on Saturdays.

1956

A new type of investment was available for the first time in Jersey. Premium Bonds went on sale and although demand at the main post office was less than expected, sub post offices did good business. Georgetown Post Office sold nearly £1,000 worth of bonds on its first day.

1967

Deputy Vernon Tomes presented plans to the States for the development of Fort Regent. The anticipated cost being £2.65 million, the House voted unanimously in favour of the project, subject to a feasibility study, and also ordered £100,000 to be available if things went wrong.

1974

One of Jersey's leading politicians, Senator Wilfred Krichefski, died while en route to the airport. This was fitting as he, more than anyone else, was responsible for the Airport's development. His car was involved in a head-on collision with a lorry after the Senator had suffered a heart attack. Senator Krichefski was one of Jersey's longest serving States members. First elected to office in 1945, his service was rewarded in 1958 with an OBE.

13 December

1948

The newly constituted States met for the first time. Senators and Deputies gathered in the House but the Jurats and Rectors no longer joined them. One of the first matters dealt with concerned the work on St Ouen's sea wall. Work by the Germans had disrupted the bay's balance, but nature seemed to be putting matters right more quickly than States contractors, so the work was stopped.

1961

Dr G Godber, Britain's Chief Medical Officer, published his annual report which said that Jersey men had the highest lung cancer death rate in the world. Island woman were also suffering an exceptionally high rate of the disease. Pointing out that Jersey had no air pollution, Dr Godber noted that the Island consumed more tobacco per head of population than anywhere else and he recommended a change in smoking habits by reducing consumption or preferably stopping altogether.

1971

A chapter of Island life ended when a sentence of 30 years imprisonment was passed on Edward John Louis Paisnel, who had been found guilty of charges of rape and indecent assaults on, among others, local children. Dubbed the Beast of Jersey, his nocturnal activities had caused fear and alarm throughout the Island for over a decade. When eventually apprehended for a motoring offence, a search of his Grouville home revealed a secret room and a quantity of Satanic regalia. Paisnel served the bulk of his sentence on the Isle of Wight and died soon after being released.

1977

Two thousand people gathered in the Royal Square to protest on behalf of pensioners. The States had in recent years given all OAPs a Christmas bonus. This year, however, the £10 was not to be forthcoming. States Members were jeered as they arrived for their sitting. Some chose not to run the gauntlet and arrived early, while others entered the Chambers via an alternative entrance.

14 December

1699

Having originally introduced import duty to fund the building of St Aubin's harbour, the States decided to continue the charges to fund the building of a harbour at St Helier.

1965

The States debated the proposal to allow jet aircraft to use the airport. By the narrowest of margins, 25 votes to 24, it was decided to allow BUA four daily flights until March 1967. The BAC 1-11 jets had been objected to by many St Peter residents and the four plane ruling was a compromise.

1970

King Street was made a pedestrian precinct on an experimental basis. The idea had been around for many years but it was a change in the law that had finally allowed the road's closure. On the first day shoppers were very positive about the move, but shopkeepers were less sure. By the end of the year there were no plans to end the experiment as there had been no major complaints. The only comment had been that the scheme should be extended to include Queen Street and Bath Street.

1972

The States voted in favour of Senator J J Le Marquand's proposition to introduce a £10 Christmas bonus for all pensioners. It was decided not to apply any means test as this would cause administration problems, although it was hoped that the more wealthy would decide not to claim the extra cash. The scheme was to cost the Island £100,000 and although opposed by the Finance and Economics Committee, it was passed by 28 votes to 12.

1985

Former St Peter Constable W P Le Marquand married for a third time, his bride being 49-year old Yvonne Emery. The 78-year old had served over 50 years in the Honorary Police, and had spent 22 years as the Father of the Parish.

15 December

1651

The garrison lead by Sir George de Carteret, which had been under siege at Elizabeth Castle since October, finally surrendered to the Parliamentarians. The terms of surrender were very generous to Sir George but less generous to his men.

De Carteret was given £1,800 along with free passage, possession of all his land, belongings and a ship, the *Scout*. In fact he left with his entire fortune intact and no punitive action taken against him. The ordinary soldiers had, on the other hand, lost almost everything.

As Sir George set sail for St Malo, a great crowd gathered to witness the historic event. The Parliamentary commander, wishing to disperse the assembly, fired a cannon at them, killing a horse, but not its rider.

1917

The price of the *Jersey Evening Post* doubled from half a penny to a penny. The paper was a broad sheet made up of one sheet folded, giving four pages. The cover was mostly made up of adverts, with world news more in evidence than local events. Earlier in the year the price had doubled in an attempt to reduce sales of the newspaper, as paper was in short supply due to the war. But that price increase had been withdrawn after only one month.

1956

Travellers flying to Jersey from London with BEA were surprised to find themselves being broadcast by the BBC on 'Turntable Travel'. Douglas Flemming moved among the passengers, asking for record requests which were retrieved from the BBC record library and played on the air.

The pilot, Captain Dell, chose Sylvia Magano singing 'Anna', while Bryan Harrison of Samarés Manor picked Handel's 'Water Music'. The half hour broadcast went out live, although a similar programme had been recorded in case of technical problems.

16 December

1869

An offer by Mr Pickering of the Jersey Railway Company to build a seawall from West Park to St Aubin for the sum of £30,000 was considered and later agreed by the States. The intention was to back fill in the area behind the wall for a distance of 90 feet, 30 feet of which would be used by the proposed railway and the remaining 60 feet for a carriageway and promenade. The building of the sea wall was important to the railway as the tracks would run very close to the high tide and would be in danger of being washed away in a storm. However in 1873 the railway company decided to abandon the sea wall project as it would cause them a heavy loss. It was left until 1879 when the State's Committee of Defence started the construction work themselves.

1954

The 84% turn out of Grouville electors showed just how keenly the position of Parish Constable was being fought and at the end of the day only 32 votes separated the two candidates. Harold Brée and Commander Le Cras only had to wait 30 minutes as the votes were counted, when Brée was declared the Constable with 455 votes. Crowds had jammed the parish hall for several hours prior to the count and surrounding roads were blocked with traffic.

1959

The States decided to set up a special committee on building costs after it was revealed that the cost of building States flats had risen from £2,014 to £2,932 in three years. Housing was being built at Town Mills and was proposed for Great Union Road. Wages were increasing and it was said that a skilled craftsman could earn £12 per week, although this alone could not account for the 50% increase in construction costs. Deputy Venables pointed out that States houses were finished to a higher standard than those in the private sector and, although not in favour of building substandard units, he suggested that the quality of the present ones was too high. This was not the first enquiry to be made into building costs and was not to be the last, with one being set up on average every 15 to 20 years.

17 December

1862

The foundation stone of the Masonic Temple was laid on this day.

1889

Workmen for builders Messieurs Woodsford and Harris discovered one of Jersey's finest archaeological artefacts on this day. They were building a house in Lewis Street when they uncovered a gold torque which dated from the Late Bronze Age. It was of British type and the terminals at the end had been broken off and it had suffered other damage.

1896

Philippe Pinel, the King of the Ecréhous, died on this day, aged 76. He had lived on the reef since 1848, along with his wife, making a living through fishing, basketry and vraicing. The seaweed was dried and then burned, the ashes being a valuable fertiliser in the days before chemical growth promoters. Pinel had become something of a celebrity and a photograph of him posing proudly with a basket for Queen Victoria has often been reproduced. Sadly, Pinel did not die on his beloved reef. When he was found to be ill he was taken to the General Hospital, where he later died.

1960

The Royal Court declared the election for St Peter Parish Deputy which had been held on 9th December null and void and ordered a fresh contest to be held in January. There had been two candidates for the post, sitting Deputy Simon and W P Le Marquand. When the votes had been counted W P Le Marquand had won by 444 votes to 442.

However, nine ballot papers had gone missing during the poll and the returning officer, Jurat Syvret, was not happy with the situation. When the matter was brought before the court its unanimous decision was that the secrecy of the election had been compromised and that the vote should be retaken.

18 December

1920

Jean Jousset's business was photography and it was world-wide. One of his American clients was found in possession of some of Jousset's 'obscene' prints and the Jersey authorities were informed. Jousset was charged under the 1908 Post Office Act for sending his wares through the post and while awaiting trial his mail kept rolling in. Hundreds of letters containing postal orders were intercepted. Jousset's organisation was quite sophisticated, with each person having code numbers and corresponding in code as well.

1933

Jersey Airway's first commercial flight left Jersey for Portsmouth from St Aubin's Bay. The timetable was arranged around the tides because unlike Jersey's earliest aircraft arrivals, the new planes could land and take off from the sands. After operating eight seater De Havilland DH 84 Dragons for a year, the expanding company began using 14 seater Expresses and after twelve months 20,000 passengers had been carried.

1943

Under existing laws tobacco could only be grown with a licence. There was, however, no penalty for those who ignored the rules. On this day a tax of 1 shilling per plant grown was introduced which was expected to bring in several thousand pounds worth of duty. At the same States sitting which saw this tax come into being, income tax was raised to four shillings on the pound but a move to make taxpayers declare all their sources of income was rejected.

1973

Lord Coutanche, the Island's wartime Bailiff, died on this day. He had held office for 25 years and was 81 when he died in a local nursing home. In his time he had greeted a number of Royal visitors on the Island's behalf and was generally held in the highest regard by Islanders. To commemorate Jersey's 25th anniversary of Liberation a special issue of stamps were produced, one of which showed his portrait.

19 December

1649

The States decided to reduce the number of taverns in town to six. By 1797, however, at least 100 inns were trading.

1899

Members of the East Lancashire Regiment left Jersey en route to South Africa to fight in the Boer War. The soldiers received a rousing send off. Thousands of Islanders cheered them on their way as they marched down from Fort Regent to their ship at the Victoria Pier. Flags and bunting festooned other ships in the harbour. An appeal launched by the Bailiff to supply the troops with pipes and tobacco had reached over £110, as well as a large quantity of cigars and cigarettes which had been donated. There was also a Transvaal war fund and donors could specify if they wanted their money to go either to soldiers, widows and orphans, the sick and wounded, disabled soldiers, or wives and children of soldiers. The total in this fund was £284 so far.

1941

Mr Le Marquand of Springside Poultry Farm was charged with selling eggs at double the allowed price. During November 150 eggs had twice been sold to a member of the German forces and the receipts from the transactions were produced as evidence against him. The charges were brought not by the Jersey court but by the German Field Commandant. A fine of 100 Reichmarks was imposed, with a sentence of 10 days imprisonment if the fine was not paid.

1961

A short service of dedication and consecration marked the opening of Jersey's crematorium. Sited at Westmount, the £35,000 building was intended to look solid, although the architect did wonder how to make the chimney fit in. The furnace was gas fired and it was claimed that up to six services could be held each day, although only four a day were envisaged.

20 December

1901

A daring thief robbed Mr H S Godfray's till. Trading from 11 Library Place, the shop was a 'fancy warehouse' from which Godfray had just popped out to deliver to another trader across the street his copy of the *Evening Post*. In these few minutes, three at the most, someone stole £19 in gold and £5 in silver from the shop till.

1956

The JMT announced the scrapping of special concessionary fares for school children, which had been introduced in 1952. From the beginning of the next year children would pay half the adult fare for their bus journeys, doubling some charges. Previously the maximum return fare had been 7d. Now a trip from St Ouen's Church to the Weighbridge and back would cost 9½d instead of 4½d. The changes were being introduced because the buses ran at a loss in the winter.

1958

The Opera House closed down as a cinema. The last film shown was 'Strictly for Pleasure' starring Tony Curtis and Janet Leigh. Having opened as a theatre in 1900, the building had later been adapted to film. However, with over 10,000 televisions now in Island homes and with four other movie houses to compete with, the Rank Organisation had decided to close the Opera House down, leaving the building's future uncertain.

1961

Old Victorian and film star Kenneth More returned to the Island to be the guest of honour at the Old Victorians annual dinner. More had left the Island to seek fame and fortune in 1932, having developed a love of the stage while at the college, to which, he told his audience, he owed everything. During the evening More autographed menus at £1 a time, raising £146 towards the Worrall Memorial Swimming Pool.

21 December

1895

Paul Hodienne and his wife Julie, a French couple, went before the Royal Court, charged with running a brothel from No 3 James Street. Paul admitted his guilt and claimed to have forced his wife to run the brothel, therefore, he hoped, absolving her of all guilt. After a complicated legal argument, the Bailiff rejected this ploy and Julie had to take responsibility for her actions. The couple both pleaded guilty and were sentenced to one month's hard labour and five years banishment. Their two children were also to be repatriated.

1901

An accident occurred on the King Street-New Street junction. A carriage driven by Mr D Squibb was at the junction when one of his horses slipped on the 'pitching which is terribly and dangerously smooth'. The horse was severely injured, so Mr G Le Couillard of Cattle Street was summoned to shoot it. The carcass was then wheeled on a trolley to the parish yard.

1907

Francis Ferdinand Maurice Cook was born on this day. His father moved in the world of London art and it was perhaps inevitable that Francis Cook should be drawn to it. As well as being an artist in his own right, Cook was also a collector. In 1948 he moved to Jersey, bringing his collection of paintings with him. A year later the greater proportion of them were destroyed in the Le Gallais fire, where they had been in storage. Cook later acquired a disused Methodist chapel at Les Augres and converted it into a studio and gallery for his own works. After his death in 1978, his widow donated the Sir Francis Cook Gallery, along with over 1,200 paintings, to the Jersey Heritage Trust.

1938

The heaviest snowfall for many years brought the Island to a halt. Milk was rationed, schools were closed, deliveries ceased and a series of minor accidents were reported. In St Helier a soup kitchen was set up. But the thaw soon set in, turning the snow to slush.

22 December

1906

The Bailiff gave his judgement on a long-running civil case. Private Alfred Biggs was suing Lieutenant Colonel T Nock Bagnall, Vingtenier Militaire George L Sinnatt and Sergeant Moy for wrongful arrest and imprisonment and he was demanding damages of £100, with £25 costs.

The incident started when Biggs' rifle had been rusty and had required cleaning, for which he should have been fined 2s 6d. But instead he had been ordered to appear at the Arsenal. When he did not, he was fined for his non-appearance and ordered to appear again. When he again failed to do so his arrest was ordered. In an escalation of alleged offences and penalties, Biggs was imprisoned. He escaped and when he was recaptured he was imprisoned for a longer time.

The Bailiff, much to the military authority's dismay, found for Biggs, ruling that the three men's actions had been illegal. Bagnall was ordered to pay £5, Sinnatt to pay £1 and Moy 1s compensation, as well as costs.

1952

Hedley Maillard was elected Senator in a bye-election caused by the resignation of R Carson. The term remaining was eight years. The two candidates were Maillard and Deputy C P Rumfitt. In what was described as a poor turnout, with only 30% of St Helier's electors voting, Maillard won by 590 votes.

1960

Thieves blew open the safe of Orviss' main store in Beresford Street using gelignite. Once the explosives had blown the lock between £200 and £300 had been taken. But a second safe, although tampered with, remained intact. Although the thieves got away with a good haul, they had overlooked £150 which remained unseen in a drawer of the ruined safe.

But the firm's troubles were not confined to the break-in. The following day a fire broke out, destroying Orviss' supplies of turkeys, geese and ducks which had been due to be delivered on Christmas Eve, as well as damaging property and other stock.

23 December

1591

The Royal Court was so concerned by the amount of witchcraft practised in the Island that they ordered anyone found seeking the assistance of warlocks and witches to be imprisoned in Mont Orgueil Castle for a month on dry bread and water.

1916

Philip de Ste Croix, the lightkeeper on Elizabeth Castle's breakwater, drowned. Supplied with fuel and light, de Ste Croix had two rooms out on the islet and his job was to keep a light burning as a shipping aid. Once the light was lit, he was not allowed to leave his post. On this occasion he set out for the harbour in a rowing boat. Tidal conditions swept him around the La Collette area and his body was later washed ashore at Grève d'Azette. His boat had been old and rotten and although the inquest jury had returned a verdict of accidental drowning, they also criticised him for leaving his post.

1976

Islanders saw Channel Television's first colour broadcasts on this day. A camera, valued at £40,000, had been loaned to the company by RCA, an electronics company, to brighten up the viewers' Christmas. Continuity announcements and some news was to appear in colour. However, this would only happen when RCA did not require the camera themselves.

1977

The face of Grève de Lecq changed overnight when one of the Island's landmarks was destroyed by fire. The building which dated from the late 19th century had originally been called the Pavilion but had become Caesar's Palace in the early 1970's.

After the fire the night spot reopened, staging cabaret entertainment as before. However, by the 1990's tastes and circumstances had changed and the 1994 summer season was cut short. Caesar's Palace has ceased to be one of the Island's premiere cabaret venues.

24 December

1787

The season's spirits were dulled for residents of St Helier as they were inundated by floodwater. At this time there were no proper drains and streams still flowed through what is now the heart of town.

1875

Sir John Le Couteur died on this day. Le Couteur had initially chosen a military career and as a Lieutenant in the 104th Foot, while still in his teens, spent three years fighting alongside Sioux Indians during the American War of Independence. Once the war had been lost, he returned to his native Jersey, taking a keen interest in local affairs. While on the St Brelade Roads Committee in 1824 he persuaded his fellow officials to adopt McAdam's road making system, making the parish one of the first places in the world to have tarmacked roads. Among his other achievements were the introduction of a lifeboat, the building of a road to link St Aubin and St Helier and the building of the parish arsenals. He was also closely associated with royalty, being friends with William IV and highly regarded by Queen Victoria.

1903

John Le Brocq faced a choice when he appeared before the Magistrate, either pay a £1 fine or spend Christmas and three more days doing hard labour in prison. Le Brocq had been found guilty of brawling in a railway carriage after a fellow passenger had objected to his drunken singing. Le Brocq did not pay the fine. At this time the court sat both on Christmas Eve and Boxing Day.

1974

A Dart Herald owned by British Island Airways crash-landed at 7 pm while attempting to land. It came in on one engine and with its undercarriage not in position. Coming down on the grass verge at the eastern end of the runway, the plane spun around and slid 200 ft backwards before coming to rest on a minor road, having crashed through the perimeter fence. All 53 people on board escaped unhurt. The incident lead to a review of airport boundary safety.

25 December

1650

Philippe de Carteret, later Sir Philippe, was born in St Ouen's Manor on this day. When he was 26 he married 12-year old Elisabeth de Carteret. The marriage contract stated that 'on the day of the marriage the bride's father shall pay to the groom's father £1,000 sterling'. It went on: 'the said Elisabeth shall immediately after the marriage return to her parents and remain with them till she is fifteen years old'. A further £1,500 was to be paid to the groom's father at a later date. One of the marriage conditions was that if 'Elisabeth survive her husband, she shall receive one third of the revenue of the Manor'.

1883

In the early morning of this Christmas Day Alfred Le Masurier and Mary Ann Noel were married in St Luke's Church. They were both 20 years old and 74 years later they were celebrating another wedding anniversary, making them the longest married couple in the Channel Islands.

1933

Neomie Hepburn was knocked down and killed at Charing Cross when she was hit by a Safety Coach. John Romeril, who had been driving the bus, was suspected of being drunk but insisted that he had only had port wine and a drink or two at dinner. He claimed to have felt a bump and stopped the bus, whereupon he found Hepburn lying in the road. One witness told the inquest that the woman had run straight into the bus. Having heard all the evidence, a verdict of accidental death was returned.

1944

Despite the desperate shortages of food the German occupying forces were sitting down to a fine Christmas feast. Over 2,000 chickens had been requisitioned and it was recorded that 'meals are as opulent as in times of peace'. It was also noted that the loss of 2,000 chickens was 'an unpopular measure'.

26 December

1836

A museum was established in St Helier. It only functioned for six years but while in existence the Jersey Athenaeum offered the facility of a reading room.

1869

Onslow Clarke was charged with throwing snowballs. He had launched the frozen projectiles against the house of Mr Luard, who had come out and threatened to shoot him if the windows were struck. Clarke took no notice and was arrested after Luard was himself hit with a snowball.

This was not an isolated incident. Two officers had been similarly attacked at Fort Regent and as they were on duty they had been unable to retaliate.

When the Clarke case went to court it was thrown out as witnesses alleged a case of mistaken identity.

1898

Jersey Railway opened the tunnel at St Aubin. The railway line to the west of St Aubin had had some very tight curves in it and the tunnel was built to straighten the line and do away with the most dangerous bend. The project took only 18 months from decision to completion and although enormous amounts of rock had been removed to build the line, this is the only time that tunnelling rather than a cutting was constructed.

1922

Jersey's first public baths were opened at No 18 Gloucester Street by Constable Pinel, who took the inaugural immersion - in private. The facility contained 20 baths and the company running it hoped to introduce Turkish and saltwater baths in the future.

A large crowd gathered to watch the band at the opening ceremony and raffle tickets were sold a 2s each. The first five tickets drawn entitled the holder to a bath once a week for a year, the second five received a bath a week for six months.

27 December

1810

An Examiner of Imports and Exports was appointed. Smuggling was still a profitable pastime for an island of seafarers and big profits could be made landing tobacco in both France and England. Brandy was another favourite cargo and boats with false bottoms were built to fool customs officials.

1909

A new roller skating rink opened and was enjoyed by thousands of people. The New Olympia saw 700 people paying admission on this first morning, using skates on the specially constructed floor. The arena was lit by electric lights and was heated with radiators, keeping the damp winter weather at bay. Music accompanying the skaters was provided by a band dressed in scarlet and gold, who played from the musicians' gallery.

1979

The Bailiff's Chamber confirmed that local cinemas had been told not to screen Monty Python's Life of Brian until a panel had viewed it to see if it's AA certificate was appropriate. A double A rated film allowed ages 14 and over to see the film and the panel were to advise if an X certificate was more appropriate, or even if it should be shown at all. In the event, Monty Python refused to allow their film to be shown with an X rating, which meant that Islanders had to travel to the more liberal Guernsey to see this classic movie.

1983

Vandals used the Christmas holiday to cause some of the worst malicious damage the Island had seen. Les Quennevais School, Fort Regent and the Sugar Basin Cafe at Beaumont were among those hit. But the worst damage of all was at Mont Nicolle School. Televisions and radios were smashed, glue and ink had been dashed over furniture and floors, and other machinery was wrecked. The following day two boys, aged 12 and 13, were assisting police and a large amount of the goods stolen from the schools had been recovered.

28 December

1648

Trinity Church is obviously unlucky when it comes to lightning. The steeple had been struck in 1629 and again in 1646. Although on previous occasions damage had been done, the strike on this day caused far more destruction. The bolt had smashed the south-west side of the steeple almost down to the bell, all but one window had been broken and the roof badly damaged. The lightning had also struck a nearby house, smashing windows, and had killed a calf.

1751

An Act of Parliament was registered in the Royal Court so that Jersey's calendar stayed in line with Britain's. It had been decided that the following year should start on 1st January instead of 25th March. At the same time the calendar would be corrected of the inaccuracy of the early astronomers so that 3rd September 1752 would became 14th September 1752.

1963

As a result of a challenge a man climbed the 450 ft high television mast at Frémont. With him was a decorated Christmas tree, which he left at the top. This festive activity was not appreciated by the authorities and a prosecution for trespass was threatened.

1988

Teams of transplant surgeons arrived in the Island to remove organs from John Ryan and Anthony Fortune. Both young men had been declared brain dead, Fortune from a brain haemorrhage and Ryan following an accident with a lift. Both had been kept alive on life support machines at the express wishes of their families until their organs could be used. The surgeons were due to return to the mainland as soon as the procedure was completed and then carry out transplant operations on waiting recipients. The law allowing this to happen had been brought in on 12th April 1985 as the result of a road accident in which Jason Wright had died.

29 December

1927

An advert offering a £25 reward for information about the poisoning of a valuable French bulldog on Christmas morning appeared in the local press. It turned out not to be an isolated incident as more owners of pedigree dogs came forward, their animals having been killed. A number of prize-winning show dogs had died in what appeared to be a deliberate campaign.

1929

Lady Houston, who had lived at Grands Vaux, died. This wealthy, and slightly eccentric, woman had financed a British entry for the Schneider Trophy so that they could compete in this international flying competition. The aeronautic advances she funded lead directly to the development of the Spitfire which proved so successful during the Battle of Britain.

1944

An enquiry was held into the death of John Larbalestier. In November, John, his brother Bernard and their friend Peter Noel had, like a number of others, tried to escape to France. Disaster overtook them and the attempt ended with John drowned, Bernard missing, presumed drowned, and Noel imprisoned by the Germans. The jury returned an open verdict.

1976

An injunction to stop pigeons in the Royal Square being culled was presented to the Bailiff's Chambers. The Public Works Committee had employed Rentokill Ltd to dispatch 300 birds before Christmas. After 99 pigeons had been killed John Berger had halted proceedings with an injunction. This was later lifted but now Berger was trying again. The trapped birds were taken to the Animals' Shelter to be injected with pentobarbitone, which was said to be painless, but Berger considered it to be cruel. He proposed that when his property in Waterworks Valley was repaired he would house the pigeons there.

30 December

1896

A meeting was held at St Ouen's Parish Hall to discuss the adulteration of butter with margarine. A similar meeting had been held in St Peter on 16th December. The meeting was of the opinion that the 1894 Margarine Act was not satisfactory. Suggestions were made that all margarine should be white so that it could not be mistaken for the butter. At this time butter was made on farms and, with no enforced weights and measures law, it was possible to sell short weights or add the cheaper margarine to the butter, thus increasing the profit, a practice apparently widespread in other parts.

1929

The film The Perfect Alibi caused a stir in Jersey. Starring Chester Morris, it was the first talkie to be screened locally. The review acclaimed it a great success, with fine acting and a number of thrills. However the American accent obviously grated a little, being described as a 'nasal twang'.

1959

The *Chronique de Jersey*, the Island's last French language newspaper, ceased publication. It was originally one of many local French publications but after 145 years it was no longer viable.

1972

The film Jeremiah Johnson, starring Robert Redford, was showing at West's Cinema and the 8 o'clock screening was the picture house's last. Having opened in 1923, it was later refurbished to compete with the Forum Cinema. The building's twin towers dominated the Bath Street-Beresford Street junction. Once demolished, the site was to be redeveloped into a shopping centre.

1983

Linda Quenault lost control of her Triumph Dolomite near St John's Church. The car struck a bank and a tree before flying over a wall to land among the gravestones. The car was written off but its driver, who was seven months pregnant, only received minor injuries.

31 December

1811

The ever expanding Methodist movement opened the chapel at Six Rues. It remained in use until the 1980s, when the church and hall were sold off. The congregation had diminished to single figures.

1849

By this day over 250,000 tons of granite had been quarried, transported and deposited during the construction of St Catherine's breakwater. A rubble mound more than 200 ft wide was tipped until it reached low water level. On top of this foundation two skins, up to 14 ft thick, of dressed granite were built and in-filled with more rubble. The breakwater is 2,300 ft long and forty ft high. By the time it was completed it had swallowed over 750,000 tons of stone.

1910

A ketch, having arrived from Ipswich, was unable to get into her allotted berth, so she laid her mooring chain alongside the quay. When the crew went to secure the vessel their 10 fathoms of chain had been stolen. That the thieves took the chain and not the cargo is explained by the fact that the ketch was carrying manure.

1914

The court martial of a civilian named Edwin Single took place at the Grand Hotel. He was found guilty of spreading false reports likely to cause alarm and sentenced to 14 days in prison without hard labour. The Lieutenant Governor, however, commuted the sentence and he was released the following day.

1965

The Parish of St Helier became the owner of the Town Hall, the title having been transferred from the States. The Hall had been built by the States in 1872 as a police station, with the Constable of St Helier being allowed use of part of the building for public administration. As the police and fire services who had originally been based in the building were now sited at Rouge Bouillon, the Hall could be used solely for parish affairs.

Bibliography

Balleine, G R, A Biographical Dictionary of Jersey. Staples Press:
    London: 1948
Balleine, G R, The Bailiwick of Jersey. Hodder and Stoughton:
    London: 1951
Bonsor, N R P, The Jersey Railway (J R & T). The Oakwood Press:
    Surrey: 1962
Bonsor, N R P, The Jersey Eastern Railway and the German
    Occupation Lines in Jersey. The Oakwood Press: Oxford:
    1986
Carman, WJ, Channel Island Transport. Private publication: 1987
Chevalier, Jean, Diaries. Copies can be found in the Sociètè Jersiaise
    Library
Corbet, Francis L M, A Biographical Dictionary of Jersey Vol 2. La
    Société Jersiaise: Jersey: 1998
Davies, William, Fort Regent. Private publication: 1971
Davies, William, The Harbour That Failed. Ampersand Press Co:
    Alderney: 1983
Davies, William, The Coastal Towers of Jersey. William Davies/La
    Société Jersiaise: Jersey: 1991
Foley, L A, Raising a Clameur. Foley Publications, St Helier: Jersey:
    1999
Ginns, Michael, Transport in Jersey. Walters-Rutland Publications
    Co: London: 1961
Grimsley, E J, The Historical Development of the Martello Tower in
    the Channel Islands. Sarnia Publications: Guernsey: 1988
Hillsdon, Sonia, Jersey: Witches, Ghosts and Traditions. Jarrold
    Colour Publications: Norwich: 1984
Holmes, Dennis, Ready Aye Ready ... The St Helier's Fire Brigade
    1900-1950. CTV Publications: Jersey: 1988
Jean, John, Jersey Sailing Ships. Phillimore & Co Ltd: Sussex: 1982
Lake, Chris, The Battle of Flowers Story. Redberry Press Ltd: Jersey:
    1989
L'Amy, John H, Jersey Folk Lore. La Société Jersiaise: Jersey: 1971
Layzell, Alastair, Announcing the Arrival .... CTV Publications:
    Jersey: 1987

Lempriere, Raoul, Customs, Ceremonies and Traditions of the Channel Islands. Robert Hale Ltd: London: 1976

Le Ruez, Elizabeth, The Jersey Cow ... and its Island Home. Royal Jersey Agricultural and Horticultural Society: Jersey: 1992

Le Seelleur, Kevin, Channel Islands' Railway Steamers. Patrick Stephens Ltd: Wellingborough: 1985

Mayne, Richard, Mailships of the Channel Islands. Picton Publishing: Wiltshire: 1971

Mayne, Richard, The Battle of Jersey. Phillimore & Co Ltd: London: 1981

Moignard, Ian G, The History of Jersey's Lifeboats. Ashton & Denton Publishing Co (CI) Ltd: Jersey: 1975

Rybot, Major N V L, The Islet of St Helier and Elizabeth Castle, Jersey. States of Jersey: Jersey: 1968

Rybot, Major N V L, Gorey Castle. States of Jersey: Jersey: 1978

Sinel, Leslie, Jersey Through the Centuries. La Haule Books: Jersey: 1984

Sinel, Leslie, The German Occupation of Jersey. La Haule Books: Jersey: 1984

Slade, Edouard, Pictorial History of Aviation in Jersey. Private publication: 1964

Syvret, Maguerite and Joan Stevens, Balleine's History of Jersey. Phillimore & Co Ltd: West Sussex: 1998

von Aufsess, Baron, The von Aufsess Occupation Diary. Phillimore: Chichester: 1985

A number of local newspapers were also used, including:
The British Press and Jersey Times
The Chronique
The Jersey Evening Post
The Jersey Independent and Daily Telegraph
The Jersey Times